DATE DUE

JOSTEN'S 30 508

architecture
and THE SPIRIT OF MAN

architecture
and THE SPIRIT OF MAN

by JOSEPH HUDNUT

GREENWOOD PRESS, PUBLISHERS
NEW YORK

contents

contents

part one

ON TRADITIONAL AND
MODERN ARCHITECTURE

CHAPTER ONE

what buildings are beautiful?

WHEN I was very young—five years old, as I remember it
—I heard my mother say that she had engaged a *perfectly
beautiful laundress,* and being by endowment curious of femi-
nine charm I hid behind the kitchen sink to have my first look
at beauty.

My first look and my first disenchantment. The face of my
mother's laundress was as yellow-red as the soap which she
exercised upon my jumpers and my stockings and her figure was,
like that of her tub, round, stable, and very wide.

My mother had spoken in a metaphor, inaccessible to my
understanding. She had used the word beauty to signify not an
attribute of the laundress but a quality of workmanship for which
the laundress, irrespective of her appearance, had become an
embodiment. That which was called beautiful was neither the
laundress nor the objects of her laundering but the performance
to which these were machine and medium, a performance made
express and visible in the comforting crisp cleanliness of linens,
pajamas, towels, and pillowcases. The work done was well done;
the task and the process were perfectly mastered; the end was
attained completely and without excess; and my mother, perceiv-
ing this unity of intention, method, and product, cast over all
of these the aureole of beauty.

In my mind the basket of my mother's laundress, thus filled
with the magical effects of the art of laundering, stands as type

and symbol of all that universe of beauty which is identified with skill in making and doing: the beauty entangled with our delight and surprise and wonder at man's ingenuity and invention and with the release which a fragment of perfection brings into our imperfect world.

In the basket of my mother's laundress, awaiting my tardy recognition, lay the silver saltcellar made by Benvenuto Cellini, the *cadenza coloratura* of Lily Pons, the tenth-inning three-bagger of Ted Williams, the sonnet that Keats composed for Fanny Brawne, the exquisitely timed bomb that burst above the roofs of Hiroshima. In that basket lay the splendor and ever new adventure of Fifth Avenue: the sapphires in the window at Tiffany's, the black-and-gold chocolates at Rosemarie's, the subtle bathing dresses at Bonwit Teller's, and at Brentano's the gem-encrusted missal from the cloister of Saint Benôit-sur-Loire. The Lincoln cabriolet, custom-made and sleek and driven by a smart chauffeur, lay there and the hat of the delicate lady who rode within. The gilded Sherman and his fragile angel were there and the Nymph of the Fountain who takes her eternal bath under the thousand eyes of the Plaza Hotel; and in that basket lay also the chiseled façade of the New York Public Library, all garlanded with Gallic imageries, innumerable of molding, console, and plump baluster, of naiad-filled spandrel and foliated keystone, of chaste goddess, stern lion, and leaves of the lush acanthus.

To the majority of men living in this our mechanized world such beauty, immediate and virginal, returns all that could be asked of architecture. Architecture, except as it is sometimes colored by history, consists for most of us of buildings built of fine materials, sound in techniques, and brave in ornament and invention. The architect is supercraftsman and jeweler, scenic artist and pleasure merchant. He is a beautiful architect whose storehouse is most completely stuffed with styles, precedents, decorative amenities, and the amusing novelties which are mistaken for genius.

The role is a pleasant and rewarding one; to refuse it would be to extinguish our profession; nor is there any morality or logic of design which demands of us so inhuman a sacrifice. It happens, nevertheless, that there are other measures of beauty in architecture. One of these measures is that afforded by architectural *form*.

The New York Public Library is not, as I have hinted, one great confusion of ornamental episodes. Any one who looks even hurriedly at the New York Public Library can hardly fail to be aware of an order in the disposition of its parts. A central pavilion pierced with three deep arches anchors the building to the fine terrace upon which it stands; from this pavilion two peristyles march equal distances right and left and end in identical little temples; and the blithe ornament dances across the marble walls in rhythmical ecstasies. The intention of the architect was clearly so to relate all of these that taken together they would present a unity; and if we are persuaded of that unity, finding it complete and without adventitious parts or discordances, it may happen that we will find in such unity a mode of beauty.

Form is a name which we give to a harmony thus apprehended among a variety of elements. The Sistine Madonna carries Her Child at the center of Raphael's canvas; the curtains part right and left to admit Her to our earth; the sky on all sides gives an increase of radiance; the saints kneel at either hand; and even the angels worship in a symmetry. So Lincoln, seated in his temple, framed by systems of peristyles, steps, reflecting basins, and disciplined foliage becomes an element in a pattern whose beauty, surely, transcends even as it includes the beauty of Doric columns carefully copied from the Parthenon and of marble block set exquisitely on marble block.

We do not need to be told that color and sound, idea and

image, constructed fabric and enclosed space exist not singly but in combination, yet our attention is not always centered upon their relationships. There is an art, sometimes called architecture, which consists in conceiving, developing, and establishing such relationships. The apprehension of that art carries us into a realm of beauty which—if for no other reason than for the sake of my exposition—may be conceived as apart from the nearer landscapes of craftsmanship. Until we have become interested in form, until that interest controls our perceptions of buildings and our thought about them, we will know very little about buildings. We must see buildings, as we are taught to see pictures, as networks of relationships: relationships not only of line and plane and shadow but of solids "occupying space and with space around" in which stone and steel, mass and ordered space, color, light, and texture are brought together and arranged in consciously controlled patterns.

That way of seeing demands obviously some expectancy of a beauty to be unfolded in buildings and it demands also the firmness of attention which such an expectancy might provoke and maintain. Relationships do not leap into our vision as do color, light, and technical dexterities; they are not always accessible to the passive mind indolent of new knowledge and experience; nor do they always force themselves upon those scientific eyes which are focused upon the processes of art, upon the way things are done and the way things work. You have to care about relationships to see them; you must search them out, establish them in the mind, hold them there as you might hold the invisible structures of mathematics.

We must not expect that everyone will thus take the trouble to acquaint himself with form. We are, as a people, too preoccupied with technologies, with ways and means, with promises of comfort, to bother about this etiquette of architecture. We deny ourselves the beauty of form, being absorbed in those

practical matters which make true judgments of value imprac-
ticable.

This explains in part our present dislike of Renaissance architecture, which rests upon contemplation and scholarship, which
takes for granted a process of learning, which yields its secrets
only to minds disciplined to discrimination and expectant of
subtleties. The masters of the Renaissance addressed their façades
to that aristocratic mode of seeing. Sanmicheli, for example,
assumes that you will look beyond his bold and original outlines
to the harmonies into which these are divided: to the nice adjustments of voids and solids, the musical progressions of window, arch, and column, the contrast of rusticated basement
against the elegance of classical peristyles, the enrichment and
accent of his careful ornament. The Empire State Building can
be taken in without time or effort: taken in, swallowed, and
digested in twenty seconds.

Form demands a principle and its principle must be operative
within an area defined by a habit of seeing and of understanding. Each of the great traditions of architecture arrived at such
a synthesis. Each has its plan of organization and its peculiar
components of form selected from the complex totalities of
buildings. Each developed its ideal of form as much by exclu-
sion and repression as by emphasis and elaboration. The large
effects of Baroque architecture, for example, are paid for by
some deficiencies in the treatment of surfaces and materials—
this *theater* could not attain its splendor in an architecture too
solicitous of refinements in proportion and of perfect control
in line—nor could the Renaissance architect guard his serenity
and elegance in the presence of cataracts of light falling over
undulating walls.

Our standards of excellence in form will thus change with our
interests: with the character and range of those buildings which
arrest our vision. Form cannot in practice comprise all the ele-

ments of a building. On the contrary form cannot be defined except in its relation to the fact of selection and to the mind which selects, arranges, accentuates, represses, and distorts.

No art offers the form-giver so wide a range of selection and combination as the art of architecture. Space, for example, except as space may be represented in painting and in the theater, is the almost exclusive possession of architecture: that defined and controlled space which may be shaped and arranged, which may be channeled through nave and aisle, gathered together in crystalline stars, or made to flow upward into sunny domes. Space may be static and universal as it is under the air-borne dome of Sancta Sophia, dramatic as it is in the vast reaches of Versailles, or filled with luminous splendor as it is at Amiens. Structure also is our peculiar province. Only the patterns of architecture may comprise the effort of columns to sustain a pediment, the thrust of buttresses against a wall, the weight of a tower against the earth, the energy of a steel frame. The thousand arches which in the Colosseum lifted the populace of Rome above the arena may exist in the mind as elements of form as distinct as the oval façades which hide them from our view; and the great vaults which hold the dome of Michelangelo above the grave of Saint Peter enter into and sustain the grandeur of the whole, not by their shapes and proportions merely, but by the tremendous energies arrested within them. The resources of form in architecture include these living forces; include also the colors, textures, and ornaments which enrich the surfaces of buildings, the sculptures, paintings, metal grills, and wood carvings which stand against them, the light which plays over them and reveals them; and form in architecture may also include the terraces and walled areas upon which buildings may stand, the gardens which surround them, the squares and streets laid out around them, and the city into which their rhythms may be made to extend. The Washington Monument includes the Mall, the patterned groves of trees, the Lincoln Memorial, and the distant Capitol; the Salute is a water flower which draws its life from the blue sea of Venice; and the dome of Saint Paul is an equestrian statue pedestaled upon the red roofs of London.

Our modern form—assuming that we desire form and are able to achieve it—is not likely to be compounded of all of these elements. Our architects also will proceed by selection and emphasis. That which will guide them will be the mind of our era which with its thousand uncertainties and irrational preferences is yet for architecture the final arbiter of beauty. Architects, more than any other artists, lean upon their clientele; and architects, like all artists, live upon applause.

Form is dependent, more than any other mode of beauty in architecture, upon these changing valuations. That beauty which is identified with technical skill—the beauty of materials, of crafts, of the ornaments which are the products of taste and invention—provokes a more universal admiration; the beauty of form must be more often sustained by knowledge, fashion, and a disciplined vision. That is a circumstance equally annoying to the academician in search of standards and to the philosopher in search of truth, but it is a circumstance fundamental in the experience of beauty. We have to open the stubborn eyes of our students before they will see any beauty in the form of China or Egypt, nor is there any pioneer in the long evolution of architecture who did not need his apologist and interpreter.

There is a third mode of beauty in architecture—one not irrelevant either to technical excellence or to excellence of form and yet not inseparable from these in the mind. People who are indifferent to form in buildings and who take little note of methods and ornaments in buildings may nevertheless have feelings about them. In a great chimney embraced by snug roofs overhanging casemented windows we may feel that security, love, and loyalty which are inseparable from remembrances of home. In a church covered with lichen and set among ancient trees we may feel the frailty and brevity of our lives. We say that the chimney *expresses* the home, the church expresses mortality, meaning that these structures convey to us the mood of those who built them or perhaps the intentions of their builders to evoke these sentiments in us. So the Lincoln Memorial expresses the character of Lincoln; the Taj Mahal expresses the splendor and mystery of India; and the Chicago Opera House expresses the decadence of the art of the opera. Often we find such expressions beautiful. They may afford us a beauty which may be and often appears to be quite apart from the experience of form or the recognition of skill.

Such beauty has its origin in associations. Architects design in associations in much the same way as writers think in metaphors; they are the colorations which energize the meanings of architecture. The open hearth, for example, confirms the· idea of home so persuasively as to be mandatory in the art of the most audacious of functionalists; the spire signals not less certainly the immanence of the faith out of which it rose; and no honest-to-goodness American would for a moment entrust his money to a bank whose temple is unprefaced by four columns of unembezzleable granite. For my part, I shall always refuse to believe in the worth of a Raphael unless I must climb at least forty marble steps to reach it.

The people cling to these symbols and have every right to do so. The sentiments they evoke are not always profound but they are often real. Not that such sentiments are wholly innocent; and yet they are less implacable enemies of form than they sometimes appear to be. They provide architecture with that base of popular interest and feeling—with that *story*—which is essential to architecture in a democratic scene. We should be careful lest in destroying sentiment we destroy that base. I am by no means sure that the standardizations of prefabrication will prove less oppressive to our art than the standardizations of sentiment which they promise to overcome or that the new stories which they tell will promote a deeper understanding of form. It may be moreover that the consciousness of emotional values in traditional architecture which is witnessed by neo-Gothic churches, Roman banks, and Cape Cod cottages prepares the way for the emotional content, if such there be, of modern architecture. Who shall say that the happiness the heart discovers in its environment is less important than our art; and above all, when that happiness—if indeed this be happiness—is multiplied one hundred and forty million times.

Count me as a Victorian if you will but I confess that I like a story in everything: in church and skyscraper and suburban house, in the Temple at Sunium and the quaint Asphalt Manufacturing Plant of the Borough of Manhattan, in the chairs of Alvar Aalto and the sculptures of Alexander Calder, in sunset, sea, and parallelogram. This would be a dull world if we were to divorce story from our judgments of architectures.

Now there is more than one way in which a building can tell us a story; more than one way in which it can set forth a sentiment. Buildings may address us more directly than through associations, more dramatically than through symbols, and they may do this without a negation of form. Buildings may, for example, speak to us in patterns shaped by the life they were meant to shelter, by the uses to which they are to be put. That life and that use may be our life and our use and buildings may in that way tell us stories of that unique and unprogramed world which surrounds us today and for which no symbols have as yet been invented. Buildings may tell us stories about the present, stories charged with truth and made the more eloquent by that sweet ornament.

I think that that is what Louis Sullivan meant when fifty years or more ago, in a city spellbound by the World's Columbian Exposition, he made the famous pronouncement which ever since that time has directed the eyes of architects from symbol and association to the beauty of realism. *Form follows function.* The form of a building must be a consequence of its purpose. The form of a building must tell the story of its life, of its inward activities and outward affiliations. Whatever idea may be the generator of a building—the idea of family, of government, of manufacture—that idea imposes upon that building relationships peculiar to itself and these relationships, clearly established, are the deepest source of architectural character.

The principle was not new. It had been known to the Egyptians, was the basis of architecture in Greece and Rome, was creed and foundation of practice among the cathedral builders, cardinal in the art of Michelangelo and Mansart, accepted and followed in the prim buildings of our Colonial ancestors. It had been formulated moreover in the writings of a dozen essayists and was in the eighteenth century a familiar cliché of architectural criticism. But words have little force and usually little meaning apart from the persons who speak them and the circumstances under which they are spoken. That which gave wings to the words of Louis Sullivan was the confusion of tongues which at that moment oppressed our land. The White City, innocent enough as pageant and scenic architecture, fatuity and mockery as contemporary ideal, gave uncontrovertible emphasis to his passionate protest and above the roofs of our great cities a thousand skyscrapers lifted their tortured heads to din the moral into our ears. The creed of Louis Sullivan became a guide for our seeing, a measuring rod for our judgments.

Thus it happens that we often find a peculiar beauty in those buildings which, either through palpable adaptations to function or through the selection and emphasis of those elements of form which are most pertinent to our present culture reveal the thought and activity of our own time. We understand such buildings as the containers of our society and that content shines through their visible shapes and gives them meanings intimate to ourselves. Thus illumined they capture the imaginations of men who live in this present world more surely than those buildings which seem to have been shaped by the ideas and functions of the past.

The command of such buildings is vastly enhanced by an awareness of a thought and activity still operative in architecture: by the assurance which they give that those ideas which surround and channel us not only shaped our buildings into what they are today but are today shaping them into what they will be tomorrow. When we are conscious of a participation of idea and form in the art of architecture, a participation which is active and before our eyes, which is in process and not soon to be ended, that consciousness gives to buildings a dynamic character denied to those buildings which announce a completed cycle of thought and experiment. Function and form, idea and expression, progress together and together share a modernity which is advancing towards a newer modernity.

People who have felt the grandeur and promise of our era and who have given themselves to its proud pageantries often entertain a sentiment for modernity, more essential to our art, I think, than aesthetic preference or reasoned opinion. To such the measure of excellence in architecture will be the measure of its intimacy with that sentiment. They will perceive, below the novel forms and materials of our new design—too often traps for the imagination—the operation of those ideas and feelings to which these are language and clothing. When, for example, our architects discover a lyricism, hitherto unrecognized, in plate glass or exploit with subtlety the rhythms of flowing space—so that our houses open their hearts to sunshine and to nature— these people will look beyond such outward changes to the changing demands and new understandings in the pattern of the family which, if not creators of the new architectural forms, were certainly essential to their acceptance and currency. There is an art of living, of which we are all practitioners, which across the centuries created the family and within that frame developed—is developing—ways of life congenial to many different climates and scenes. That art also determined—is also determining—the form of the house, constant of theme, innumerable of appearances. That art is sometimes the genesis of a moving beauty not always revealed to those whose eyes are fixed on the anatomy and the envelope of buildings.

That which is true of the house is true of every structure planned for human use: of school and hospital, church and university, city hall and theater, and the buildings of commerce. Our schoolhouses throw down their classical walls not because classical walls are illogical to steel construction but because classical walls are an embarrassment to that new relationship of the school to the democratic process which is transforming, not the schoolhouse merely, but the school; and a corresponding relationship, together with the urgencies of our sciences, has prompted the university and the library to forget their ancient symmetries. From new orientations of idea, not from changes in architectural taste, spring the cold invigorating winds which tear from the sides of skyscrapers their armor of arch and column, overthrow the heavy domes of our capitols, arrest the spires of great cathedrals, spatter with green squares the fevered slums of our cities, and reshape even our factories to the needs of the humanity they shelter beside their machines.

Our buildings are live creatures and submit impatiently to the imprisonment of our traditions. They are growing creatures, changing constantly with change of purpose and method, and they change also with our reassessments of relationship and responsibility in the structure of society. They change with economic change, with the rise and fall of political doctrines, with the standards, rituals, and conventions of social behavior, and with our knowledge of right and wrong. Our architecture receives all of these, the multiplex currents of our civilization: receives and channels them and is molded by them.

Our buildings are beautiful when they take part in that evolution. Our buildings are beautiful when they are plastic to new circumstances, however uncongenial to antique precedent; when they are organic to our present life whatever its conflicts and inconsistencies; when they exhibit a need to reconcile new uses and new feelings with uses and feelings continued from the past. Buildings are beautiful, as soldiers are beautiful, when they show the signs of conflict and of victory.

Shall we conclude then that there are degrees of beauty? Since skill and technical competence, form, story, and contemporary meaning, are all modes of beauty shall we assist our judgments with a little ladder of judgments, giving perhaps a higher value to the beauty of truth than to the beauty of sentiment, a higher value to form than to story? Philosophy above feeling, feeling above knowledge, knowledge above pleasure? I do not believe that such judgments are useful or that they can be true. Aestheticians who write libraries to define a word and those great minds who have tried so valiantly to fit beauty into their systems of philosophy sometimes arrive at their grains of truth through such distributions of emphasis; but to the artist beauty will not lend herself to such assessments. Beauty is a relationship between the self and whatever qualities of the known world are experienced by the self. In that relationship there can be no values other than those established by the self. To each of us, then, his own measure of beauty.

If there is one kind of beauty which is universally experienced —and one which in many ways is peculiar to architecture—it is that beauty which time builds into the things made by man. There is in buildings which have withstood the siege of the centuries a magic which is irrespective of form and technical excellence and which is everywhere acknowledged. The temples of Thebes, the pyramids of Yucatan, the Roman arches across the Gard: these, the wreckages of distant worlds, are radioactive with a long-gathered energy which cannot be explained by the laws and practices of our design. On condition that these relics are genuine, that they are not pretenders and false witnesses to the present, they will speak to us of an inheritance which is an inalienable part of ourselves. They are witnesses of an adventure which we shared, which we are still sharing, with the millions who came before us; nor is such beauty inconsistent with the beauty of modernity.

I hope that my readers will understand that I am not inflicting upon them that old saw about architectures expressing civilizations. So long as warlike people build castles and devout people build temples architectures will express—or illustrate—civilizations; but the truism is not so profound as to need more than a million restatements. I am thinking rather of buildings as fragments of time, of time crystallized and made visible and charged with time's bittersweet power to touch the heart, and I think that that power has less to do with the circumstances of history than with the fact of history. We recognize in old buildings that stream of life of which we also are parts; we know its pathos and its consolations; these buildings belong to us.

When we see the Parthenon we see it, not as type and crown of Athenian imperialism—still less as the triumphant crest of an architectural style—but as a shrine bathed in great renowns and stirring events. The applause of the theater carved in its pedestal still reaches us, and the sound of the waves against the thousand ships that were counted in the Bay of Salamis. The earth is strewn with such splinters of ourselves. We may if we wish live again in the Alhambra, world of fragile arch and cool patio; in Salzburg where Mozart still plays to the prince-archbishop the first of his symphonies; in Bath still vocal with the urgencies of Sir Anthony Absolute; in Independence Hall still informed with the reasonable spirit of Franklin. Who shall say that such beauty is not authentic to the many-faceted art of architecture?

Architecture has in it this virtue: it proclaims not only the splendor of the earth's successive cultures but of human culture as a whole. Architecture writes the story of humanity not in episodes only but in its totality. The theme which with infinite variations threads that long narrative is also the theme of architecture which holds before us in its thousand scattered symbols the never attained ideal of peace on earth. The buildings which witness the great traditions of architecture, the temples, cathedrals, palaces, and cities—vast complexities of space and light, of structural weight and energies, of utilities and mechanisms, of carvings and color, of story, idea, and genius—are affirmations of man's authority however brief over his environment, of his capacity for pattern and reconciliation, of his ability to overcome the discordant and hostile forces which array him or press upon him from within.

Standing in the transept of Chartres I could believe that man —whose armies blacken the earth, whose engines of destruction ride the distant-margined seas—this savage whose single bolt destroys a city and all who live in it—may yet build for himself a home symmetrical with that majestic synthesis.

That promise also is beautiful.

CHAPTER TWO

the obelisk of general washington

WHEN not long ago I was in our national capital I had some words with the great obelisk which stands at the end of the Mall.

Said the obelisk: I am General Washington. I am the Father of My Country.

Your country, indeed, said I. My memory is not so short, my good sir, that I have forgotten your Egyptian birthplace. For how many centuries—was it not twenty at least?—did you stand at the rim of the Lybian desert before the alabaster altar of the sun-god Re, pretending to be *his* symbol? Were you not afterwards seen in Rome where for fourteen hundred years you frequented the circus of that disreputable little boot, Caligula? You know how you made the innocent Middle Ages believe that you held the ashes of Julius Caesar; and when young Domenico Fontana with the aid of eight hundred horses moved you to a place of honor before the Basilica of Saint Peter you announced yourself with cool assurance to be the type and vicar of the First Bishop of Rome. Did I not also meet you in Paris at the very center of the Place de la Concorde, guarding the memory of that most crimson of harlots, Madame la Guillotine?

There is really no limit to the effrontery of these obelisks. They will recite any story, confirm any lie, exalt any authority. In spite of all I said the imperturbable monument faced me down, declaring itself the perfect simulacrum of our first president, and I heard a young lady who stood near me, a graduate of the Yale School of Fine Arts, assure the obelisk that it is beyond any doubt the most WONDERFUL and BEAUTIFUL and SUBLIME thing in the world and that it certainly teaches a marvelous lesson in democratic simplicity especially to foreigners and especially to Prussians who however would probably not profit by it. The obelisk, which meanwhile had captured the red sun of Virginia, blushed.

At this point I must pause to eat some of my words. Of course I know that the obelisk has every right to represent Washington, having been authorized to do so by act of Congress—although there is somewhat more of Washington, I think, in the mansion and garden of Mount Vernon—and of course I know that the obelisk is beautiful, that title having been conferred on it by the acclamation of the American people. I have committed this bit of lese majesty, not to defy these self-evident truths, but because, momentarily and for my own purpose, I want to clear them away. I invite my readers to look beneath the clothing of symbol and sentiment which we have projected upon this versatile cosmopolite and see the obelisk as object and architecture unveiled of these fond radiances. I want to make the obelisk a peg—no mean peg, to be sure—on which to hang some comments on that classical principle of form, the principle of Egypt, Greece, and Rome, which forms so large a segment of our architectural inheritance, and, more specifically, upon the relevance of this principle, so persistent in past architectures, to the architecture of this our present world.

I can imagine no more perfect representative of that principle. The obelisk has, in the first place, that weight and mass and vastness of scale, originating in stone construction, which was developed by the architects of the Mediterranean into a language of supreme energy and power. The obelisk has also that simplicity of shape, definite, firm, and immediately to be apprehended, which gives to the classical masterpieces a universal

relevance not unlike the abstract figures and syllogisms of mathematics—so that wherever they appear—in New England, in South
Africa, in the Argentine—they seem to be at home, their home
being the world. Here, finally, is that patterned environment,
that wide geometry of terrace, avenue, reflecting basin, and
subordinate temple, which so often gives grandeur to those
buildings which follow the tradition of Rome—so that the obelisk,
having the quiet strength of a mountain within its heart, the
purity of a star in its outward plane and silhouette, yet gathers
to itself the splendor and circumstance of vast symmetries reaching out around it.

That *power* which is inherent in great mass and weight is a
resource which architecture alone among the arts possesses. The
immense oval of the Colosseum, the inhuman accumulations of
the pyramids, the precipice of wall which masks the butte of
Saint-Germain-en-Laye: these have in them an authority scarcely
less tyrannous than that of the mighty kings who raised them
at such great cost amid the fragile landscapes of our civilizations.
Music, drama, sculpture have each their grandeurs but not this
visible force, this immediate ascendency over the mind, which
awes and humiliates the individual man even as it affirms the
permanence of his race.

The obelisk at Washington has no other originality than that
of size and weight. Senmut, architect and lover of Queen Hat-
shepsut, praised her ancestor-god with an obelisk one hundred
feet high; Bernini, who may be called a specialist in obelisks,
entertained a lady of the fashionable world with an obelisk of
silver to ornament her dinner table; Robert Mills, architect of
the Washington obelisk, extended the pattern high as the heavens.

Bigness is thus seen to be a mode of invention—not to say of
genius; but it is not bigness alone that gives power to the conception of Mills but bigness combined with solidity and weight.
The Eiffel Tower is as high and yet has little authority either

as architecture or monument. The Empire State Building is big enough, Heaven knows, and yet it seldom impresses itself upon our imaginations with that sense of dominion, of ascendancy, which we feel in great structures of stone masonry. Against these airy creatures, these cages of metal provisionally defended against the corrosions of time, we cannot measure our own strength or our season; they bring us no immediate apprehension of the energies, mechanical and remote, which went into their making. Standing before the Washington obelisk we are aware, not of its form merely, not its great height merely, but together with these we feel the pressures of its innumerable strata, one against another, and the accumulated burden which they lay upon the unseen foundations.

There is an aristocracy in such constructions. They unite our unrooted lives to the established past: to the past through which they have endured and to the future in which they will endure. They assure us of a pageantry of civilization in which our own is but an episode. The *monument* rests solidly upon the earth and will not be dissolved; time is fused into it and is its quality; its message is eternity even as it anchors great dignities and stirring events against the inconstancies of our memories.

To what degree will our modern technologies of building admit such consolations? Our steel structures, if we understand them correctly, have relatively neither mass nor weight; nor do they possess in the nature of their materials and processes that scale of effort by which we translate the energy which created them into human energy. We cannot balance them against our human strength. A machine intervenes between our strength and theirs. Nor does steel, however alloyed or defended against the weather, persuade us of its everlastingness—a quality still less to be recognized in buildings whose suspended walls enclose compositions of "flowing space."

I think therefore that the peculiar grandeur of that monumental form which has its source in great weight and mass or in the play of solid shapes set in space will be denied our new architecture. If we address our buildings to eternity—supposing that we shall again yield to that flattering impulse—we shall probably do so in a mode not fundamentally different from that of classical architecture.

Nevertheless, steel has its grandeur. Steel, in the course of time, will achieve its own quality of monumentality. It may be that our minds, saturated with the idea of steel, accustomed to think in steel, as ready to grasp the energies of steel as we now grasp those of stone, will recognize in steel a power, and even a majesty, peculiar to itself. The effort which raised the pyramids may seem less colossal when day by day the tremendous mechanisms of our new constructions inhabit our imaginations; it may then happen that the machine and not man will be "the measure of all things." It may happen also that, constantly aware of an impermanent world, knowing the immensity of the earth's cycle and the frailty of civilizations, we shall have less faith in structures made impregnable to time. Where the most solid of constructions can abide no more than a moment, the relative durability of granite, steel, and confectioner's sugar may not greatly concern us. I think it most significant of our changing valuations that we could conceive the capitol of the world in the form of a skyscraper and that we should find in a band of steel, rising six hundred feet above the river front of St. Louis, sufficient diuturnity to continue the renown of Thomas Jefferson.

I am the more persuaded of this inaptitude of the classical mode for contemporary use and expression when I remember another characteristic of that mode—one which is clearly illustrated in the Washington Monument. Not only is that structure very tall and very heavy: it is also very simple. It speaks to me not only of that which is powerful and that which is eternal but also of that which is elemental. A single crystal of stone, the obelisk ascends in unbroken inward-leaning planes unembarrassed by utility or story. Its language is direct and requires the intervention neither of text nor apology; it does not withhold itself for the sophisticated or the learned; we apprehend it at our first glance and without debate. The obelisk, sheer abstraction of a spire, is as catholic as prayer.

Shapes, and the intervals between them, are the prime substance of architecture and the important source of its eloquence. Shapes act upon us—sometimes; they "do things to us." There are shapes which invite rest and shapes which provoke movement; shapes which exalt and shapes which depress; shapes which annoy and shapes which bring us peace. There are proud shapes, confident shapes, mean shapes, and shapes which solace or accuse. The architect uses these as a conjurer uses his incantations, the sensuous vehicle of his spell.

Not that this influence of shapes is mysterious in nature—or at any rate more mysterious than all other human experiences. It has been explained to me that the authority of shapes, and no doubt that of shapes in combination, has its basis in associations. Thus the horizontal plane captures the calmness of the sea's horizon and the secret of the pyramids, goal of a thousand years of learned research, is only an echo of the mountain's eternity. But we do not defeat influences by describing them. However explained, shapes and the intervals of shapes remain the essential material of the art and alchemy of architecture. An architect who does not create his shapes, but allows them to be made for him by inherited formulas or present calculation, throws away his magic wand.

The architects of Greece and Rome created only simple shapes, serene in their universality. The portico, the pediment, the dome, the square forum, the oval arena—cube, hemisphere, cylinder, cone—each has its quiet and immediate access to the understanding, not of one people, but of all peoples. Explicit and

primary, these impress themselves upon us when we first en-
counter them in architecture as shapes already known and
inevitable. They are complete and final and, their elements
concentric about a point of rest, they are immobile. They are,
moreover, logical to stone and to stone construction, itself a
mode of building congenial to all cultures.

The obelisk, invented in Egypt, was introduced into the tran-
quil company of the Greek and Roman shapes during the Age
of Augustus and received an indisputable accolade in the practice of the Renaissance. The architects of the humanist popes
took it to themselves, delighted by its clarity and simplicity, its
sympathy for stone; and because the obelisk—an arrow aimed
at the sun, its rising contours dissolved into the sky—was in itself
neither primary nor static they endowed it with those qualities
by the way in which they used it. Placed at the center of a *piazza*,
the common possession of the palaces around its rim, the obelisk
became focus and vertical axis in a symmetrical—and immobile—
"reservoir of space." It is in that way that the obelisk in the
Piazza di San Pietro is bracketed between the great elliptical
porticoes of Bernini: a Latin commentary placed, in parentheses,
on a Christian text.

Fontana often placed his obelisks at the end of a street where
they became the "promises of rest" which closed the horizontal
movement of the palaces ranged at either side. Le Nôtre repeated the pattern at least once, using trees for the walls of a
corridor of space in much the same way as trees are used in the
Mall of Washington where the great obelisk, standing at the end
of that wide avenue, arrests the progressions of the trees which
line it and frames with them a vast arena of peace. The harmony
thus effected is not that which might arise from a similarity of
forms but rather that of movements held in equilibrium: the
kind of harmony prefigured in the Egyptian temple where obelisks, used in pairs, are placed on each side of the entrance pylon

in such a way that a horizontal progression, a "going-through," is balanced by their vertical thrusts. The pattern was repeated centuries later in the Gothic cathedrals. The progression of the temple was from light to darkness, from splendor to austerity, from substance to immateriality, and led the spirit through sculptured courts, tower-sentineled gates, and columned halls to sunless sanctuary—a richly developed theme to which the obelisk is, so to speak, ornament and counterpoint. The Christian movement is from monument to ethereal splendor. The great spires stand like archangels guarding the gate to Heaven.

I have mentioned these examples from the historical architectures not to display my learning but to make more clear the principle of formalism and to illustrate the versatility of the classical shapes as elements in form. So widespread and familiar are these shapes both in time and in space that they have come to have in the eyes of that multitude of people to whom beauty is a quality of an object a character that is almost transcendental. They take their place among those screens through which a reality, beyond that revealed by the senses, is made known to us. There is an architectural Platonism which is so nearly religious that one hesitates to comment on it for fear of being ill mannered. This is especially felt when the classical shapes are fused, as they are in the Lincoln Memorial, with a deep popular sentiment.

If in our new architecture we turn away from mass and weight, from stone construction and the monument, from the tried sorcery of the classical symmetries, must we turn also from the simplicity and lucidity of classical shapes? I can draw no other conclusion from the nature of steel and from its brief tradition; nor is there anything in the types of shelter engendered by our dynamic civilization—multiform, intricate, and individual—which promises a return to the static vocabulary of stone. Not that we shall abandon altogether the effects of primary geometry—we shall find excuses to revive these from time to time—yet it must be obvious that the dual nature of architecture, whose forms must rest upon utility and technique not less than upon expression, will prohibit their use in our general practice. The classical shapes had their provenance not less in the laws of masonry than in the laws of the spirit. We must draw new shapes from new technologies and from our new spirit and endow these with new mysteries.

In his famous essay, *Vers une architecture,* Le Corbusier tells us that the primary geometric shapes are essential to beauty in architecture—without explaining how these are possible to our modern complexity of use or to the inexhaustible invention of our machines. The thousand new functions of our buildings, ever more varied and unpredictable, compel an individuality and adaptability of form which could only be compressed into the primary geometric shapes by the most extreme tyrannies of taste and tradition. Steel has set us free to mold our buildings to that infinity of use which, disguise it as we may, is also a secret source of interest and delight; and except where they are imprisone by the regularity of streets or held within the invisible plane. thrown around them by legal restrictions our structures respona to the new—and limitless—adventure of steel. The buildings of our age will assume, are assuming, a complexity of shape not unlike that of Baroque architecture and yet without that sculptural fluidity or that exultant *ecstasy* which gave unity to its energetic rhythms; a complexity which may be also, provided we continue our present speculations into the aesthetics of structure, not unlike the Gothic complexity but without that mist of pinnacle and saint which veils the logical surfaces of the cathedrals. I cannot predict a new principle of form but I should think it strange indeed if, building with steel for a modern use, we were to arrive at the ascetic elegance of the obelisk at Washington.

The young lady from Yale whom I have already quoted reminded me at this point that all beautiful things are simple. That, said I, is a somewhat gratuitous traducement of Helen, Cleopatra, and Juliet. Anyway, said the lady, you will admit that democratic architecture is always simple.

I admit nothing of the kind. In the first place, I doubt if I have seen the democratic virtues, liberty, equality, fraternity, expressed in architecture—unless it be in Cape Cod cottages—and certainly the authorities in this matter are far from agreement. Thomas Jefferson, for example, who may be presumed to know something about democracy, crowned our newborn government with the dome of the Pantheon and, no doubt to assure its immobility, balanced in colonnaded pavilions on either side of it the Senate and the House of Representatives. At the University of Virginia he housed the professors in temples designed for the Olympian gods—a remarkable demonstration surely of racial toleration, but not, I think, of popular sentiment. William Morris, equally an authority, proposed as democratic expression a revived medievalism, having conceived Gothic architecture as an art of craftsmen; and I know an architect in Wisconsin who, in a torrent of exposition, has discovered the very essence of democracy in his own romantic genius. I should not be surprised if our democratic architecture, assuming that we ever have such a thing, will be the most chaotic and perverse of all architectures. It may be indeed that there is a paradox hidden in the expression *democratic architecture.*

I suppose that the matter should be decided by a democratic process, that is to say, by a referendum to the people, and if that were done it is certain that the obelisk would carry the nation by a large plurality. Not, however, the obelisk which stands at the end of the Mall. The obelisk which we would elect president would be that other obelisk which rises amid the undulating meadows of the "Monument Grounds" enfolded by random groves of trees; the picturesque obelisk which—like the spire of Salisbury over its wooded close, like the Jungfrau over the valley of the Grindelwald—offers a corner to the photographer and admires its own reflection in scenic waters as it rises, a white prism, above billowing greenery.

It could be said truthfully that the architect—I suspect that he was a landscape architect—who united the obelisk to the Capitol by the wide Mall created in effect a new Washington Monument. Without moving the obelisk he placed it at the center of a vast garden of formal splendor which, like a stage prepared "in the grand style," lifts this grave actor out of uncomfortable romance and restores to him that dignity of role which he had rehearsed over so many centuries. The obelisk was thus reinstated in the classical tradition. To understand this one has only to revisit the Monument Grounds where the shaft still stands as its author placed it on the slope of a little hill without so much as a grass terrace to tie its mighty geometry to the formless earth.

I mention this formalism of *entourage,* and contrast it with the popular taste in such matters, because that formalism is something very necessary to the classical ideal. Together with weight and mass in structure and lucidity in basic shapes and patterns the symmetry thus exhibited forms one of the three essentials in the long tradition of Greece and Rome.

It was in such a symmetry of setting that the Egyptian kings environed the obelisk at the very source of that tradition. These were not melancholy shafts of gray masonry set casually down in landscapes created by the blind artistry of nature. Quarried from huge monoliths of blood-red granite, their exquisite surfaces worked and polished, their tips of pure gold ablaze with the sun and each of their four faces carved with hieroglyphs of praise and thanksgiving, the first obelisks stood on mighty platforms of huge granite blocks surrounded by peristyled courts made splendid with the magnificent reliefs which set forth royal ceremony and divine beneficence. Thus at the outset there was established a unity of pattern which fused monument and setting; a unity continued through the forums of Rome where the rhythms of basilica and temple reach out into wide areas of organized space, through the gardens and *piazze* of Renaissance Italy, the châteaux of France, and the plan which Major L'Enfant prepared for the City of Washington—the plan which was revised a century later into the formal throne and retinue of an obelisk.

L'Enfant, by the way, would have been horrified by this revision of his gentle vistas. The "Congress Hall" and the "Presidential Palace" were to have been the monuments in his scheme, each set on its separate hill. Each was to have been provided with its separate "prospect," the one westward to the hills of Arlington, the other southward over the long reach of the Potomac, and where these prospects met an equestrian statue was to have confirmed without interrupting the equal and brotherly unison of President and Congress.

Like a great sword held upright in a buried hand the obelisk arrests the progress of that wide vista which L'Enfant would have continued into the western sun. New avenues not anticipated by L'Enfant approach it from all sides; palaces and temples —White House, Capitol, and the Memorials to Jefferson and Lincoln—acknowledge its presidency in their disposition and orientation; tree-lined aisles repeat in their horizontal perspectives its inward-leaning lines; the square waters flatter it with imitation; and around the edges of its wide estate the ranged palaces of government, dressed in the rich liveries of the Renaissance, stand at attention like regiments on parade. Let no one say that the king is naked.

From what element in our civilization rises this dominance and ceremony given to an abstraction? Can we find in our own way of life the sources out of which this synthesis developed— an explanation for so vast and circumstantial a symmetry centered, not as L'Enfant would have centered it on Capitol and White House (active and useful agencies of government) but on a pure essay in form? In our science? in our sense of evolution and of progress? our organic conception of man and society? our democratic politic and behavior? the new perspectives of our machines? In our skeptical philosophies? our ethical religions?

The great architectural ensembles of Ancient Rome, of Medieval France, of Versailles present themselves as products of growth and development. We understand them as rising out of their time, saturations of the spirit of their time. Not so this Cartesian paradise laid out at the foot of the Washington obelisk which comes out of the past to tease us with the vision of a secure system and firm faith forever passed away. We recognize the ancient principles of order, the breadth and dignity, the "unity in variety"; we perceive that the elements which these principles pull into a harmony—the temples, avenues, garden forms—are indeed drawn from the universal arsenals of classicism; but we perceive also that both principle and element have been assembled and arranged, not in response to any urgency in our civilization, but for the sake of a timeless mode of beauty which could be summoned out of the past by the conjurations of a learned architect. That quality, I suppose, is implicit in the term *classical revival.*

The remoteness of this mode of beauty from a present reality is made all the more evident by those fragments of antiquity, pieced together by those who conceived the art of architecture as an archaeological craft, which form the ornaments of its geometric cosmos and surround it, so to speak, like a chorus of ghosts. An avenue from Versailles, a peristyle from the Acropolis, a dome from Rome, a bridge from the Seine: these create for those who recognize them a synthetic atmosphere like that of a museum—as if some Henry Ford had amused himself, and instructed the public, with a collection of architectural curiosities, among them an obelisk proportioned to his resources.

I do not mean that a definite unity is not achieved in the scheme of Washington—in spite of the somewhat formidable challenge offered to harmony by a Greek Lincoln, a Roman Jefferson, and an Egyptian Washington. I mean rather that this unity is one of thought, having its origin, as everyone knows, in the private consciousness (and libraries) of architects and quite apart from the general current and surge of our national life.

There existed late in the nineteenth century a mode of valuation and apprehension among architects which bound together with secret sympathies these temples, palaces, and garden forms. Whatever their provenance they had undergone in the history-haunted mind of the classical revivalist strange transmutations, as if they had been melted there and recoined. The Parthenon, the Pantheon, the Louvre, were domesticated, informed with our own idea of monumental decorum and made to reappear as characters in the American scene. Just as the prophets and kings of the Old Testament became so much at home in the mind of Colonial New England that one might have expected to meet Ezekiel, Hosea, Daniel, or Solomon on any green-and-white common of Maine or Connecticut, so the masterpieces of Athens and Paris were made to reside among the magnificent distances of Washington overlaid with the Puritan thought of our architects. Egypt without mystery, Greece without sensuality, Rome without magnificence, Georgian London without snobbishness; of these we built our surrealist Versailles.

We ought not to despise the fine works created by men who limit their art to such perspectives, but we must recognize that art as one which at its best can express only an esoteric ideal. Neoclassicism is a philosophy, by-product of eighteenth-century enlightenment and taste, well suited to those who, like Jefferson, could deduce a constitution from a self-evident law—like Jefferson who, beginning the construction of Monticello, looked for a design in the pages of Palladio. Neoclassicism represents a return to clarity and elegance and artificiality, as if our civilization, which seeks ever new victory and adventure, the conquered wilderness and the horizons of new mountains, could be decently channeled in a sedate and stately mall leading to an abstraction.

The report of the McMillan Commission—the architects of the Plan of Washington—repeats on nearly every page the word *dignity*. They could not imagine a dignity in architecture apart from the classical tradition. They wanted to revive that tradition not because (as some have said) they were mindful only of academic values or because (as has been said with greater malice) they desired to exhibit in architectural terms the beauty of a capitalistic imperialism. No little plans were made. Their faith in the rightness and authority of the classic forms was deep and they wished to reëstablish these forms in the midst of our uncertainties and confusions in order that by entering into them we might find a new serenity—and dignity. Architecture was to create rather than to illustrate a civilized way of life; and because they did not see architecture through the glass of their time but saw it rather as an encyclopedical art, spanning the centuries, coeval to all times, they saw no reason for clouding its broad surfaces with the unquiet sentiment of modernity. Only that sentiment could have given life to their magnificent and somnambulant patterns.

I did not intend in this chapter a treatise on classical form. I have omitted from my pages many of its most salient elements. I have said nothing, for example, about classical space: the obelisk, fortunately for my readers, does not enclose space. I have not mentioned the classical colonnade: and perhaps the most surprising characteristic of the obelisk is its strange faculty of living in Washington without columns. I have not mentioned sculpture, an art inseparable from classical architecture, nor have I given more than a hint of that wealth of individuality and lyrical grace which that architecture has received from changing cultures, new climates, and the impact of great personalities.

I have tried to bring my readers not a descriptive or critical analysis of classical architecture but rather a review of those tendencies in this architecture which, it seems to me, prevent its use as a language of modernism: its dependence upon a mass and weight inconsistent with our technologies of structure, its basic simplicities of shape which deny the variety and complexity of our buildings, and that abstract and static formalism into which we cannot translate the realism and onrushing temper of our day. Nor did I wish to dissemble a sense of that loss which we shall suffer as we turn inevitably towards an architecture more consonant with our uses and our sentiment.

I could have chosen a target—Grant's Tomb, for example—more vulnerable to my pebbles of criticism than the obelisk, so laureled with popular acclaim. My frailty, my impertinence, and my mortality are patent enough beside the crushing weight of these sheer walls, this long and confident tradition, this mysterious austerity, this moving symbolism; but—as my readers may have guessed—I love the Greek and Roman masterpieces too much to wish to caricature them.

The obelisk is a stubborn antagonist. Like the stone *Commandatore* in Mozart's opera it speaks to me in a voice from another world—and I am no Don Giovanni to ask it to supper. The obelisk is a genie and, like the classical architecture it represents, can assume a hundred formidable aspects. Standing in the Mall, the dying sun at its back, it is now a bishop of the Inquisition, a stern uncontrovertible authority shining like a nimbus behind his mitered head; now it is Goliath, advancing before the glittering ranks of the Philistines, his great spear pricking the floor of Heaven; and now once again it is General Washington, his tall figure dimly seen against the campfires of Valley Forge, his fingers pressed together in prayer.

CHAPTER THREE

the glass of our time

SINCE beauty in architecture consists of a harmony between the individual self and the qualities of buildings
it follows that there could be no building which might not at
some moment be judged beautiful; nor is there any formula,
the self being so varied, uncertain and elusive, by which we
may predetermine the nature of those buildings which fate may
cover with that sudden and evanescent mantle.

It would be useless then to set up standards for the measurement of beauty in buildings; useless even when these measurements relate only to that architectural *form* which among all
the attributes of art most obviously invites measurement and
codification. We might, for example, define good proportion—
assuming that we know what proportions are good—as an element
of beauty in buildings, whereupon a thousand witnesses would
appear to attest the presence of beauty in the most ill-propor-
tioned of structures. Functional fitness as a criterion of excellence
would fare no better even if we could define that fugitive term;
and as for balance, rhythm, economy, good sense, and the hundred other ideals of the academy or the market, these are clearly
all quite as impotent to capture or explain an essence of which
everyone may be separate witness and judge.

In truth all of these definable properties of buildings offer us,
when they exist, satisfactions which are essentially intellectual
in nature. Their mode of apprehension is of course an aesthetic
experience since they are made known to us through vision, but

it does not follow that they form a necessary part of that kind of aesthetic experience which is peculiar to an acquaintance with beauty. They may, and often do, exist side by side with beauty; they may indeed open the door to beauty since they lift us, when we are aware of them, out of our rooted preoccupations with self-interest and security; but beauty does not demand their attendance.

Denman Ross described the artist as one who strives for order and hopes for beauty. I think that his definition sets forth quite perfectly the part played in architecture by the classic traditions of proportion, rhythm, and unity and indeed by all the other principles through which the mind composes and arranges the parts of buildings. These are principles of order—and invitations to beauty. They make possible that experience in which we apprehend buildings, not as utilities and instruments merely, but as objects set in space, and by so doing they bring us that vivid and immediate knowledge without which beauty does not occur. They may also create an emotional state favorable to beauty, not only through the release which they afford from the urgencies of daily life, but through their comforting promises of reconciliation with an unseen longed-for order in the world which environs us. Provided that we do not accept them as code or doctrine or standard of excellence, provided that we do not substitute understanding for experience, there may be many such principles of order which might frame the path to beauty.

It seems to me that a consideration of this relationship of mind and architecture—which is at times a reasoned art—is especially pertinent to modern architecture. A clear statement of this relationship might help to dispel that mist which, perhaps because our new architecture had its genesis in revolt and theory, seems to surround our brief experiments in a contemporary vocabulary of form.

Buildings, considered as media of expression, may embody

both general and endemic ideas. There are themes which appear in all architectures and there are themes which are specific to the Baroque, the Islamic, the Colonial. The first are the persistent substances of architecture and often have for that reason a universal eloquence; the second, having their origins in nationalities, techniques, and the changing nature of cultures, form the more diverse and complex elements of expression which overlie the stem of architecture—and sometimes hide from our view its breadth and universality. These are essential since, except for them, architecture would lack that relevance to the life of an era without which it would remain, like the specimens in a museum, remote from the quickening currents of daily experience. However we may share those sympathies which are common to all humanity we are necessarily cabined by time, place, and circumstance; and architecture, if it is to command our hearts, must repeat her ancient promises in languages peculiar to each epoch in human history.

The human mind is, I suppose, much the same in all eras, being shaped by reactions which are everywhere alike and continuous; but it is subject to wide changes in emphasis. Where experience and knowledge are constantly changing both in range and content such changes are invariably reflected not only in the thought and actions of men and in their institutions but in the things they make. There exists in every epoch a collective mind, a background of general concepts in part inherited and in part formed anew by commerce with the world; a background which is not passive, not a white page merely to receive the imprint of experiences, but alert and active, and which even without the consent of conscience shapes and colors the interests and the aptitudes of each epoch and as surely directs also its ways of seeing and of evaluating whatever is made by man. We see our buildings, so to speak, through the glass of our time, set up for us by that collective mind.

It seems altogether plausible, for example, that the Greek conception of the world as a complete, fixed, and symmetrical system concentric about man should in part at least have determined the humanized geometry of the temple. Since they thought of the universe as an order accessible to the understanding the Greeks could not have found delight in a mystic or obscure architecture, still less in an architecture of realism or of passion. Infatuated with the objective beauty of the visible world, boldly seeking to apprehend nature in nature's terms, the Greeks translated their rational soul into rational philosophies and rational temples.

In the same way the medieval mind is as unmistakably reflected in Gothic architecture. In that youthful poetic world wherein each of its inexhaustible shapes revealed some new aspect of the vast drama of creation and redemption the cathedral had no other purpose than to affirm the reality of the Divine Will. That same passion for belief which directed and illumined scholastic theory and popular legend informed also each detail of an architecture which was also the most universal of architectures. The visible cathedral is the mirror of an invisible cathedral of thought.

So the seventeenth century, which overcame human misery and defeat by spectacle and formal observance, by pomp and incense and high language, which created by an act of the will an illusion stronger than reality, impressed as definitely its thought and its passion upon its scenic architecture. And where else than in the façades of Georgian houses can we read more intimately not manners, customs, and techniques merely but the very spirit, lucid, decorous, and arid, of that engaging period?

A principle so persistent in history must, it would seem, be operative today; and if a new architecture is indeed in process of formation it is probable that at least some of the characteristics of that architecture are being determined not merely by physical and social circumstances such as climate and available materials, the customs of the people, the form of government, the conditions of science and industry, and the perversities of contemporary genius, but also by whatever habits of knowing and of seeing are provoked by the currents of contemporary thought. We have not explained our new architecture when we say that it will be specific to our day—that is to say, conformable to our technologies, adaptable to our uses and our way of life; it will be specific also to whatever may be the pattern of contemporary idea. It will be shaped as inevitably by whatever vision we may form of the structure and movements of the universe, by whatever explanations of human experience we may accept, by whatever hope or despair is ours as we face the unknown and the implications of that which is known.

It will not be denied, for example, that we are living in a world infinitely more varied than any hitherto known to mankind. The worlds known to the Greeks and to the Gothic nations and even to the nineteenth century were narrow in range beside that vast stage which the telescope and the microscope, the dynamo and the radio, have set anew for the human drama; nor does this transformation include merely physical discovery, our enlarged knowledge of the surface of the earth, of the illimitable spaces in which it moves, of the infinities of life beneath its appearances, but also an awareness of the complexities of its social and economic patterns and, even more, of the diversities and subtle movements of that which we call consciousness.

There are those who, dismayed by a Nature so irreverent of human institutions, take refuge in one of those systems of surmise, whether rational or mystical, by which our fathers made their worlds ordered and comprehensible. These will take refuge also in the staid oracular shapes of neoclassic architecture. Others there are who dare to live in a modern world, confronting with a new vision the actualities of our time and place, the genuine culture of our day. These will not turn their faces from that magnificent pageantry to which our new knowledge invites them. Far from denying or disguising that knowledge they will find a positive joy in the very ferment and multiplicity of form in which the life principle is seen to be manifest. Those who are still in search of ultimate truth will still find pleasure in the contemplation of philosophic principle; but where men have, for the time being at least, renounced that search, seeking in man's natural home the materials and methods of his making, there they will find contemplative satisfactions in the forms shaped by the incessant changes of our enlarging environment. We are not so compartmentalized as to admit a wide separation between intellectual and aesthetic ideals; these are, in truth, one and the same; and that artist who is impatient with the recurrent images created by classical authority has arrived at his intuitive creed on the same currents which have carried the scientist, and often the philosopher also, beyond the boundaries of architectural dogma.

I think that this awareness of multiplicity, both in the human and in the nonhuman world, explains in part the development of an architecture which is based, not upon authority or principles of form arrived at through aesthetic speculations, but upon the frank acceptance of the widest individuality in the species of buildings. We are impatient of all codes and precedents and systems of form; we delight in variety and complexity; our architecture is as unprincipled as nature. This exploitation of new materials and techniques—of steel, concrete, plate glass, machine-made installations—could not have so stirred the imagination of our time if this exploitation had not had some forerunner in the general experience. These new shapes of buildings are in their way visualizations of the thought of our time: of a thought never divorced from the advancement of technologies. Technologies are consequences, not causes, of ideas.

If then the column and the arch are disappearing from our current vocabulary of architecture; if portico and Gothic tower, symbol and type of the classical modes of thought, are taking their places among the youthful antiquities of our towns and villages; if, impatient of copybook and formula, we look for individual character in buildings, seeking to establish new relationships of mass and space and line from their specific techniques and multitudinous programs; then it may be that all of this represents, not the confusion of architecture, but an integration of architecture with a new principle of life. The ancient longings remain, continuing beneath our complexities an eternal search for absolute values. When we return to them we shall do so, not to imitate their traditional clothings, but to express them in a living language.

We shall understand this new language more clearly if we consider a second characteristic of the contemporary mind: I mean our ever present awareness of change and growth both in our environment and in ourselves. The multiplicities of the non-human world are themselves conceived as consequences of an incessant change and growth of which we also are consequences. In everything that we undertake we are reminded of that long chain of evolution to which our least significant act seems bound. In all that we build, whether for ourselves or for the future, we accept as certainties the factors of movement and unpredictable event.

Locke compared the world to a watch. The Maker had fashioned it, complete and perfect, and having wound it up left it to continue forever its nicely calculated movements. The precise planets should proceed forever in their majestic revolutions and on earth the life of man should admit an ebb and flow as definite and as rhythmical. The metaphor was characteristic of eighteenth-century thought, sure of some reasonable and mind-comforting order beneath the unstable appearances of the world.

Our experience admits no such rationalization. Not the heavens only where suns and systems forever form and dissolve; not the visible surface of the earth merely in whose ferment life assumes ever new transformations; but in human societies as well there is constancy neither in outward aspect nor in knowable principle. The repeated triumphs of our invention transform our most daring imaginings into sudden realities; the dimensions of our universe and of our experience change almost daily; and the foundations of belief and of confirmed habit which sustain our institutions must be rebuilt after crises ever accelerated in their recurrences. We are borne forward on a fierce unceasing current for which we find no reasonable explanation but to which we give ourselves without fear, being confident of its grandeur and the ever increasing splendor of its pageantry.

Our imaginations outrun even the rapid pace of our expanding experience and are constantly building for us a wider universe. Only yesterday we lifted our first airplane into the sky; instantly the oceans and the deserts are made swift thoroughfares; and tomorrow armies will be air-borne across the width of continents. Yesterday we spoke from house to house, from city to city; then the voices of the world came to us at the touch of a button; tomorrow we shall be present at the distant conferences in which the crises of the world are resolved. We learned in our laboratories to break apart the atom; today we find in our hand the power to shatter the cities of the earth. In California a great silver eye looks out beyond the edges of space to show us a thousand new suns whose paths we shall chart tomorrow.

Men who live in such a world cannot keep their eyes upon the past. Their habit of seeing no less than their habit of thought will be biased by an acceptance of movement and hazard: of movement and hazard away from that which is fixed, certain, and finished to that which is on its way. They will be solicitous of promises in things seen. Not the full and perfect flowers of the ancient cultures but rather the new buds of our own culture in which growth is implicit will arrest them; they will recognize with delight whatever is unfolding and becoming.

Those buildings which capture us today have in them an element of expectancy. They exist not in space merely but in time. They are going somewhere. Our interest follows the origins and development of new forms, the exploitation of new techniques and materials, and adaptations to new purposes. We look for and approve the experimental process, the procedure by trial and error, and even when our buildings reaffirm an ancient principle they must assure us that it, too, is directed towards discovery. Where the end is new experience we condone the awkwardness of the first essays; we are as ready to applaud a prediction as an accomplishment. There is no *event* in a plaster Parthenon.

The most characteristic motives of contemporary architecture may be explained as a search for the forms which contain the future. Those walls built of glass, the consequence of new industrial processes, capture us less by their crystalline grace and splendor than by that which they promise us. They are windows opening into the coming world. Like the architects of the fifteenth century who built whole cathedrals of glass we are intoxicated by the promise of glass—as if a new color had suddenly been laid upon the palette of a painter. That could not have happened if we had not been, perhaps subconsciously, in search of just such an escape as that which is in the nature of the glass wall: the escape from that idea of permanence and conviction which is in the solid wall of masonry, from that *monument* which existed not in our architecture only but in our thought. The movement of our mind was already entrained towards an architecture which we felt, however vaguely, should be etherialized and not massive.

If this is true, then it explains in part the efforts of architects to make of space—of that new space which is enclosed by thin membranes hung on metal frames—an important medium of their art. Far from dismay at the loss of the monumental theme we are only too eager to exploit this inviting quality of space, so hospitable to new idea. Nor was it through caprice that architects began to imitate the structural effects developed in steamships, but rather because the ship designer, having never lived in the shadow of the monument, developed by a process unretarded by the academy a free and spontaneous character in his metallic enframements. That the architect, however reluctantly, recognized in steel and in space enclosed by steel a new province, that having recognized it he entered into it with delight, that he forged from that unprecedented technology a new arsenal of formal elements is, I think, persuasive evidence that architecture, whatever may be its other and conflicting movements, accompanies science in its beautiful and forward march.

If I may continue my analogy I should like to suggest still a third way in which our modes of thought influence our judgments of architecture. We think of the world not only as multifarious in nature and in a state of flux but also as a world which is an organic world; or, if not itself organic then made up of a large number of organisms. We conceive all things as belonging to a system, an organized whole, and as being each, according to the principle of its being, made up of correlated and coöperating parts. The infinite forms which life assumes on our planet constantly change and develop but they do so, not by accretion or dismemberment, but through alterations in their structures.

Of all the consequence of the theory of evolution none has been more fateful than the belief that man himself is a product and a part of nature, that he is himself the consequence of organic changes, a biological creature in structure and habit, in ideals and moralities and social relationships. This conception of man has in our time permeated every phase of human thought.

It conditions every valuation, translating into biological terms every problem of ethics and politics, of social order and economics. Unless there is indeed a realm of art alien to that of nature it would seem inevitable that this awareness of man's intimate identity with the nonhuman world should temper also our judgments of architecture.

We have in this era a very special way of looking at buildings. Our habit of vision includes not their outward aspects only but the *organisms* which these shelter and disguise: their skeletons, whether wood, stone, or steel, the ordering and shapes of the spaces within them, the pressures and resistances of the life that flows through them, and even the mechanical veins that energize them with electricity, heat, and water. All of these may enter into our apprehension of a building and become as essential to our notion of its form as are the arrangements of its outer shapes, the disposition of its planes, the color, textures, and silhouettes of its enclosing walls. Buildings may exist in our consciousness as things more akin to biological creatures than to inert objects raised stone above stone and submissive to the laws of physics. We think of them, not as appearances formalized, but rather as energies interacting and arrested.

Thus our modern house is known to us not as a formal pattern or as a symbol—although it may be both of these—but as an apparatus of wood and glass and brick fitted to our daily use. We know the nature of these materials, massive, cellular, brittle, transparent; we know the ways they are put together and the ways they react upon one another; we know the ways in which they enclose and fashion our rooms and our furnishings. We perceive also that these physical and tangible elements of our house are parts of a wider pattern, that they have assumed their shapes and taken their places in response to the requirements of a way of life to which they are frame and instrument; they are related organically to our lives.

Like the modern house a skyscraper may be thought of as having a character analogous to that of a live creature. The architects of the first skyscrapers, aghast at the monotonous interiors, the endless repetition of uniform cells, strove by every means to dissemble the facts of their structures; any masquerade seemed permissible rather than that such dreary reiteration should be confessed. The idea of organic order in architecture had gained a wide currency before we were able to see these cathedral towers and campaniles, these temples piled on temples, as the aesthetic aberrations that they are. That the public has at last recognized the excellence of those skyscrapers in which the special energies of that difficult contraption have been exploited is a striking evidence of the changing sovereignty of contemporary idea in the art of architecture.

This tendency to apprehend an organic character in buildings, which had its origin in our conception of the nonhuman world, is closely associated with still another habit of thought and of vision characteristic of our time—the fourth, and last, which I shall consider in this chapter. The changes which take place in our buildings as these conform more and more to our new needs and desires take place on a field far wider than architecture. Our modern buildings exhibit in their forms a wider event and interest than the event and interest comprised within their walls; they hold before us, as in a mirror, our growing conception of human society itself as a society having an organic character.

We are each day more conscious of a participation in great tides of human behavior. We are aware with increasing clarity of the collective destiny which we share on earth: of lives to be lived, of happiness to be attained, as parts of a social whole. It is certain that we shall include the arts, since these are at once cause and consequence of civilized living, among the significant factors in that general life; and we may expect architecture, so long torn from its setting at the heart of society will reassume its ancient role as interpreter of the communal spirit. And even if we despair of an architecture thus restored to dignity we must at least recognize in our judgments of architecture a social relevance each day more evident. We admire with lessening fervor private comfort, self-expression, and the splendor of individuals; and even as the medieval burgher turned to his cathedral and the Greek citizen to his temple so we turn to programs of construction which are collectively undertaken, finding in these the valuations and intentions which open a path to beauty. Even in our appraisals of purely formal qualities we are apt to admit a prejudice to those enterprises which lift and sustain the happiness of populations.

That prejudice is not inconsistent with a prejudice for variety and individuality of character in buildings. Social purpose and conformity do not imply generalized form or absolute law; on the contrary the range of architecture is diversified and enriched by wider companionships and collective enterprise. Architecture, which gains its authority from a free accommodation to the necessities, habits, and feelings of those whom it shelters, aggravates rather than diminishes its store of patterns in the service of our complex society. That society is not guided by academic usage or precedent; nor are there any standardizations prescriptive to men in association.

Every architect will remember the plan for the rebuilding of Paris offered by Le Corbusier. With a ruthlessness somewhat excessively heroic Le Corbusier proposed to destroy a wide section of that crumbling city in order to make room for the good life of the future. I do not suggest that such a city is possible—still less that there is a race of men fit to live in it—but I think it significant that the Utopias of architects should be thus dominated by a concern for social regeneration. That concern is evident in all the evolving shapes of our new architecture, in our new schools and hospitals, in housing projects and garden cities, in our immense parks and widely scattered playgrounds; nor should I omit from the category of architecture the mighty utilitarian projects of our day undertaken in the public interest, the colossal bridges, harbors, and irrigation projects, nor fail to claim these as further proof of new vision and appraisement.

The intellectual forces continue on these new fields their ancient battle with material ills not from compassion merely, not from a love of order merely, but in the daring faith that by an alteration of our environment our human nature, itself created by environment, may admit a further alteration. No doubt our cities, biological in origin, will remain, like the hives of bees, submissive to biological law; but they will also be malleable to the reshapings of science and to the ministry of the arts which have supplemented and illumined science. Therefore I do not despair of planned cities; by which term I mean cities molded by that communal intelligence which seeks through a recognition of the relation of man and society to bend natural law to human betterment. I am sure that our architecture will alter and renew itself with a constant reference to the promise-crammed art of city planning.

I have heard modern architecture defined as an architecture of flat roofs, unshadowed walls, and plate glass: as a new *style* made up of new technologies, the new shapes which these engender, and newly coined theories of design. This is, I think, a superficial definition which takes into account only the surface phenomena of architecture. No one will deny that buildings are in one sense modern when they embody modern methods in planning and construction and are adapted to modern use; but there is a deeper meaning of the word modern which has escaped us if we are unaware of that need for a new expression, that desire to realize our present thought in these tangible patterns, that *sentiment for modernity*, which exists below these the practical components of our art and to which technologies, patterns, and precedents are—often subconsciously—materials and media. The master architect of our era is that sentiment for modernity: I mean that understanding and acceptance of the world which science has created for us, that positive delight and participation in its multiplicity, its splendor, and its unfolding. I think that that sentiment will pervade and illumine our cities, no less than our buildings.

Before the collective and anonymous mind of our era our architects lay their inventions and their theories. Some of these, congenial to that mind, are accepted and developed; others are at once rejected; others are carried forward for a short distance on the stream of our consciousness and then forgotten. Modern architecture is not invention although it is more fecund of idea than any which has preceded it; modern architecture is not caprice although it is capable of fantasy and absurdity; modern architecture is not genius although it is not without its heroes and its prophets. Modern architecture is a crystallization of modern thought and feeling.

We may be sure that our civilization, which is one of majesty and great breadth, will ultimately make itself known in a new principle of architectural order. It is probable that that order will be one which will admit the widest range of functional and evolving shapes, which will acknowledge the organic nature of all buildings—being wedded to a technological grandeur surpassing all previous architectures—and which will, above all, proclaim the social nature of an art made inseparable from the collective welfare of mankind. There will be many who will find that principle beautiful.

CHAPTER FOUR

the last of the romans

EVER since Thomas Jefferson, in 1785, sent from France his model of the *Maison Carrée*, we have been trying to create an American architecture by the imitation of European master-pieces. Today, after ten thousand experiments, the futility of this process is not yet amply demonstrated; one more effort was needed, it appears, if only to prove the hardiness of the neo-classic thesis. The National Gallery of Art combines again the portico of the Temple of Diana and the dome of the Pantheon.

Winckelmann, who invented the Greeks, invented also the idea of a beauty untouched by time and place. When he had abstracted from the lush Apollo Belvedere and the rounded Niobe that world of "noble simplicity and tempered wisdom" which he called antiquity, architects, imitating this imitator of imitations, abstracted from the gorgeous Parthenon their white and absolute temples—and made these the pure symbols of the most turbulent and scandalous of nations. The theory of a universal architecture, of an ideal beauty composed of column, arch, and dome, a beauty realized once for all by the Greeks and Romans, was thus offered to the triumphant rationalism of our young republic. Jefferson, the American exponent of France, a builder of constitutions, as ready to follow up his deductions in art as in politics, found no difficulty in accepting an architecture which could be proved to be beautiful by the syllogisms of authorities. An international style, based upon the study of the antique—generalized, documented, unweighted by reality, the work of aesthetes rather than of builders—became the *American style*.

Since Jefferson's day the idea has undergone periodic reconstructions. Like the Greeks of Winckelmann it preserves in spite of the assaults of common sense an eternal youth. Each generation returns to it in one form or another. Beauty in architecture is perennially reëstablished as a harmony of absolute forms accessible to the intelligence and embodied in the Roman masterpieces. No relation to time or place is necessary, no reference to humanity in forms thus emptied of purpose. The columns which clothe with dignity the home of the Supreme Court will do quite as well for the Archives Building or the Temple of the Scottish Rite; the dome of the Pantheon is as serviceable for a university library, a railroad station, or the pillared churches of the Christian Scientists. These suffer differences in arrangement, not in response to use or structure, but in accordance rather with the rules of a game intelligible only to the players—the peculiar solace of architects in a world too uncomfortably transformed by the cumulated successes of science.

I can understand the seduction which such a theology of architecture exercises over the minds of those prepared for it by that discipline in irrelevancies which, until recently, went by the name of architectural education; but I have never been able to explain its hold upon the imaginations of the rich and the great of our day. That men who have participated as leaders in the rise of American industry, who have shared its magnificent upward progress, its ceaseless and inexhaustible ferment, should turn for expression to the pale temples of an imaginary Greece is, I think, one of the strangest phenomena in the psychology of idealism. I should suppose—unless indeed, as some believe, our ideals are necessarily our complementary opposites—that such men more than any others would wish (to borrow a phrase from the *Poetics*) to attain and make evident in art that form towards

which their own age—the age they have created—is moving. Is it
not reasonable to assume that when after a lifetime of effort
and success they felt at length the need of a monument, they
would wish to continue into whatever constructed forms they
might essay at least some aspect of that world of which their
own lives had formed so plenary a part? I can guess at the mind
of Jefferson, "violently smitten with the Hotel de Salm," to whom
the temple was both discovery and adventure, but I cannot explain the complacency of the Virginia legislators, willing to compress their explosive energies in that tight little box which the
American ambassador sent them from Paris. I think that I can
catch some hint at least of the mind of McKim and share the
delight which must have been his when he arranged the peristyled terminal of the Pennsylvania Railroad; but the mind of
the Pennsylvania Railroad is beyond my reach. The railroad,
I think, could have had no secret joy in neoclassic abstractions,
still less in pale translations of the garish vaults of Caracalla.
Was it prompted, then, by modesty or shame thus to cover its
iron bones with the debris of an ancient civilization? Or by a
clandestine pleasure in the vision of those unhappy beings who
for generations must carry their baggage across those vast unnecessary vistas? And that princely person who crushed the
Harvard Yard with the prodigious peristyle and steps of her
library: what was there in his life so apposite to the Corinthian
mode that he should wish to leave unexpressed, not himself
merely, but that America of which he was so characteristic and
notable a part?

Of all types of buildings the museum of fine arts has offered
the most favorable field for this pious collaboration of wealth
and power with the priesthood of the Roman tradition. The
museum, born in a palace, nevertheless built its first homes—
in Munich, Berlin, London—out of the pages of antiquarians;
and from that day to this its blank walls, its static functions,

its learned and leisured attributes have invited the attention of classicists, impatient even of windows. We know, for example, with what intransigeance these have exercised their art upon the Metropolitan Museum of New York: the preface of mighty steps, arches, and columns; the terror-inspiring vestibule; and then the interminable stairway which, I am sure, leads like those of the Mayan and Cambodian temples to some gruesome sacrificial platform. The architect of the Brooklyn Museum wept when the director, insensitive to the dignity of exterior steps, removed these and admitted the public directly to his exhibits; and Philadelphia, which always thinks in superlatives, has pedestaled its museum upon a mountain at the base of which not one but three mighty flights challenge the knees of the hardy visitor, his soul being kindled by as many porticoes.

Forty granite steps of majestic width lead up from the Mall to the main entrance of the National Gallery of Art. They are placed there, not to be used, but to be admired. They are there in accordance with the rules of the game "for their own sake." A mighty portico crowns these steps: that too exists for its own sake, as does also the stupendous doorway, disdainful of human ants. For their own sake the great *vérde* columns of the central rotunda appear to sustain the weight of an angle-iron Pantheon and sumptuously cage the blithe little Mercury of Giovanni da Bologna. For their own sake were built the huge vaults, plaster on metal lathe, covering the nave-like corridors which lead right and left to the girder-supported gardens which nurture, not trees, but columns.

The columns, for their own sake, support nothing. Across the wide spaces which separate art and reality a sacred forest invites at every step the astonishment of the visitor, seducing him with expense and weight, crushing him under its firm assertion of authority. All of which adds nothing of delight or value to the objects exhibited: nothing, that is to say, which could not have been added simply, directly, unpretentiously, at one fourth of the cost.

What is a museum? Surely not an opportunity merely for the virtuosity of architects. A box, then, for the display of curiosities and susceptible therefore of rich encrustations? A theater built for our entertainment and therefore congenial to the flattery of bronze and marble? Perhaps an apparatus of the schoolmasters, to be made less tedious by a coating of gilt? Those who think thus have never known a museum or felt the genuine magic that a museum may enfold. What is a museum? An invitation to a voyage; a window opening on the music of other times and of other spirits; a *means* always, never an *end*. The beauty conserved and guarded in the National Gallery of Art is made less, not more, accessible by this clamorous prelude; nor does the high language of neoclassicism assist in any way the quiet happiness to which that beauty entreats us.

Museums of art, although addressed as a rule to the use of other generations no less than to our own, are yet serviceable buildings. The source of whatever dignity they may attain is service, the inevitable source of all dignity in architecture. I mean, of course, not practical service merely—although that is included —but also whatever service architecture may render the spirit of man. I know of no one who would approve a stark utilitarian building on the Washington Mall; still less an undistinguished building for the collections of the National Gallery of Art. But where has beauty ever been discovered in an architecture which was not a social form, grown out of social needs? It is that which the temple itself teaches us and which Greece and Rome would teach if we could but see them clearly. This temple reaffirms that lesson even now when it is torn from its setting and made the frontispiece to a museum gallery. If we were not atrophied to the meanings of form we could not bear the dissonance so clearly proclaimed in these opposed shapes.

The trouble is that we are thus atrophied. Because we have been taught that architecture is something embedded in history, that it is something precious, imported, and remote, this art which might illumine our lives does not even impinge upon them. In this mist of make-believe we have never experienced architecture. We have never learned to discover the genuine power inherent in useful space and the energies of constructed shapes, or to know that form—which is indeed the syntax of architecture—must nevertheless be developed from, not added on, to these.

Not the tradition of the temple codified in his books, but those facilities in which function is fulfilled—that is to say, the exhibition galleries—should have been the first concern of the architect of this building. That these should be clear, luminous, and peaceful enclosures, arranged in a rational order easily apprehended, is a principle which ought not to have needed a demonstration; nor should it have been necessary to remind the architect that these enclosures, welded into an organized crystal of space, unified by harmonious shapings and rhythmic intervals, by developing and unfolding sequences, should form the heart of his pattern. Yet we have in the exhibition rooms of the National Gallery neither order nor sequence other than the primitive order of the *enfilade*. The areas left over at the edges of the grandiose center are partitioned into *salles carrées* as if these were slices cut from a cake. Casual in the extreme is their relationship to the pomp and circumstance which they surround.

The expression of purpose is as little evident on the exterior as on the interior. Where no form exists in the interior it is scarcely possible to establish that conformity of outward aspect and inward purpose which is the first essential of a genuine architecture. Nevertheless, if the long wings had expressed even the rabbit warren that is inside them, they would have been more evocative than in their present role as the awkward acces-

sories of a temple. They would have then our respect if only by
a blunt truthfulness: all the more so if the steel framework could
have been set free from the oppression of the heavy masonry
forms which deny the true nature of its lithe energies. I think
that an architect must be somewhat naïve who supposes that the
public will find in massive windowless walls of marble an expression of the conserving and guarding function of a museum.
The public is not so innocent as to have failed to guess at the
steel fabric which these mask or to know that the building will
endure only so long as this endures. And those heavy interior
partitions which appear to support arches of such a prodigious
width and weight: that visitor is incurious indeed who is not
aware of the hollow pipes and conduits with which these are
stuffed. What is there so shameful about steel? Or about those
felicitous mechanisms threaded through this structure which
bring to every corner clean air, even temperature, security from
moisture and accident? Are not these the true conservators and
guardians? I understood the pride of the engineer who showed
me in the attic the superb structure of his roofs and in the basement the miracles of his machines, and I marveled that an architect could ignore elements of expression so evocative. By this
I do not mean, of course, that pipes and conduits should be
everywhere visible, but only that their presence should be confessed—that the fabric of our building should be illumined by
the wonder of our mechanical progress. But there is no precedent for that, I suppose, in the Parthenon.

It is said that we are bound to this dissimulation by the conditions of our site. There is a "prevailing style" in Washington to
which architecture is chained; our fathers cast the expanding
organism of the government in this iron mold and that mold must
not be shattered. What then is the prevailing style? Two thousand years separate the Egyptian monument of Washington from
the Doric temple of Lincoln; and seven hundred years more lie

between Lincoln and the imperial symbol which quaintly canopies Thomas Jefferson; and a span of another sixteen hundred
years lies between Jefferson and the Georgian White House.
There are nine different styles of architecture in the Triangle;
nineteen face the Mall from the Folger Library to the heights
of Arlington; and the National Gallery itself is compounded of
at least three.

Nor is the character of this building imposed upon us, as is so
often said, by any sanction discoverable in the magnanimous plan
of L'Enfant. The garden forms of L'Enfant—a Mall surrounded
by planted areas—were never intended to be crowded with structures so vast as to defeat a parklike quality in the ensemble; nor
did his scheme admit any building so grandiose as to challenge
the supremacy of the Capitol. Garden and city were to be parts
of a single design; and no greater reproach can be made to the
National Gallery of Art than the evident fact that not only does
it shatter the balance and scale proposed by L'Enfant but also
that it blocks forever one of the avenues which might have assisted the unity of the central garden form and the vaster dimensions of the growing city.

A cold invigorating wind is blowing these days over our national architecture. A new temper, impatient of make-believe,
of professional hocus-pocus, of an art existing "for its own sake,"
is everywhere felt. I find, I hope not entirely as a consequence
of wishful thinking, some hints of a coming change in the buildings built for the use of our government; and that change is foreshadowed by our judgments of buildings already built. People
seem to admire less fervently such aberrations as the Archives
Building; a strange silence even now surrounds the Jefferson
Memorial. Architectures are born sometimes from that concord
of spiritual experience which is engendered by crises faced and
collectively overcome. Surely the time cannot be far distant
when we shall find the means to open this city of Washington,

symbol and temple of the nation, to the rekindled soul of America.

Yesterday, when I passed the mighty steps of the National Gallery of Art, I thought that I could discern over its doorway the inscription, dim but growing slowly distinct: ULTIMUS ROMANORUM.

CHAPTER FIVE

the gothick universitie

IN London, in the year of our Lord one thousand eight hundred and thirty-six, a decorative designer, whose reputation was meager and by no means impeccable, published a book of engravings which was destined to people with antique spires a thousand cities of England and America. In that year, in that slender bitter volume which he called *Contrasts*,* Augustus Welby Northmore Pugin transformed Gothic architecture from a romantic plaything into a flaming creed.

The acid power of pictures to kindle the heart has seldom been more urgently demonstrated. A crabbed little tract, whose dialectic was chiefly that of ingenuous drawings, converted instantly both the Roman and the Anglican communions. The Roman Church, Who

> . . . never knew
> Till Mr. Pugin taught Her
> That orthodoxy had to do
> At all with bricks and mortar,

was now to believe that Gothic architecture (which had never appeared on the banks of the Tiber) was indeed Christian architecture; and as for the Anglican Church, had she not just remembered after a century of Enlightenment, that she too was Catholic? Gothic architecture, which had once clothed her ancient

---

* . . . or a parallel between the noble edifices of the middle ages and corresponding buildings of the present day, shewing the present decay of taste.

dogma with splendor and warmth and eager color, became from that moment the robe of her happy repentance.

This sudden conversion, this impetuous rediscovery of the "Christian centuries," had been prepared for, to be sure, by a clamor outside the vestry walls which after a hundred years had reached a crescendo too strident to be ignored even by this, the most conservative of institutions. The Church had resisted that clamor stoutly. She was indeed the last to share the Gothic mood (as she will be the last, no doubt, to escape it) and her precipitant surrender is by no means the measure of her intransigeance.

The first Gothicists were the poets. Milton struck the opening chord, at once solemn and introspective, that was to awaken more than one echo, not wholly Augustan, at the court of Queen Anne—

> In these lone walls . . .
> These moss-grown domes with spiry turrets crowned,
> Where awful arches make a noonday night
> And the dim windows shed a solemn light.

From that time on every poet found in the medieval treasury precisely that which he sought there: Wordsworth, sweet lessons of simplicity and peace; Keats, rich harmonies of sensual delight; Coleridge, transcendent unities of experience and intuition; and each and all an escape from that "extinct world, deserted of God" into which they had been condemned by an outrageous Fate to live. The picture makers and story makers, the gardeners with their "venerable ruins" and the philosophers with their "natural men," joined the growing chorus, to which the architect acceded almost the last of all. And if at length the architect did accede it was not through disloyalty to his Italian master; it was because his client, being more the poet's client than his own, insisted upon "crenelated and melancholy towers" and because the rulers of England, rebuilding the House of Parliament, specified the "grandeur and pride" of an Elizabethan composition. After that the Church, which had held out bravely for the arid, uncomfortable, and elegant architecture of the Georges, yielded; Gothic architecture was to be, not sentimental merely, not picturesque and natural merely, nor yet merely sublime—but Christian.

We perceive now that this conversion of the Church to Gothic architecture was the final and critical episode in a prolonged struggle to escape from a world made too actual to be endured. We see now with what pathetic eagerness men had for a hundred years grasped at that mirage which their romancers had conjured from the medieval legends, from moldering castle towers, and from the traceried tombs that lined the abbey walls. A far-off remembered radiance had grown slowly brighter until it filled the northern sky with the clear majestic colors of chivalry, adventure, and faith, and in the shadows that oppressed a disillusioned England—England after Waterloo, the England of Bentham, the brutal stupid England that made Shelley shriek with indignation—men looked up from their ledgers to catch, with a growing fascination, the shimmer and stir of antique pageantry, the gleam and movement of Catholic pomp, the glory of knightly war and the pathos of great renowns—of Arthur and Tristram, of Abelard and Jeanne d'Arc—forever passed away. Gradually the colors and the movements assumed a unity. Gradually the fragments evoked by written word, by music, by picture, and by architecture crystallized into a pattern. In the midst of their disordered and futile world men beheld at length a design for life which rose above them in clean firm lines like those of a cathedral—a nobly imagined hierarchy of beings human, angelic, and divine ascending in well-ordered gradation from peasant and citizen, vassal, knight, and king, through priest and abbot and pope, to a perfect culmination at the feet of God.

Into this *summa* the Church must inevitably enter. In this dream world her sovereignty was manifest, and the belief that the glorious vision evoked from the past might by an act of faith be made real became at length too compelling to be longer resisted. The magnificent idea could be lived again, not merely commented upon, the pattern of scientific rationality overcome by simple processes of make-believe. Let us invite the audience to cross the footlights, to enact with us the lofty comedy whose fulfillment it desires, and if high language, costume, and a noble setting are needed for that ardent illusioning, clearly it is for the Church to supply them. Henceforth her mission was undebatable: to take the Middle Ages out of the hands of romancers, and to make it a part of her ancient, indissoluble creed; to lead the world back to Gothic architecture. The vast fabric of routine and casuistry, of artifice and decorum, which had long been the support of Georgian architecture, undermined by a slow insistent infiltration of romance, now crashed to the ground. The irony of Pugin was the push needed to effect that irrevocable collapse.

Architecture tells us not what men were at any period of history, but what they dreamed. Architecture cannot be explained by social and political circumstance; it is made out of the longings and the starvations which the soul has endured. Desire, and imagination, have a curious way of making men accept as beautiful the shapes which are merely mean to our dispassionate eyes. It is only so that we can account for Victorian Gothic. By the aid of these strange symbols copied from the relics of a dead civilization our grandfathers did actually lift themselves out of their time, they did actually enter that vague preposterous world which they believed to be medieval.

On plate eight of that naïve explosive book called *Contrasts* there are pictured two gateways, each an entrance to a university. To the left is drawn that "noble Roman arch" which Sir Robert Smirke, architect, had just completed as a frontispiece to the new King's College in London; to the right is drawn the ogived archway which leads, amid an effulgence of traceries and crocketings, into the ancient cloister of "Christ College," Oxford. Look upon this picture—and on this. To the left is the rational principle expressed in abstract geometry: cold intellect impotent before the problems of the soul. To the right is the Catholic principle expressed in the dynamic energy of flowing and dissolving forms and sumptuous ornament: the aspiring spirit that ennobles the hearts of men. The architecture of reason—the architecture of faith.

A seasoning of malice gives point to this sermon in stones. It was not the judicial temper surely that framed the "noble Roman arch" with the meanest of mean shops, peopled it with the joyless, ridiculous costumes of the 1830's, and sentineled the sidewalk in front of it with cast-iron gas lights which, being "functional expressions of modern processes and materials" could be proved, by a process of rational deduction, to be supremely beautiful. It was not the judicial temper that evoked beyond the Gothic arch the sweet escape of the antique cloister, its quietude and peace, and the grave beautiful rites of the ancient Church whose robed and ordered ministers, at once joyous and devout, carry in solemn procession the symbols of her ancient tradition. The moral is laid on with a trowel: "Cheap knowledge, lectures mechanized . . . Professor Gab on the Superiority of the People . . ." We are to understand that it is not only Georgian architecture that is pilloried but the social order in which such an architecture is possible. We are shown the way of escape from an unendurable scheme of things—from a dull and complacent civilization, hospitable only to ideas, deaf to human anguish. From this the way out lies—through the Gothic gateway.

It is not by accident that this gate leads into a university. It was the university that created the medieval order—or, at any rate, gave it significance; the university therefore should be itself the first symbol of its recovery. The university should purge itself back to Christianity by means of medieval structure and ornament.

It was thus that the Gothick Universitie took shape in the Victorian mind: the university of escape. The familiar concrete world might not enter here, where faith and not science is the important fact in life. It was to be a picturesque university, with a tangle of turret and crocket and piled-up battlement; a romantic university, fraught with the spell of ancient happenings and the thronging ghosts of quaint personages; a natural university, ignorant of the staid rules of Vitruvius; but most of all, a Christian university, which should provoke once more the sanctity and power of that vast tradition by the simple process of actualizing its externals, by raising "in lofty pillars and the branching roof self-poised" a simulacrum of the forms in which a departed spirit had once expressed itself.

The quest was beset with infinite difficulties not apparent at its inauguration. The spirit of ancient Cambridge was coy, it seems, even to the wooing of so fervent a devotee as Sir Gilbert Scott; and no angel appeared at Oxford even when John Ruskin with his own hands shaped a clustered pillar of the New Museum. The "restorations" of these moldered quadrangles served only to give them a questionable authenticity. Nor have we on this side of the Atlantic, where there has developed a science of counterfeiting not less complete than that of Vignola, been wholly successful in creating new Oxfords. But we have at least struggled manfully. An avalanche of documents, photographs, measurements, and exhortations has overcome the ineptness which spiked with the late Gore and Vanderbilt Halls the yards of Harvard and Yale, a perfect Magdalen Tower now rises a hundred paces from the Midway Plaisance, and the eleventh-century battlements of West Point, bristling with machine guns, rise like those of Mont St. Michel to a climax splendidly consistent. Ye

spirit of Ye Olden Tyme could not escape so apt an entangle-
ment as that spread around the sweet white temples of Princeton
should she yield for a moment to their dulcet seductions.

In the year one thousand eight hundred and ninety-seven, a
new group of university buildings was proposed for the Island
of Manhattan. If in that year Charles Follen McKim, architect,
had not possessed his unequaled powers of persuasion and if,
as might well have happened, Rome had not yet taken command
of his imagination, this island should now be crowned with the
greatest of Gothick Universities.

Shall we try to imagine what might now be the aspect of that
narrowly averted Columbia?

With walls and towers the Rock of Morningside would be
girdled round. In a majestic march (for McKim's was no mean
scale) their mighty machicolations should frown over the Hudson's heaving tide and across the wide plain of Harlem. Above
this solid cincture, like the lances of knights assembled for a
tourney, should rise two score of delicate spires, fretted with
broken shadows, trembling with tumultuous cataracts of light.
In that gallant company the Riverside Church and the Cathedral
of St. John the Divine should find themselves unexpectedly at
home (may I be present at their jousting!) and the fragile cloisters of the Union Theological Seminary should find a sudden
quietude denied by auto and subway viaduct.

In the shadows of these spires and strongly contained within
the heavy *enceinte* a hundred narrow uneven streets should
tumble about over the surface of the huge rock, leading by devious routes and dark from the portcullised gates to the vast bulk
of the square library which, shining with a thousand heralded
panes, spiked with great finialed turrets, and filled with ancient
books "more aromatic than stores of spice," should dominate the
crest of the citadel. Between these streets, in the dense spaces
packed with a motley of hostels, taverns, shops, warerooms and

houses of every kind—from the great houses of the Jewry, tall and nobly built, to the mean squalor of the Court of Miracles—there should be strewn the green square cloisters of the fifty colleges, gracefully arcaded with ribbed and traceried bays and guarded by the sheer buttressed walls of lecture halls, of chapels and refectories, of the latticed casements of the dons.

Throughout these streets and cloisters (for we should not do this thing by halves) there should move perpetually a costumed humanity, fitted to the architecture. The fifty thousand students should wear their bottle-green cloaks fur-trimmed, with great length of sleeve, their shoes tippeted in cerise and blue, their waists girdled with wide enameled belts from which thick knives should be pendanted; and, disdaining the tonsure, they should wear their hair long and curled, their beards fiercely pointed. The scarlet-capped doctor, whose sleeveless coat is lined with miniver; the master, green-tabarded and yellow-stockinged, wearing the blood-red gown which Puritan austerity had not yet turned black; the gold-laced beadles, the sober priests and the plumed soldier should add a rich variety to the busy streets to which all manner of men accessory to a university— the stewards, the shopkeepers, the servants, and the peddlers— should form an audience. The President, preceded by his eight archers in their purple liveries and followed by his mace-bearer, his *chambrier*, his dozen pursuivants, should twice each day survey his wide emperies; as should also the deans, to each of whom three halberdiers, in the velvet of Valencia, should be assigned. The students, encountering them, should pull their hoods over their eyes and tuck their two thumbs into their belts, as etiquette prescribes.

Nor should there be wanting those lesser buildings and persons needed to complete our picture. There should be no lack of gay taverns and bright shops, fraught with all store of wares, of workrooms for the parchment-makers, the illuminers, the copyists, the binders; and there should be booths innumerable where are sold the woolens of Ghent and the metalware of Cologne, damascenes from Cordova and Baghdad, dinanderies and the tiles of Ecouen, paxes from Castile and games of backgammon; and there should be seen in the streets juggling, games, cheats, fools and rogues, and that of every sort. No doubt there should be brothels, too, and dens of every iniquity, and, at the foot of Morningside Drive, below the apse of St. John, where once the elevated trains made hourly their circling flights, there should be set up the gallows where should be hung until dead whosoever should deserve the good bishop's stern displeasure. Their withered bodies, executed I trust in papier-mâché, should picturesquely dangle there—

> Round are they tossed and here and there
> This way and that at the winds' sweet will.

That is what might have been Columbia had Charles Follen McKim, in the year one thousand eight hundred and ninety-seven, yielded to the Gothic nostalgia—if he had not felt the robust influence of Richardson, if he had not breathed the enrapturing air of Rome. There are even now fragments of this unfamiliar Columbia, of a size quite ponderable, scattered about the edges of the wide forums; let us not imagine that they may not yet overcome the Latin pattern. Have we not seen in Piranesi the fate of the Colosseum and the Theater of Marcellus? The steps of the Library may yet furnish the blocks for a Cistercian convent whose rose-colored campanile, dedicated to San Clemente, shall lean against a white, complacent, and ruined dome.

We shall not be free from this menace until men shall cease to believe that there are moral values in architecture. To destroy the illusion so impregnable in the public consciousness that one architecture may be more Christian than another—that God is more pleased with gargoyles than with antefixae—we need some great poet, like Ruskin, able to offer our world a new and more commanding vision. The poets, who created this mirage, alone can dissolve it.

If I were a poet, I would try to evoke, in whatever compelling metaphor and meter I might command, the vision of that Columbia which shall arise in that happy time when our minds have become clear of both Amiens and Rome. If I possessed the astringent pen of Pugin, I would add a new page to the volume called *Contrasts*. I would place, beside the picture of the Gothick Columbia that I have just drawn, the picture of a university that looked, not backward, but forward.

Then I should draw a picture of a university wholly conscious of a present heroic mission. Unconcerned with antique rite and privilege, with custom, manners, scenes, and precedents, that university should be unmistakably addressed to a present task, declaring in every line of its external form its commanding place in the scheme of things around it. There should be no part of its architecture, covering the heights of Morningside with new miracles of steel and glass, that did not affirm its kinship with the great city at its feet, no detail of structure or of ornament that did not find its excuse for being somewhere in that mighty heart. My towers should be brothers to the towers that leap heavenward in crest after crest across the plain of Manhattan; my streets should live with the same swift currents that throb through the vast arteries that thread their bases. The patterns of my façades should repeat the million eyes that catch the sun along the cliff of Riverside Drive; they should confess their harmony with the frail ocean liners in the river below, with the grace of airplanes, with the colossal energy that bent the steel bow of the Hudson Bridge against the wall of the Palisades. "I want this university," said McKim, "to face New York." My university should take New York into her arms.

This I would do if I were a poet, and I should persuade all

who listen to my voice that there lies here at our feet something beautiful to be expressed. I would tell the architect (for, being a poet, I should be privileged to preach to architects) that he has no business in this world if he cannot discover that beauty. It is for the poets to tell us that life once was beautiful.

I know of few places more pathetic than the campus at New Haven. That vast well-meant extravagance, that futile grasping at an ever fleeting illusion is pitiful in the extreme. If this were a theater, or if these towers stood eternally amid the harmonies of great music, I might consent to the spell to which they entreat me; perhaps then I should hear behind their vaulted archways the voice of the Angelic Doctor making eloquent the ancient Hall of the Dominicans or listen to the anthem of pilgrims before the shrine of St. Julien-le-Pauvre. But not here, amid these firmly built façades, clearly revealed in the light of noon; not here where the Gothic cloak is thrown over buildings fashioned for a present use, where gargoyles and niched saints ride the tops of concrete girders, where elevators, conduits, and pipes for plumbing are threaded through antique buttresses. Not in a scenic ensemble held against the sky by whatever ingenious fabric of beam and strut or executed with whatever subtleties of imitative skill and bewildering scholarship.

My university, should I build one, would be a Christian university: not made Christian by a mummery of trefoil and canopied niche, but made Christian, as were Oxford and Salamanca and Paris, by the immanence of the Divine Spirit within its walls. The men of my university, being Christian, should pray each day and this would be their prayer:

Give us the courage to be men of our own time; give us the light to see clearly the task that we have to do; give us the faith to believe that great things can yet be accomplished—and preserve us, dear God, from the *Gothick Universitie*.

CHAPTER SIX

picture, sentiment, and symbol

WHEN at a tender age I began the practice of architecture I accepted, being in those days without conscience, a number of commissions for churches. I built many churches. I call this my Early Christian Period.

At first I built stone churches in the Gothic style. As I look back upon these I find them more Goodhue than Gothic: the point is that I believed them to be Gothic. I held that faith not merely because I shared at that time the generous illusions of the Gothic Revivalists but also because I was very young. *Folie de jeunesse.* I believed that Goodhue was carrying forward the tradition of Canterbury; and indeed he was doing so, but in a manner which I had not as yet understood.

For several years the beautiful little temples of Goodhue and Cram reappeared, somewhat faded to be sure, on my drafting board and were retranslated into three-dimensional pictures in stone, complete with the lush ivy which cloaked the Goodhue buttresses and the birds which at his invitation quaintly nested in the towers. I could never manage his romantic old graveyards. There were never any rude forefathers picturesquely to molder there.

I might have gone on indefinitely building these pictures, had it not been for my clients. My clients were not indifferent to the felicities of this, my private Heaven, but they were equally conscious of a useful task here and now to be performed, and they could not always understand the way in which that task shat-

tered the romantic pattern which had taken so firm a possession
of my imagination. They wanted, for example, an expansion of
the educational and social facilities for which the Gothic tradition offered no precedent. They wanted modernizations in planning and simplifications in ceremonials which threw my compositions completely out of balance; and their disinclination to pay
for masonry vaulting was positive in the extreme. I blamed, not
the Gothic tradition or my own misconceptions of it, but the
intransigeance of my clients for the disasters which followed.

I have confessed my sin not so much to obtain absolution as
to point a moral. I was not, I fear, the only architect to design
pictures rather than buildings. I hope that no one will think
that I admire less sincerely the form and the tradition of Gothic
architecture—and yet I am not sure but what the program of my
clients might have formed a better foundation for my art. At any
rate, I am sure that it would have formed a better foundation
than that excess of pictorialism which was the almost universal
anodyne of architects in that day.

It should be understood that I am thinking not so much of the
habit of seeing buildings pictorially as of the habit of designing
them pictorially. As long as there are Cook's Tours and castles
on the Rhine, people will look for and find picturesque charm
in buildings; and why not in buildings near to our homes? People "of good taste and an Anglican inheritance," for example, are
sure to desire such qualities in a country church. They will take
pleasure in the scenic effect of a rambling parish house set
against the bolder masses of tower and transept, in a spire rising
over great trees, in splashes of light on textured masonry. Such a
manner of seeing does not necessarily prohibit an apprehension
of the more austere and sculptural values of buildings—of those
"patterns of solid form set in space with space around"—provided of course that the architect has created such values and
made them accessible.

The trouble is that many architects, at any rate at the time when I was an architect, did forget to create such values. The completed picture leaped into our minds almost before the first line had been put on paper and continued its subconscious tyranny over plan and structure; and no theme of architecture, unless it be the skyscraper, was so vulnerable to that tyranny as the church. We thought in pictures, remembering the gray abbeys of Picardy and La Beauce, and built our churches out of the pages of our sketchbooks.

In that way we often sacrificed not only the energies of three-dimensional pattern but also the vitality and command which buildings have when their use and social reference are firmly established in their outward shapes. I do not think that churches are an exception to that principle, so fundamental in all architecture. Churches, in spite of the slow changes in ceremonial usages, can be alienated from their environment as readily as any other buildings by qualities of design. The tower of Norwich rising over a Nebraska prairie, a fragment of Aquitaine under the elevated railway: these do not (I hope) clarify the relationship of the Church to contemporary society.

Incidentally, this tendency to pictorialism encourages an insidious type of merchant-architect. I know an architect, successful in the practice of church building, who can develop a dozen pictures from a plan common to them all. He enchants building committees by dressing up his project as if it were a paper doll, or a congressman running for reëlection, in a succession of costumes, Georgian, Lombard, and Provençal; and if by chance your taste is for the modern, the heterodox fellow will at no extra cost offer you his wares trimmed in cantilevers and corner windows. I am constantly surprised by the number of styles in which he can be insincere.

I have seldom seen a church which was pictorially designed that did not suffer also from an excessive tincture of romantic sentiment. There is a language of form by no means doctrinal in nature which has come to have a wide currency in this country, a language made up of architectural elements used without respect to their meanings as architecture. That awkward buttress placed where no buttress is needed with intent to give an air of rural ingenuousness, the turret through which the lone sexton climbs into the belfry (the electrical machinery being out of order), craftsmanship expensively homespun and windows quaintly paned: these are fragments of romance too blurred by associations to play a part in an architectural ensemble. We cannot see them objectively.

I know a woman who, having seen in Normandy a massive pillar of stone, insists on sitting behind one in Potawatomi, New Hampshire. She is firmly persuaded that there were no sermons in the Middle Ages (the best argument I have heard for medievalism), and if Abelard himself were to preach in Potawatomi she would hear him from behind her pillar, his kindling voice tossed about among the facets of sexpartite vault.

Of all architectural forms, the spire is, I think, the most sentimental: not perhaps the majestic spires of cathedrals in great cities, but certainly the smaller spires which people our thousands of smaller cities. I spent all of one summer designing a spire—and unless an architect has designed one he can have no idea how exacting are the requirements in mass, transition, shadow, and silhouette—but I am sure that the citizens of the town in which it stands have never looked at it. They know through associations that a church ought to have a spire; they *feel* its presence; it comforts them with the knowledge that everything has been done properly. Perhaps that is all we should expect of a spire.

There are architectural clichés as well as verbal ones: preserved sentimentalities which become the small change of church design like the thousand and one pietisms of ecclesiastical conversation. These are so familiar that we no longer take any note of them. They are like the prayer which was pronounced each Sunday by the minister who, when I was a boy, was always our guest after the morning service. My mother would load the table with good things to eat—a goose when geese were in season and a roast, a spiced ham, fruits, vegetables, and sweets— and then Dr. MacConochie, folding his hands across his generous waistcost, would say, in that same voice in which the raven spoke to Edgar Allen Poe, "Oh Lord . . . For these few morsels of which we are to partake . . . we thank Thee . . . And may they sustain us, Oh Lord, until the evening repast . . ."

"Few morsels!" my mother would say afterwards, "Few morsels! . . . a whole jar of my best crabapple jelly!"

My mother did not understand that "few morsels" and "evening repast" were stylistic elements wholly devoid of contemporaneousness. They were used in precisely the same sense as the homely trimmings on the church built for Dr. MacConochie in our Michigan town by an expensive Chicago architect. It took the good Presbyterians thirty years to pay the mortgage on that "humble edifice."

Picture and romance, even when used in large doses, seldom destroy completely an architectural pattern. Symbolism, however, is another matter. I mean, of course, the excessive use of forms having a doctrinal significance and especially the tendency to discover such meanings in this or that type of building construction.

There is a kind of architectural as well as ecclesiastical obscurantism and these sometimes get so mixed up together as completely to defeat all apprehension of structural or spatial pattern. The Church speaks to us in symbols and has of course every need to do so, and yet I could wish sometimes that these might be used with a greater understanding of the equally evocative language of architecture. There is a sense in which a church building is itself a symbol, one of its functions being to play a part in ceremonial, but I cannot think that this circumstance justifies all that is implied by "diacritical design."

We architects and not the clergy are to blame for the notion of architectural style as symbol. We are prone to evangelize our clients, to indoctrinate them in some architectural creed. We have told them unblushingly what is and what is not Christian architecture—as if it were not *their* business to tell *us*. The clergy have proved to be apt pupils.

Now we are hoist with our own petard. That instruction which we gave the priest, the priest now repeats to us. Questions of architectural form and technique, which ought to be the prime business of architects, are lifted into the field of religion and resolved by considerations wholly alien to architecture.

Not long ago when I visited the Cathedral of St. John the Divine I asked one of the young men attached to that cathedral to explain the purpose of the transept, then under construction. He said in reply that the transept would pull into harmony the existing nave and sanctuary (a striking example of our renewed belief in miracles) and would also give the cathedral plan the shape of the cross, a symbol which by its permanence and grandeur would confirm the faith of thousands.

Now it seems quite evident that these two purposes, either of which would obviously justify the expenditure of a million or two of charitable dollars, have very little to do with each other. The first is architectural in intent. It is concerned with relations of space and of mass and with an objective, or sensible, unity. The second is pure spirit. The relation between them, that is to say between architecture and symbol, is not a necessary one. One could exist without the other, surely. It should be possible to disentangle them.

You cannot argue with symbols. They find their way to our hearts immediately or not at all. Suppose, for example, I should crown the rock of Morningside with a swastika of giant size. No architecture, I think, would make you love it. You would destroy it. I might tell you that its proportions are exquisite, that its form and rhythms invite you to the most abiding of contemplative pleasures—you would destroy it just the same. —My dear sir, my swastika is skillfully made of priceless materials: of chrysoberyl, of fine gold, of the very best creamery butter. —To hell with it, you would say. —Sir, all the scholars of Columbia University have conjoined to make my swastika the most perfect exemplar of Moresque art. —Smash it, and smash it quickly.

No architecture can protect a symbol; nor is there any symbol which owes its life to architecture—still less to any particular style of architecture. If we love a symbol we will call it beautiful; if we hate it, no art can make it less hateful. The soldiers of Cromwell wept with joy as the lovely windows of Litchfield crashed under the blows of their vengeful lances; and Ferdinand, Most Catholic King of Spain, did not perceive until he had destroyed half of it, that the Alhambra was harmoniously built and full of grace.

It should be understood that I admit picture, sentiment, and symbol as fountains of architecture. I would have people more, not less, sensitive to the pictorial qualities of buildings and I should think it strange indeed if sentiment and symbol were not integral to objects so intimately fused into human life. To be afraid of sentiment is to be afraid of life.

It happens, nevertheless, that there are many kinds of picture, sentiment, and symbol. Some of these obscure architecture and defeat its eloquence; others seem to make architecture all the more evocative by their presence. We may, for example, project upon buildings pictorial relationships which spring into our minds from associations which are wholly irrelevant, except through the inconsequential caprices of the memory, to the building which stands before us; but we may also create for ourselves and out of that building a picture which will confirm rather than destroy its essential character. In like manner we may pour over our new building a sentiment distilled from the past or draw from it the more genuine sentiment of its purpose; and we may crown it with symbols which are living or dead, which reaffirm or deny the meaning of its architecture.

People sometimes ask me to describe the kind of church I would build today, assuming that I were absolutely obliged to build a church. I should like to answer: a church charged with whatever sentiment might be entertained by my client. I am by no means sure that I should not build—only, I hope, with greater competence—in the Gothic style, just as I did thirty years ago. I should not hope to give my building a modernity of expression unless I were sure of a modernity of sentiment shared by those for whom my church is built.

I am sure that I could not make my church modern by means of glass blocks and corner windows, nor could I ask my client to believe that flat roofs, giant cantilevers, and machine-made ornament will bring his building, or his religion, into harmony with our age; nor should I find it my duty to astonish him, in the name of architecture, with parabolic vaults, floating walls, and chapels lifted on *pilotis*. Without a Christianity informed by that same sentiment for modernity which nourishes our modern architecture—I mean a Christianity integral to our world, *secular*, militant, and clairvoyant—we will not get very far in church architecture with our new vocabulary of shapes. It is not enough that such sentiment should color the creed of an architect.

An architect who had built many fine churches once wrote in one of his essays: "The difference between Hudnut and me is that he thinks there is something fine about this modern world —I don't."

There were many other differences between us, for he was one of the most distinguished of American architects; but I think that he expresses with great clarity the essential difference between traditional and modern architecture.

I do not question the sentiment which is raising great medieval cathedrals at Washington, at Liverpool, and on the Rock of Morningside. Sentiments about buildings do not have to be rational to be genuine. That is a truth, by the way, which is quite as apposite to Cape Cod cottages as to cathedrals; and indeed I think it a happy augury for architecture that people should care enough about that art to ornament our bleak cities with splashes of medieval splendor and to wreathe them with white romantic cottages. We have less to fear from such constructions than from that acrobatic modernity which imitates, without knowing the meaning of any of them, every *coup-de-maître* of Le Corbusier.

My students sometimes believe that a sentiment for ancient and modern buildings cannot exist side by side in the same mind. Actually the existence of the one implies the other; and those persons who understand modern architecture best and who have been most deeply touched by its achievements and its promise are almost always those who have approached it through the disciplines of history; nor is it necessary that we should erase from our minds all romance, all make-believe, all unreasonable delights in order that we may love that which is real and present before us.

When I was in Cleveland recently I was shown a section of that city occupied by immigrants from the Ukraine: a square mile or so of squalor extending westward from that deep valley, filled with steel and fire, which cleaves the city as if it had been struck a savage blow with a great axe. At the edge of this valley a church, brought here surely from the Black Sea, lanterned the sky with five golden onion-shaped domes; while below it, tumbling down the slope of the valley, there lay a housing project newly built by a government solicitous of social re-generation.

Now, I am, I believe, thoroughly persuaded of the rightness of modern architecture. My interest in the evolving patterns of our buildings seldom deserts me and I take infinite delight in the discovery of a contemporary spirit working within them. Nevertheless I did not observe the plan or the structure of that church. It may or may not have been logical or correct. I saw it, as I am sure the people who live about it see it, as picture, sentiment, and symbol. As picture, a spot of color giving life to a dull landscape; as sentiment, a splinter of sunshine from distant fields of wheat; and as symbol, a flag raised by sailors adrift on a wide and uncertain sea. I am afraid that I did not look for either function or form.

In truth, the church, with its five shining crosses, half Greek and half Tartar, almost seduced me from the housing project I had come to see. It was only after I had walked for some time among the neat row houses each with its hedged garden and its view, examined in detail their honest reticent shapes set in space and sun, and talked at the community house with the women who were there sustaining our civilization, that it occurred to me that here also were buildings illumined not less than the gilded church by purpose and faith. Here also was picture, sentiment, and symbol.

We have built and are building great hospitals as precise in function as the scientific instruments which are used within them. The poorest patient may there receive without cost all that modern medicine can give to the wealthiest. We have built schools and colleges to which every boy and girl regardless of race or economic status may have equal access; recreation centers and parks free to all the people; housing projects and garden cities; stadia and halls for sports, music, and public assembly. We intend to build at no late date new cities planned for human happiness. Sometimes by means of a clear adaptation to function and by the logical use of techniques peculiar to our age, or by that clairvoyance to which architects sometimes yield themselves, we have succeeded in capturing in their outward forms the spirit which created these new structures: I mean of course the Christian spirit of our times.

If now there were a church which by the same means affirmed its unity with that spirit; a church which, careless of doctrinal disputation and ancient privilege, made its present purpose express and visible in the unequivocal language of modern structure; which illumined that purpose with picture, sentiment, and symbol drawn not from the researches of antiquarians but from the life that flows around and through it; well, then I might call that church good architecture. I might even call it Christian architecture.

CHAPTER SEVEN

architecture and men of science

I HAVE a friend, long experienced in hospital management, who showed me recently the blueprints for a new hospital which he intends to build. The plans were drawn without the services of an architect. The physicians and nurses, it appears, know what they want; the engineer and the contractor know all that is necessary about steel and brick; and the manager knows about organization, coördination, and executive competence. "This building," said my friend, "is going to be so functional that we won't have to have an architect."

I must say that I was somewhat disturbed by this remark. I have in recent years given some encouragement to the doctrine of functionalism in architecture and it was certainly not my intention to promote the extinction of my profession. It seemed to me, as I thought it over, that my friend the hospital manager had offered my creed a somewhat formidable challenge, a challenge which I ought not to ignore. What architecture is possible in a hospital? What has art to do with medicine? Is there any common ground upon which science and beauty meet and have need of each other?

It will be admitted that the cause of architecture is in a perilous state if such common ground does not exist. There can be no doubt about the rise of science and of scientific thought to supremacy in our present culture nor any doubt as to their continued triumph. The arts will not flourish in this world if science has little need of them.

The remark made by my friend the hospital manager—no scientist, to be sure—seemed to me to bring this problem into sharp relief. A hospital is a home, and an instrument, of science: of a science close to the general mind and widely understood both in operation and objective, a science applied to human life. Why not then make the hospital a little basket in which to throw some comments on the relationships and responsibilities of artists and scientists? Perhaps that will help to untangle that prickly bundle of ideas which occupies a corner of the public consciousness under the general label *functionalism.* If I may judge by the outward aspects of recent hospitals our scientists have taken that facile doctrine to their hearts with an appalling zeal.

Now I shall put aside for a moment all consideration of the architect as technician. I am aware that my manager-friend challenged the architect not only in his role of form-giver and artist but in his role as technical expert and executive; but I shall assume that the architect's proved competence will suffice to meet the second of these challenges. When people have built a few hospitals without architectural service there will be little need for further discussion. If architects are content to be technicians merely they may let the argument rest at that point.

I am going to assume that they will not let the argument rest at that point. I am going to assume that architects are artists— and not ashamed of it. Taking for granted that they are rightly employed in the building of hospitals as planners, engineers, and experts in mechanical installations, may we hope to find in hospitals, and in all of those buildings in which the scientific spirit must prevail, some scope for that art of expression, integral to planning and construction and yet distinct from these, which deserves the name *architecture?*

To come back now to that disturbing comment, *This building is going to be so functional that we won't have to have an architect,* let us see just what is implied. Architecture, clearly, is conceived here as something added on, something not essential to the completion of the building. Architecture is ornament, style, sentiment, good taste, fashion, precedent, scholarship, or decent respect for one's neighbors, but in any case it is not understood as something inherent in the nature of the building. Architecture is understood as something having its source not in the thing to be done, the idea to be expressed, but in some climate or realm of idea outside the hospital. It is meant to satisfy, not doctor and patient, but some vague authority to which both are alien.

There is a good example of such a hospital in Manhattan, beside the East River—a good example of a good hospital given an apocryphal character by the "architecture" added on to it in the name of taste. It is a well-built building, competently planned for the very exacting services of a great medical center, but it appears that the architect could find nothing in his magnificent theme which could be expressed in his art. Therefore he added something on, something brought to New York from distant Avignon. For the outward forms of his hospital he took as his model the mighty donjon and towers, the heavy walls and pointed windows, of the medieval palace built there by the popes of the thirteenth century. These borrowed elements he embedded in the steel frame of his scientific instrument in the hope that the relics of a departed civilization might afford the people of New York those contemplative satisfactions which are, alas, prohibited by our contemporary civilization.

I am not sure that this *architecture-added-on* embarrasses in any way the efficient operation of the hospital. Perhaps it is indeed an innocent whimsy giving pleasure to romantic minds outside the hospital and no hindrance to the serious work within. On a rainy night, under a waning moon, the firm somber mass of Avignon contrasts pleasantly with the confusion of the river front. Just the same, it must be evident that the relation of such an architecture to the active science it encloses must be somewhat tenuous. It does not surprise me to learn that some doctors of medicine feel that they can get along without it: not that they wish to get along without beauty but because they are somewhat impatient with this kind of beauty.

I am sure that doctors do not wish to get along without beauty and I have noticed that their idea of beauty is sometimes very like my own. Only a few weeks ago I overheard in a hospital— at the moment when I was slowly regaining consciousness after an operation—a conversation which it seemed to me threw a most engaging light upon the understanding of art in the medical profession. A young interne is questioning my nurse:

The interne: Has he come out of it, Sugar-plum?
The nurse: Not yet, doctor. Numb as a nail.
The interne: Queer dick, isn't he?
The nurse: I'll say, doctor. Absolute nuts about art, beauty, and all that.
The interne: Plump as a pullet outside and tough as all Hell inside. But, Sweetheart, you should have seen the Old Master open him up. My God it was beautiful!

Except for the use of the word *beautiful* to describe an operation this conversation is, obviously, irrelevant to my theme; but I must say that I found that word—which seemed to belong to my private vocabulary—decidedly arresting when used in this way. I assumed that *beautiful* was not used in a technical or professional sense. I assumed that my doctor meant what he said, the only safe assumption with doctors, and I resolved that, once free of ether, I would explore this meaning.

The doctor meant that there was in the performance of this operation some perfection of technique and procedure beyond the strict routine sanctioned by the known laws of biology and chemistry. Into this routine the Old Master had introduced an unusual precision and sureness, an exceptional elegance and distinction, and these were introduced not as things added on in the name of taste but as inseparable parts of the work to be done and the means which were essential to that work. Beauty was the consequence of that way of working. Beauty is form imposed upon external data whenever the need for a perfection beyond necessity guides the hand of the worker.

Now I am by no means sure that my young interne meant all of this or that my nurse understood all that he meant her to understand; but that is what I mean and what he ought to have meant.

To be a beautiful hospital, a hospital must first be a hospital. A hospital must be first of all shaped for the life which it is to contain and for the requirements of whatever structure envelops that life. That life and that structure may nevertheless be guided in such a way as to lift the forms which they create above the dull compulsions of circumstance. Few techniques, whether of medicine or of building, are so absolute in their demands, few economies so rigid in their limitations, as to leave no opportunities for proportion and rhythmic relationship, for selection and emphasis in arrangement and distribution in line and color, in shadow and silhouette; nor are there any patterns of useful space which could not be made, without loss of usefulness, concordant with the basic laws of form.

These are the genuine processes of architecture. They are prompted by that same need for perfection which guides the practitioner of a science, whether it be medicine or engineering, when, without forsaking the firm bases of his practical skill and experience, he yet brings into his practice that imaginative command of means and expediences which lifts that also into an art.

Most scientists, I think, are aware of this imaginative quality in their practice and will admit its analogy to modern architecture, and yet it may seem strange that I should invite them to accept a responsibility for beauty—if I may again use that much-abused word. Their cares are sufficiently numerous and, confronted with issues of wide import to the welfare of populations, the matter may not seem of supreme importance.

It happens, nevertheless, that the practice of science does not occur in a private world shut off from general current and circumstance—although I sometimes think that this fact is overlooked in the education of scientists. The practice of science is not bounded, as some suppose, by that physical world, part nature and part artifice, which is made known by our five senses —and by the twenty-one additional senses which we have invented. The practice of science takes place in the midst of a structure of idea and thought and feeling, a structure built out of vast complexities of social, political, and spiritual values: the structure we call *civilization*. The practice of science reaches out into that fabric; and that fabric in turn lays hold of science; lays hold of it and channels it and determines its utility and power.

Whatever therefore concerns that general cause concerns also the scientist. Whatever influences may be at work to sustain our civilization, to give it firmness, direction, and consequence, concern him. The balance and strength of political structure, order and justice in our society, well-being and progress in our economy, security in our national life and the educational processes which continue and enlarge our culture: these are not to be separated from the cause of science. Nor are these abstractions, little bundles of idea to be put into some remote compartment of the mind separate and apart from science, but parts rather of that same good life to which science is addressed. Science progresses beside those who promote the general and social health.

Thus it happens that the practitioner of science cannot fail to acknowledge two loyalties, which are parts of a common loyalty.

His immediate concern is with his profession, with the public welfare; yet, even when he is most preoccupied with these, when his techniques are most exact in method and purpose, when all of his faculties and all of the intricate apparatus of his profession are brought to bear on the one thing there and now to be done, he is also engaged in a wider service in which each individual act, each individual sacrifice, is a cumulative and integral part. Around every scientist, in each commonplace and habitual exercise of his art, stands the general envelope of humanity from whose cause his individual service gains its dignity and its meaning.

How could it be thought then that scientists should be unmindful of architecture? Architecture is one of those means by which our universal need for order and harmony is realized. Architecture is one of those means by which men enlarge the world by adding to it the qualities which satisfy that need for order and harmony. There is no mystery about this—none, that is, which does not exist in all human experience. In proportion as we desire a satisfactory pattern in life—a balanced and complete civilization—so we will desire to bring into that pattern the arts which enrich it. In proportion as we understand human life we will understand the power of art to illumine and expand that life. Certainly architecture, which is a kind of clothing wrapped about the dry bones of our institutions, must stand first among the arts: the arts which environ the sciences not less surely than they guard all other aspects of our civilization.

There exists in the public mind a certain prejudice respecting this matter. People are too ready to think of the practitioners of the sciences—among whom I include doctors of medicine—as persons standing somewhat apart from that general fabric of moralities, amenities, and emotions which we call the culture of our era. Scientists themselves sometimes imagine their realm as abstract, eternal, exempt from history, romance, and religion.

They forget that science and the products of science are just as integral to each culture as are philosophic thought, politics, or music. The sciences and the technologies of the Middle Ages, for example, complement the religion and the statecraft of that period: we could scarcely imagine the Crusades without the catapult, or the textiles of fourteenth-century Flanders without the dikes and canals which sustained that industrialized art. So our present thought, our politics, our manners, our picture of the world are bound up with the airplane and the printing press.

To be persuaded of this, we have only to recall those essays in fiction in which the technologies of one age are transferred to another. The Yankee at King Arthur's court was a monster of more frightful mien than the Minotaur or the Great Worm in Siegfried. The Minotaur and the Great Worm were rounded by the ideas which had nourished them; they were in a sense *natural*, being the products of their environments. The Yankee, opposing his Colt revolver to the lance of Lancelot, was an abomination, a hideous rent in a tapestry woven by Time. The atomic bomb is our Minotaur, created less from the sciences than from the imagination of this land; and who shall say what spoil of beauty may yet lie in his dark labyrinth?

Of course, if we think of architecture as a clothing brought into our civilization from some more picturesque age—an anodyne for eyes unable to look at the present—I see little in it to deserve the respect of scientist or physician. I should think that these might rightly wish to dispense with a masquerade which obscures or denies the relevance of a hospital to its great and immediate purpose. Suppose, on the other hand, that there were architects who wished to state that purpose in their constructed forms; to set forth in the language of architecture the *hospital idea* and to do this in such a way that all who saw the hospital should perceive the idea within it and know that this was one with those great ideas which light the path of mankind in this our confused and uncertain culture. I think then that fewer doctors of medicine would be willing to dispense with architecture.

Our architects will find that hospital idea, not in the libraries, but in the hospital itself. In the things that are done there lies the thing to be expressed. This marshalling of science to the relief of human suffering, this generous strict coöperation of men and skills, this vision free of substitution and imposture and confusion—these are themes more noble than a wilderness of stylistic romances. Not by affectations of scholarship, by extravagances of ornament, or by stark asceticisms of shadowless walls will we make this theme eloquent but rather by our understanding and clear statement of purpose, to which is to be added, by the well-tried expedients of our craft, that good form in mass and line and plane which affirms the harmony of this purpose with a deeper ministry.

We must remember when we design a hospital that there are degrees of beauty not possible to every type of building. A cathedral is made more beautiful than a garage by merely being a cathedral. An exalted idea will sometimes overcome the most devastating of architectural incompetencies. I do not think that any hospital could be as beautiful as a cathedral, but I think that a hospital might come nearer to that beauty than is now thought possible. Certainly the idea which lifts from our soil these our machines of mercy is not wholly alien to that idea which once lifted the vaults of Amiens and Paris.

I happened to see recently a description of the ancient hospital which the Bishop Maurice de Sully, and after him St. Louis, rebuilt in the twelfth and thirteenth centuries on the Ile de la Cité in Paris. This description, written in medieval Latin, has been translated into modern French. The author, who had himself seen the hospital many times, gives us a vivid picture of what must have been a very beautiful hospital.

The Maison-Dieu—the original French name for a hospital—
lay along the shore of the island to the south of that open space
in front of the cathedral which was called the Parvis. It extended
parallel to the river in the form of a series of long narrow halls
opening into each other in much the same way that Pullman
cars open into each other in a modern train. Beginning at the
Rue du Petit Pont, which bounded the Parvis to the west, these
halls reached eastward beyond the façade of the cathedral and
flanked the nave of the cathedral as far as the southern transept.

Each hall was assigned to a special class of patient: to those
suffering from fever, to those suffering from wounds, to women
in childbirth, and to the pilgrims. Some halls were of two stories
and all had accessory rooms such as chapels and offices. The
walls were of stone, discreetly ornamented with pinnacles and
traceries. The windows were pointed and divided by stone bars
into many panes and the wooden roofs were high and gabled.

The well-organized interiors of this hospital must have presented striking pictures of an aspect of medieval life not often
described in our textbooks: the beds, forty or more in each hall,
ranged along the walls and separated from each other by low
screens, the wide aisles which marked the long axis of each hall,
the painted windows admitting splashes of colored light and
overhead the great oak trusses of the steep roof.

Everywhere was an incessant activity. Here the black-robed
nurses and the younger novices, dressed in white, moved "as if
to unheard music"; here were the more stately *médecins* in their
scarlet robes, the *barbiers*, who were the surgeons in those days;
here the priests who performed the offices of the Church, the
chaplains who heard the confessions of the dying, the servants,
valets, and students from the Ecole de Medicine recently established on the left bank. From the south were heard the voices
of the river and of the wind in the linden trees along its bank;
to the north the gray towers of Notre Dame announced the

hours of canticle and prayer; and above the long aisles the roof spaces were filled with sunlight, fresh air, and the beautiful spirit of charity.

Jean de Jaudun, *docteur de l'université* of the College of Navarre, to whom I owe this description, sums up his memorandum in this arresting phrase:

"It seemed to me that the art of medicine and the art of architecture are here made one in the service of God."

When we look back to the thirteenth century our eyes are no doubt blinded by that romantic light which our poets—and I am afraid our architects also—have cast over that colorful age. There appears to have been at that time a unity of life and thought, pervaded by ideals of universal scope, expressed in an art of universal splendor, which in our imagination overcomes all that we know of the cruelty and ignorance which attended it. Our present civilization seems broken into pieces.

Our individual lives seem also broken into pieces, each piece separate and widely apart. Each of us leads, not one life, but a dozen and we lead these all at one time, so that those ideas, valuations, and modes of agreement which belong, let us say, to family life are quite separate from business life, and those which belong to science cannot be conceived as valid also in art.

This is the great illusion of our age. The Industrial Revolution, the greatest event in human history, shattered our civilization into these fragments, setting its elements moving in these contrary directions, uprooting the authorities which bound it together, creating and dissolving new pictures of the world. Our vast technologies pile complexity on old complexities unguided by philosophy or moral law; our economy diverges ever further from our culture; and art, once inseparable from science, is reserved now for those moments when science can no longer be endured.

Of all the arts architecture has suffered most from this disintegration. Without a firm tradition, without popular understanding or aristocratic clientele, without coherence to the changing technologies of construction, our architecture is set adrift from its time. We look backward to the Gothic centuries for the principles of our art and for the masterpieces which we cannot hope to emulate. Medicine, on the other hand, marches with the empirical spirit of our age and is continuously served by the investigations and multiplex inventions of our scientists—so much so that we have almost forgotten that medicine is an art.

Now I do not believe that doctors and architects could, through some new understanding and sympathy, stay this onward rush of our civilization towards that perfect chaos which is its obvious goal; nor is it likely that beauty, even if allied to medicine, could hold a plea with the destructive forces which assail our time—still less with the terrible engines, and still more terrible misunderstandings, which the great wars have brought forth. We might nevertheless raise a standard to which (in the words of Washington) others might repair. We might make our hospital a symbol for those who would resist this cultural anarchy. We may be sure that there are many thousands who await a standard and a symbol. If each of the five hundred new hospitals which are now projected by our government were to be a beautiful hospital—not prettified with ornament, or streamlined, or made goofy with Colonial sentimentality, but dignified rather by the form and pattern of its high purpose—then a new light should shine across this land. A new light and a new hope.

I do not believe that those doctors of medicine who are to guide this program of our government will be indifferent to architectural excellence in the new hospitals. If they know the nature and true source of that excellence they will wish to renew that partnership, tried by long usage, with the architect whose healing and rebuilding is addressed, like theirs, not to physical sickness only but to that sickness which has invaded the world.

Our two arts are ancient ones; they belong not to this present merely but to history and the future; their unity should be confirmed and reanimated by this new promise of service. We wandered, scientist and artist, together into this our iron arena; we face together its strange confusions, its barbaric energies; and we must find our way out together. Together, I think, or not at all.

grand compositions

MR. Mies van der Rohe has prepared a general plan for
the new buildings of the Illinois Institute of Technology:
a modern version of those "grand compositions" which from time
to time have added brief periodic splendor to the dreams of
American universities. The architect, in his role of pattern-maker,
has joined the present facilities of a training school for engineers
to its future facilities so that all of these exist in his imagination
and upon his drawings as parts of a single work of art, complete
and timeless in its perfect symmetry. The workshops and foun-
dries, the life-filled laboratories, classrooms, gymnasia, and libraries are by the magic of art made the materials of a harmony
as ethereally classic as a symphony of Haydn.

Thus hope springs eternally in the architectural breast. Ever
since that day upon which Joseph Jacques Ramée laid out his
neat scheme for Union College—and no doubt long before—
architects have thus played with universities, corseting the body
of a live and unpredictable creature within firm frames of brick
and architectural idea; and thus they have prefigured growth and
development, resolute to impose upon future generations whatever ideal of form might be current in their day. In every instance the live creature has refused the mold; or, if temporarily
bound, has broken through its architectural shell into great
splashes of dishevelment and stylistic chaos.

If precedent is a guide in these matters the Illinois Institute
of Technology will never inhabit more than a fraction of the

crystal house which is now prepared for it, each element of which depends so much upon its relevance to its neighbors and to the geometric spaces which these organize. Some new Gothic Revival will upset this quiet synthesis; some masqueraders from a more boisterous society of modernists will join this *ballet mécanique*. Such has been the fate of all architectural Edens.

The University of Virginia—no Eden, to be sure—may be thought an exception to this law; but we have forgotten the monstrous building which in Victorian times leaned against the round library. That building was by the grace of God burned; and yet the architects who restored the library, and who surely ought to have known better, closed the fine axial vista which had welded the Lawn to the distant hills. That is a serious impairment, altering the character of Jefferson's design more radically than do the acres of dull buildings which now surround it. These are forgotten inside the quiet Lawn.

Jefferson's classicism, in spite of its Palladian origin, is strongly tinctured with showmanship. Indeed it is at times pure theater. The group at Charlottesville is a setting rather than a shelter: a courtly stage for an academic comedy; scenic architecture worthy of Serlio or John Nash. It does not depend, as does the group proposed in Chicago, on nice adjustments of plane and mass and space; it is, like all things baroque, less absolute in its theory, more hospitable to architectural strangers. It will suffer less from change and addition.

Baroque? What could be more baroque than the housing of university professors in the temples of the Roman gods? I was once a professor at Virginia and I know how a god can be uncomfortable.

The perfect exemplar of a patterned university is no doubt Columbia: an academic city, classic in its unity and completeness, set down in the conglomerate of New York, a perpetual reproach to the unquiet confusions which surround it. Descartes imagined such a city, a "perfect city, geometric and regular" in which all accident is foreseen, all growth completed. He would have contained the world itself in such a pattern.

On a pedestal of granite enough vast to delight the soul of Piranesi, above a stairway that Le Nôtre might have designed, the architect of Columbia raised his perfected Pantheon. Around it, in studied subordination, Roman *palazzi* dance eternal quadrilles amid *cortili* that are themselves consummate architecture; and had the group progressed to completion the colossal ballet should have advanced right and left of the domed library to enclose, amid a splendor of balustraded terrace and fountain, of wrought grille and chiseled sculpture, a forum not less majestic than that which Augustus laid before the Temple of Mars the Avenger. Variety in unity: the tried receipt. Each building, each open space, an individual design, and yet all pulled into unity by vista and contained plaza, by the planes that answer each other in direction and proportion, by the horizontal line threaded through and around, by harmonies of scale, color, and texture, and by the solemn presidency of the great dome, acknowledged by every element in the ensemble.

Sixty years have passed and the scheme, still unfinished, has suffered many and grievous mutilations. The temples which were the necessary frames for the central dome exist only on paper; the forum is a dreary playground; to the south a dormitory-skyscraper lifts its jejune head, upsetting the intended eurythmy there; and, most serious blow of all, the library has deserted its Pantheon at the university's center of equilibrium and in a new and ornate palace challenges the supremacy of the dome which was once its crown. Such are the inevitable impacts of events upon an architecture of abstractions. To endure, a monument must be finished at a stroke.

That is why Princeton, where the principle of unity is picture and sweet clutter, will suffer less from the malice of time. The buildings at Princeton were not planned so as to strike the eye as parts of one great ensemble; they reveal themselves one after another as one walks through a tangle of enclosed quadrangles. A general composition is created from a sequence of visual images laid one over another. Because one style of architecture— collegiate Gothic, if you please—is repeated in each of these images a unity is achieved: a unity less definite than that of geometric relationships in mass and line but less likely to be blurred by the intrusions of incongruous buildings. Where the whole is planned accident the planner can admit some accidents which are unplanned and safely leave to his successors the privilege of an occasional whimsey. When for example you have to build a new general library, huge in scale and as intricate in organization and operation as a Diesel engine, you have only to pour over it some archaeological sauce to bring it into harmony, at least skin-deep, with all that has gone before.

For my part I rejoice that neither Columbia nor Princeton has respected too piously its master plan. What are these plans but crystallizations of past usages and ideals? They contain no prophecies other than that of events already in course of development. The unforeseen necessity, the new interpretation of duty and relationship, ought by every law of casualty to demand adaptations unprovided for in a master plan. Let's not be afraid of such adaptations; they are evidences of new life and give new life to architecture. The urgencies of the present are better architects than our academy or our visions of Ye Olden Tyme.

I salute the Massachusetts Institute of Technology. When in 1909 they moved across the Charles they built for themselves a palace which perfectly conformed to the classicist's dream of a university. No Roman emperor ever imposed his will more tyrannously upon space and peristyle. That palace, unfinished today, will be left unfinished. When after many years M.I.T. resumed its program of construction, those in authority there acknowledged, not without courage, alumni being what they are, the rightness—and the necessity—of that change of program. The new buildings, except for a pious dome laid on the new School of Architecture, were designed, strange as that may seem, in accordance with new technologies of planning and building. Tech poured only a little of its new wine into its Alexandrine bottle and then looked about for more crystalline receptacles.

That does not seem to me, as some people have suggested, a betrayal of architecture. The new policy is not only good sense but the policy which will make possible an expression in architecture which may be genuine to a contemporary university. Stylistic conformities, aesthetic dogma, and precedent have too often stood between us and that expression, and will surely do so again if we admit their tyrannies. We pay too high a price for these, not only because they deny us those advanced techniques of planning and construction which are surely as appropriate to a university as they are to department stores and the buildings of the United Nations, but also because they have defeated that very eloquence of form for which they were intended.

If my readers will now tolerate a didactic interlude I should like to examine briefly some of the premises which, it seems to me, underlie this problem of form in grand compositions.

It must be obvious that the buildings of a university would not of their own accord fall into a symmetry such as that proposed for Columbia, nor would they without the promptings of some other force than practical necessity group themselves into the picturesque pantomimes of Princeton. The School of Law would not "naturally" inhabit a building proportioned precisely like the School of Journalism nor would these two from motives of politeness move to positions equidistant from an imaginary axis; and so far as I know there is nothing in the nature of Princeton's classrooms and dining halls which might provoke spontaneously the silhouettes of Compton Winyates. Clearly these forms and arrangements were imposed upon these universities by some regulating will, some conscious control and direction, which had another end than stability, convenience, and economy.

I think that it is probable that the end to which that will was directed was expression: the expression of an idea, the *university idea*. These buildings and groupings of buildings were to be shaped and arranged in such a way as to confirm that idea, to make it intelligible, to give it dignity and eloquence. The principles of form in these universities, so sharply contrasting the one with the other, were means to expression, not ends in themselves.

Form is a medium through which some of those meanings we have discovered in experience can be made known to those who look at buildings: not made known merely but made active and persuasive in their consciousness. People who build universities usually believe in them; their requirements in architecture will not be satisfied by convenience in plan and economy in operation or by the perception of organic relationships in the structure and function of buildings, but by the way the university idea is given definition and force. Form is idea made visible. The origin of form is faith: faith in the worthwhileness of human nature, in the dignity of man's enterprises. Form may be an accident; form may be logical consequence; but form is more often a philosophy.

There are many philosophies. Most of us today are persuaded of a functional basis of form in buildings. That is because our era has become saturated with technological thought; because we have made of our world one vast machine and are at every moment aware of its structure and its pulsations. We cannot apprehend the form of anything that is made by man except with reference to the way it is put together and the way it works. The power of form to enhance the quality of our lives must rest upon its identity with our lives: upon identity therefore with organism and function. That which is true of buildings is true of groups of buildings whenever, as in a university, these are united by the invisible threads of purpose and use. Not the individual buildings—library, dormitory, laboratory—must acknowledge in line and plane the task they have to perform, the methods by which they were built, but these must also be clearly revealed in the pattern of the university as a whole.

These are true principles—or at any rate are at this moment true for us; but in what way are they relevant to the buildings of Princeton and Columbia? Shall we condemn the architects of these universities, who were like us in search of a clothing of form for their idea, because they failed to exhibit in their work contemporary techniques in planning and construction? For my part, I could forgive them that failure considering the time and circumstances which surrounded them if only they had indeed fitted their designs to the living idea which they were built to contain. These buildings were not in truth fitted to that idea. They were the molds of other ideas into which the university idea was, by an act of violence, made to conform.

In the arsenals of architecture there are many such molds, beautiful grooves waiting each for its idea. Sometimes architects go about searching for ideas with which to fill a mold (brought home perhaps from Italy or London) and at other moments, when by chance they entertain an idea of their own, they reverse the direction of their search and look for a mold that is ready-made and convenient. When it happens that no perfectly fitting mold can be found it is always possible to reshape an idea—to leave out a part of it or graft upon it some adventitious material. There is something of Rome in Columbia, something of Oxford in Princeton, and if we ignore that which is contemporary in these institutions, if we disentangle from them that which is vital and in evolution, they will fall neatly into the brick and stone baskets waiting to receive them.

Ideas, alas, are restless things. They will not remain long within a mold. Ideas are active to build, urgent to give vitality to that which is built. We know how they can shatter a grand composition.

Can we hope then to create a pattern of buildings which could express in the language of architecture the meaning and direction, the social attitude and content, of a university? Could there be such a thing as form in the totality of the buildings of a developing institution?

No one can predict even approximately the requirements of tomorrow's university. No *program* is possible which extends beyond a dozen years.

There are now enrolled in American universities more than two and a half million students. The University of California has 60,000 students; Boston University has 25,000; New York University 70,000. What will happen to this growth when, as seems likely, the federal government makes available free scholarships to all qualified students? Jefferson thought that a university might have four hundred students.

How many among these two and a half million students are preparing for the learned professions, once the sole purpose of a university? And, by the way, *are* there any learned professions? What has become of that Christian sentiment which once filled the air of universities? of those aristocratic standards of genteel culture now that the university is an instrument of democracy? of pure science in the vast training schools for doctors of medicine and for engineers? of the humanities crushed under the weight of the social sciences? No one can say what will be the new relationships of the university to the society which nourishes and uses it; and no one can predict what miracles our new materials and construction methods will engender in the buildings which will shelter it.

Our form, if there is to be a form, must be a function of time: of an idea operating through time. The form must be a developing form, the form of a growing organism, a form which lies partly in the past and partly in the future. The university will never be completed. It will be forever on its way. Its form will be forever plastic.

Our problem is clearly to express that idea which is constant to a university, the idea which guards and makes available the funded knowledge of mankind, but to express this in a form which will not be overcome by the incessant and incoherent changes of our time. There lies the secret of form: to capture that inward essence, to make it reappear in each element of our developing pattern amid new utilities, plans, methods, techniques, and ornaments; to open a channel for it which shall remain open through time and event.

I have noticed that time, which is willy-nilly the chief architect of universities, has sometimes a subtle way of capturing and setting forth this university idea. Sometimes time imposes upon buildings a continuing character, a becoming and unfolding, which escapes the minor architects, preoccupied with that which is immediate and individual; and even when there is lacking all style and architectural grace there may be a unity more evident than that attained by those expediencies in design which are consciously addressed to unity. Even amid a chaos of styles—a mélange of incoherent and conflicting materials, scales, ornaments, and random relationships—I have felt the true nature of a university more truly revealed than in the most perfect of formal symmetries. With an invisible chain time surrounds, unites, and illumines.

Old universities are always more beautiful than new ones, not so much because they tell us stories or because the art of architecture has suffered a decay, but because they exist, not in space merely, but in time. I have always liked those two white classical temples at the center of Princeton, not only because they are admirable in themselves, but because they seem to assure me of an idea to which both classic and medieval form are but episodes. (Perhaps also because I think of them as marble peas in the slippers of the Gothicists.) In the same way Dartmouth Hall is built very firmly into the texture of Daniel Webster's college and certainly is a better reason for loving that college than the new library, pretty enough to dance at the Senior Prom and still untouched by the years; and if you have so fine a piece of architecture as that "Christopher Wren Building" at the College of William and Mary it really doesn't matter much what you may build around it.

On condition that we respect them such relics may well be the prime ingredients in a composition in which feeling rather than formal relation is the binding force. I do not mean that we should copy our old buildings. We have not respected them when we copy them: when we make them into "basic motives" which can be extended by imitation over the whole fabric of a university—as if they were pegs upon which to hang a newly invented tradition. You will not give your jewels a greater brilliance by surrounding them, as at least one university has done, with a square mile or so of paste; nor have we respected our old buildings when we "restore" them into something more elegant or romantic than could have been possible to their original builders—those sad counterfeit antiquities which delight only the garden clubs. Nor should we remodel our fine old buildings into uses for which they were not intended: as if use were not as essential to their magic as the forms which explain use. Even if they stand empty and silent in the midst of our busy campus they will serve us better than when we have rubbed off their character by filling them with modern conveniences.

At Harvard we have rebuilt the interior of Massachusetts Hall, designed as a dormitory for students, so that it may be used for our administrative offices. That little building achieved a wonderful eloquence by the simple expedient of stating its purpose. I do not say that the good proportions, the fine modeling of roof and chimney, the rhythmic progressions of the windows do not still deserve our admiration, but surely something has changed now that these shelter presidents and deans. Presidents and deans deserve good architecture, but architecture of a somewhat different order.

I am constantly surprised to find people so indifferent to such dissonances between use and outward form. I once owned an antique bookcover which had been refitted for use as a cigar box; its appearance, as it lay on my table, was unchanged; and there were those who thought that its beauty was unimpaired.

Our buildings are affirmations of character: not our old buildings merely but all the buildings which follow one after another on our campus down to that newest building into which we have built our present mood. The unity among these is the more persuasive for being subtle. The deadly uniformity of make-believe Gothic which was laid first over the University of Chicago and then over Yale has served chiefly to blot out the history of these institutions—and with history the greater part of character. The styles give more character than a style; they may reveal the life of a university, its adventures and changes of temper, the life which ought to be the substance of architecture. There is no doubt an excess of adventure and temper on our university campuses, but better that excess than the masquerade which hides all life and distorts all meaning.

We can only build in the present. Provided that our successive styles truly represent attitudes of mind which were present when they were created—or present when they were recreated— they will not defeat the unity of an institution which, by a law of its nature, must respond to the varying and successive phases of its central theme. The strange buildings which crowd our campuses—Colonial, neo-Gothic, Richardsonian, classic revival, and modernistic—are hooks into the past, each of them holding some part of that thread which binds together the history of an idea.

There is such a thread in the Harvard Yard, beginning with Massachusetts Hall, binding through feeling rather than through style the forthright forms of Hollis and Holworthy, fitted for the sober business of bringing up a literate clergy, through University, elegant witness of a secular classicism, through Weld and Matthews, nostalgic of the Christian centuries, through Sever, conscious of great events to come, to Widener, revealing the less gracious prosperity of the 1900's. These are the mimes in a play, crowded with incident, and yet with a theme clearly set forth. There are secret understandings among buildings as among men.

When I think of the effects of styles commingled in one composition I am apt to remember the central squares of Venice where basilica, library, palace, and campanile has each its individual ornament and perfection and yet all are Venice. I am glad that the Venetian architects were not "consistently Byzantine." Let's not push the analogy too far—there is something in Venice which escaped the notice of Harvard University—but the two have at least this in common: they are events, not monuments.

It is said that in the 1890's a rich and eccentric gentleman—of whom Harvard has known more than one—offered the university a million-dollar building on condition that it should be in the Turkish style. When asked, "Why Turkish?" he replied, "Turkish is the only style not already in the Yard." I sometimes think it a pity that we did not accept that offer. Turkish might have faithfully represented our soul at the end of the century.

I should be somewhat disingenuous if I were to leave my readers with the impression that the vagaries of architectural style which lend such a variety to our universities are wholly the consequences of a fluctuating academic temperament, or that a laissez-faire policy in these matters is the policy most likely to achieve an expressive form. The temperament, I think, was more precisely an affair of the architects; and the styles witness not only the requirements of our clients but the somewhat unstable nature of that art which we have exercised upon them. Indeed I think that the patience with which universities carry the burden of the architecture we have laid on them is among the most striking evidences of the vitality of universities. No other institution, unless it be the Church, has so much to forgive our well-intentioned practice.

I think that this forgiveness would not be long withheld if our clients would remember that the art of architecture no less than the art of teaching was engaged in a search for new values and new relationships. We were not anchored, like the university, in a tradition fortified by values and practices long continued, but were set adrift in the midst of confusions quite unprecedented in our art. The architectures which one after another we tried to adapt to our civilization were misfits which could not be worn for more than a generation; and yet each was at heart an attempt to discover some garment which would cover at least some part of our nakedness.

If we looked about for old molds into which to fit the crescent ideas of our time, we did so in the hope that from these molds some new tradition might be developed. I sometimes think that all of nineteenth-century architecture, and the greater part of twentieth-century architecture, is best understood as a search for such a tradition: an obstinate questioning and experiment of which the costumes of universities are, in part at least, consequence and clear witness. The Gothic Revival was the bravest as it was the most mistaken of the essays in dialectic and stone which enlivened that search; neoclassicism was only half a doctrine and half a hope for a renaissance; the rediscovery of the Colonial was an answer to a prayer more naïve but sincere; and those architects who built upon new theories and those who sought out new inventions were equally inspired by visions of a new and universal architecture, as were also those who put their faith in genius and those who were confident of genius in themselves. If I remember rightly the architects of Columbia and of Princeton were not exceptions to this generality; they too intended American traditions.

Tradition is time in partnership with architecture. Must I explain that I do not mean a style—conformities in motif and ornament and in practices of organization? I mean rather a principle of design, known and firmly held among architects over several generations, and a practice which although evolving and hospitable to invention and idea is yet steadfast in its general direction. I mean a continued understanding and consistency, a clear notion of the purpose of architecture, a definite standard in attainments.

Only with a tradition can architects work together in the making of a composition of buildings in which function and relationship change from year to year. Tradition gives our art a discipline, fuses its individual phases, mitigates its excesses, bridges its voids of inspiration.

I am not thinking of academic standards arbitrarily imposed but of standards arrived at by common consent and usage, assuming that to be possible. These should be necessarily standards capable of wide variety in their application; but their central intention should be unmistakable. I would have individuality but not the negation of authority. I would leave room for an occasional rebel, but not a rebel every Tuesday. I would admit advertisement but not an art which is all one big buzzing advertisement. I would have a religion but not an incessant multiplication of strange gods.

It seems to me that those architects who sought the principles of a new architecture in contemporary techniques of planning and construction were quite as much solicitous of a new tradition as were those who hoped to build new styles on the foundations of classicism or upon the inspirations of genius. If I have understood rightly those who initiated the "International Style" —unfortunate phrase—they never intended to invent a style. They intended rather to set forth certain principles which might form a base from which a new progress might be possible. Le Corbusier called his book, not *A New Architecture,* but *Vers une architecture;* and if his work, and the work of those who aimed at similar ends by similar means, cleared our buildings of that load of romance, antique techniques, speculative aesthetics, and cant with which we had burdened them, that was not in order that these buildings should achieve "stripped and stark asceticism, rigid and dogmatic" but that our architecture might be set free to establish on this base a tradition consistent with the genuine culture of our day.

Is it possible that such a tradition is actually in process around us? The currency of the ideas first formulated in this modern architecture encourages this daring hope; and we know how our younger architects are giving these ideas ever widening range and deeper human content. We see that variety of expression, wit, grandeur, and lyrical beauty are already welded to this iron stem to which Mr. Mies van der Rohe has added a serene elegance.

CHAPTER NINE

the post-modern house

I HAVE been thinking about those factory-built houses, pure products of technological research and manufacture, which are promised us as soon as a few remaining details of finance and distribution are worked out: houses pressed by giant machines out of plastics or chromium steel, pouring out of assembly lines by the tens of thousands, delivered anywhere in response to a telephone call, and upon delivery made ready for occupancy by the simple process of tightening a screw. I have been trying to capture one of these houses in my mind's eye; to construct there, not its form and features only but the life within it; to give it, if my readers will pardon me, a local habitation and a name.

I was assisted in this effort recently during an airplane trip to New York. As we left Boston we flew over a parking lot beside a baseball stadium and half an hour later, as we approached New York, over that immense parking area which lies back of Jones Beach. In each of these thousands of automobiles were ranged in herringbone patterns, all of them so far as we could see from the sky exactly alike, their forms except for varying fancies in streamlining and nickel plate being the perfect harvest of the technological mind unadulterated by art. It seemed to me that, parked in this way, these thousands of automobiles foreshadowed those future suburbs in which every family will have each its standardized mass-produced and movable shell, indistinguishable from those of its thousand neighbors except by a choice of paint and the (relative) ambitions of their owners to be housed in the latest model.

Now I am aware that uniformity in house design is for the greater part of mankind a condition which is often necessary and not always regrettable—a circumstance clearly illustrated by that cloudburst of Cape Cod cottages which is even now saturating our New England landscapes and which, it may be, is as distinct a forerunner of future standardizations in our houses as is the parked automobile. Just the same there is an important difference between these millions of wooden cottages and the more rigorous shapes of factory-built houses, a difference only obliquely related to materials and processes of manufacture. The factory-built house, as I imagine it, fails to furnish my mind with that totality of impression which the word house (meaning a building occupied by a family) has always filled it: it leaves unexhibited that idea of home about which there cling so many nuances of thought and sentiment. My readers may count me a romanticist if they wish—and perhaps they can conceive a home without romance?—but I do not discover in any one of the types of house prefigured in the published essays of technologists that *promise of happiness* which, in houses, is the important quality of all appearances.

My impression is obviously shared by a wide public—a circumstance which explains in part the persistence with which people, however enamored of science, cling to the familiar patterns of their houses. Among the soldiers who write letters to me there is, for example, one in Tokio who describes at some length, and not without eloquence, the many labor-saving devices, the new ideas in planning, the new materials, insulatings, and air-conditionings which are to beautify his new house and who ends his letter with the confident hope that these will not in any way change the design of the house which he expects me to build for him. He has in mind, if I have understood him correctly, a Cape Cod cottage which, upon being opened, will be seen to be a refrigerator-to-live-in; and I am by no means sure which of these requirements, assuming them to be inconsistent, is the more prescriptive. Having learned that I am an architect tinged with modernism my soldier fears that I may be tempted to suspend his house from a tree or pivot it on a mast around which it can be made to revolve or perhaps give it the outward shape of an aluminum bean, and I take it that he is unwilling that my enthusiasm for a technological absolutism should carry me that far. He would like all the newest gadgets but would like these seasoned with that picture, sentiment, and symbol which, to one writing from Tokio, seem to be of equal importance. He would have mechanization but would not, in the phrase of a distinguished historian of art, allow mechanization to take command. I shouldn't be surprised to learn that his requirements reflect accurately those of the Army, the Navy, the Air Force, the WAC, and the WAVES.

Our soldiers are already sufficiently spoiled by compliments and yet I must admit that here is still another instance in which their prescience overleaps the judgments of science. Beneath the surface naïveté of my friend's letter there is expressed an idea which is of critical importance to architecture: a very ancient idea to be sure but one which seems sometimes to be forgotten by architects. The total form and ordinance of our houses are not implied in the evolution of building techniques or concepts of planning. They do not proceed from these merely; they cannot be imagined wholly from these premises. In the hearts of the people at least they are relevant to something very far beyond science and the uses of science.

I wish to be understood in this matter. I am not excessively fond of Cape Cod cottages. In their native habitat these are quaint in form and charming in their forthrightness, and yet I find the type somewhat tedious now that it has been repeated four or five million times. I do wish that those contractors who spread their white nebulae of houses around our great cities might now and then tempt their market with some new form of sweetmeat. To speak frankly these represent a species of exploitation not more excusable than any other. Nevertheless it is a fact, patent to the most superficial observer, that millions of people find in these commutations of architecture compensations for an experience of which most of them are ignorant. They are the pale but necessary substitutes for the experience of an architecture in which emotional values are fused into technological values. Until we achieve that fusion Cape Cod cottages will take command.

Our architects are too often seduced by the novel enchantments of their techniques. I have known architects whose attitudes and ideals are not different from those of engineers; who find sufficient reward for their work in the intellectual satisfactions afforded by their inventions; who are quite indifferent to the formal consequences of their constructions—beauty being a flower which will spring unbidden from beneath their earnest feet. There are others who discover with such an excess of fervor the dramatic possibilities of concrete cantilevers and iron *piloti* that they forget to ask if these are in any way appropriate to the idea to be expressed. There are still others whose logic is so absolute that they will allow no felicity of form to go unexplained by economic necessity or technical virtuosity, nor will they permit any beauty to be enjoyed until justified as a consequence of the slide rule, and frequently her presence in their calculated halls will be acknowledged only after an argument.

Like a ministering angel the machine enters our house to give a new perspective and economy, a new range and efficiency, to the processes of daily living; to lengthen the hours of freedom; to dispel a thousand tyrannies of custom and prejudice; to lift mountains of drudgery from our shoulders. Like a herald from a young king newly crowned the machine announces a new dynasty and welcomes us to its liberating authority. Like a first breath of April the machine purifies and invigorates. Architects are right to love the machine; they could not otherwise build a modern house.

We are right to love the machine but we must not permit it to extinguish the fire on our hearth. The shapes and relationships, the qualities and arrangements of color, light, textures, and the thousand other elements of building through which the human spirit makes itself known: these are the essential substance of a house, in no way incidental to patterns of economy or physical well-being. Through these our walls are made to reach out beyond utility to enclose the ethereal things without which a house is, in any real sense, a useless object. Through these they speak to us of security and peace, of intimate loyalties, love and the tender affection of children, of the romance for which our soldiers hunger, of an adventure relived a thousand times and forever new; nor is that too much to expect of a house.

There is a way of working, sometimes called art, which gives to things made by man qualities of form beyond those demanded by economic, social, or ethical expediency; a way of working which brings into harmony with ourselves some part of our environment created by us; which makes that environment, through education, a universal experience; which transforms the science of building into architecture.

If a dinner is to be served it is art which dresses the meat, determines the order of serving, prepares and arranges the table, establishes and directs the conventions of costume and conversation, and seasons the whole with that ceremony which, long before Lady Macbeth explained it to us, was the best of all possible sauces. If a story is to be told it is art which gives the events proportion and climax, fortifies them with contrast, ten-sion, and the salient word, colors them with metaphor and allusion, and so makes them cognate and kindling to the heart. If a prayer is made, it is art which sets it to music, surrounds it with ancient observances, guards it under the solemn canopies of great cathedrals.

The shapes of all things made by man are determined by their functions, by the laws of materials and the laws of energies, by marketability (sometimes) and the terms of manufacture; but these shapes may also be determined by the need, more ancient and more imperious than your crescent techniques, for some assurance of importance and worth in those things which encompass humanity. That is true also of all forms of doing, of all patterns of work and conduct and pageantry. It is true of the house and of all that takes place in the house; for here among all the things made is that which presses most immediately upon the spirit—the symbol, the armor, and the hearth of a family. The temple itself grew from this root; and the House of God, which architecture celebrates with her most glorious gifts, is only the simulacrum and crowning affirmation of that spiritual knowledge which illumined first the life of the family and only afterwards the lives of men living in communities.

Here is that *shelter* which man shaped in the earth one hundred thousand years ago, the pit which became the wattle hut, the cave, the mound dwelling, the Sioux lodge, and the thousand other constructions with which our restless invention has since covered the earth: the *shelter* which in a million forms has accompanied man's long upward journey, his companion and shield and outer garment. Here is that *home* which first shaped and disciplined our emotions and over centuries formed and confirmed the habits and valuations upon which human society rests. Here is that *space* which man learned to refashion into patterns conformable to his spirit: the space which he made into architecture.

This theme, so lyrical in its essential nature, can be parodied by science. An excess of physiological realism, for example, can dissemble and disfigure the spirit quite as ingeniously as that excess of sugar which eclecticism in its popular aspect pours over the suburban house. A "fearless affirmation" of the functions of nutrition, dormation, education, procreation, and garbage disposal is quite as false a premise for design as that clutter of rambling roofs, huge chimneys, quaint dormers, that prim symmetry of shuttered window and overdoor fanlight, which form the more decorous disguise of Bronxville and Wellesley Hills; nor have I a firmer faith in the quaint language and high intentions of those sociologists who arrive at architecture through "an analytical study of environmental factors favorable to the living requirements of families considered as instruments of social continuity." I am even less persuaded by biologists: especially those who have created a vegetable humanity to be preserved or cooled or propagated in boxes created for those purposes. I mean those persons who make diagrams and action photographs showing the impact upon space made by a lady arranging a bouquet or a gentleman dressing for dinner or 3.81 children playing at kiss-in-the-ring—and who then invite architects to fit their rooms around these "basic determinants." My requirements are somewhat more subtle than those of a ripe tomato or a caged hippopotamus, whatever may be the opinion of the Pierce Foundation.

We have developed in our day a new language of structural form. That language is capable of deep eloquence; and yet we use it too infrequently for the purposes of a language. Just as the historical styles of architecture are detached from modern technologies and by that detachment lose that vitality and vividness which might come from a direct reference to our times, so our new motives are detached from the idea to be expressed. They have their origin not in the idea but in problems of construction and in principles of planning. We have not yet learned to give them meanings sufficiently persuasive. They have often interesting aesthetic qualities, they arrest us by their novelty and their drama, but too often they have very little to say to us.

The architects of the Georgian tradition were as solicitous as we are of progress in the science of building. They designed their houses with the same care for practical use that they spent, for example, upon their coaches and their sailing ships; and yet their first consideration was for their way of life. When I visit the streets of Salem I am not so confident as are some of my colleagues that her architects suffered from a limited range of materials and structural methods. Standing in the midst of a culture alien to their quaint formalisms, these houses yet make known to me the idea they were meant to capture. I understand them as I might understand a song sung in a foreign tongue. We are too ready to mistake novelty for progress and progress for art. I tell my students that there were noble buildings before the invention of plywood. They listen indulgently but they do not believe me.

I sometimes think that we have to defend our houses against the new prosesses of construction and against the aesthetic forms which these engender. We must remind ourselves that techniques have a strictly limited value as elements of expression. Their competence lies in the way we use them. However they may intrigue us they have no place in the design of a house unless they do indeed serve the purpose of the home and are congenial to its temper. When, as often happens, their only virtue is their show, their adventitious nature is soon realized; they are then as great an impediment to our melody as an excess of ornamentation. The mighty cantilever which projects my house over a kitchen yard or a waterfall; that flexible wall and stressed skin; these fanaticisms of glass brick; these strange hoverings of my house over the firm earth—these strike my eyes but not my heart. A master may at his peril use them; but for human nature's daily use we have still proportion, homely ordinance, quiet wall surfaces, good manners, common sense, and love. These also are excellent building materials.

The world will not ask architects to tell it that this is an age of invention, of new excitements and experiences and powers. The airplane, the radio, the V-bomb, and the giant works of engineering will give that assurance somewhat more persuasively than the most enormous of our contraptions. Beside the big top of industry our bearded lady will not long astonish the mob.

It should be understood that I do not despise the gifts of our new sciences; and certainly the architects of the 1920's made convincing demonstrations of the utility of these in an art of expression. They used structural inventions not for their own sake nor yet for the sake of economy and convenience merely but as elements in a language. Functionalism was a secondary characteristic of their expressive art which had as its basic conception, so far as this is related to the home, a search for a form which should exhibit a contemporary phase of an ancient aspect of life. To this end new materials were used, old ones discarded; but the true reliance was not upon these but upon new and significant relationships among architectural elements—among which enclosed space was the prime medium, walls and roofs being used as a means of establishing spatial compositions. To compose in prisms rather than in mass, to abolish the façade and deal in total form, to avoid the sense of enclosure, to admit to a precise and scrupulous structure no technique not consonant with the true culture of our day: these were the important methods of an architecture never meant to be definitive or "international"— which offered rather a base from which a new progress might be possible, a principle which should have its peculiar countenance in every nation and in every clime. I should not venture here to restate a creed already so often stated had not a torrent of recent criticism distorted this architecture into a "cold and un-

compromising functionalism," had it not been made the excuse
for an arid materialism wholly alien to its intention.

We must rely not upon the wonder and drama of our inventions but upon the qualities, beyond wonder and beyond utility,
which we can give them. Take, for example, *space*. Of all the
inventions of modern architecture the new space is, it seems to
me, the most likely to attain a deep eloquence. I mean by this
not only that we have attained a new command of space but
also a new quality of space. Our new structure and our new
freedom in planning—a freedom made possible in part at least
by the flat roof—has set us free to model space, to define it, to
direct its flow and relationships; and at the same time these have
given space an ethereal elegance unknown to the historic architectures. Our new structure permits almost every shape and relationship in this space. You may give it what proportion you
please. With every change in height and width, in relation to the
spaces which open from it, in the direction of the planes which
enclose it, you give it a new expression. Modern space can be
bent or curved; it can move or be static, rise or press downward,
flow through glass walls to join the space of patio or garden,
break into fragments around alcoves and galleries, filter through
curtains or end abruptly against a stone wall. You may also give
it balance and symmetrical rhythms.

If then we wish to express in this new architecture the idea of
home, if we wish to say in this persuasive language that this idea
accompanies, persistent and eloquent, the forward march of industry and the changing nature of society, we have in the different aspects of space alone a wide vocabulary for that purpose.

I have of course introduced this little dissertation on space in
order to illustrate this resourcefulness. I did not intend a treatise.
I might with equal relevance have mentioned light, which is
certainly as felicitous a medium of modern design, or the new
materials which offer so diversified a palette of texture and color,

or the forms and energies of our new types of construction, or the relationships to site and to nature made possible by new principles of planning. There are also the arts of painting and sculpture, of furniture-making, of textiles, metalware, and ceramics—all of which are, or ought to be, harmonious accessories to architecture.

I have heard architects explain with formulas, calculation, diagram, and all manner of auricular language, the advantages of the glass wall—of wide areas of plate glass opening on a garden —when all that was necessary was to say that here is one of the loveliest ideas ever entertained by an architect. People who *feel* walls do not need to compute them; and people who are deaf to the rhythms of great squares of glass relieved by quiet areas of light-absorbing wall may as well resign the enjoyment of architecture. Because they are free of those "holes punched in the wall," of that balance and stiff formalism in window openings which proclaim the Georgian mode, because we can admit light where we please and in what quantity we please, we have in effect invented a new kind of light. We can direct light, control its intensity and its colorations; diffuse it over space, throw it in bright splashes against a wall, dissolve it and gather it up in quiet pools; and from those scientists who are at work on new fashions in artificial light we ought to expect not new efficiencies merely or new economies merely, but new radiances in living.

Space, structure, texture, light—these are less the elements of a technology than the elements of an art. They are the colors of the painter, the tones of the musician, the images out of which poets build their invisible architectures. Like color, tone, and image they are most serviceable when they are so used as to make known the grace and dignity of the spirit of man.

Of course I know that modern architecture must adjust its processes to the evolving pattern of industry, that building methods must attain an essential unity with all the other processes by which in this mechanized world materials are assembled and shaped for us. No doubt the wholesale nature of our constructions imposes upon us a monotony and banality beyond that achieved by past architectures—a condition not likely to be remedied by prefabrication—and no doubt our houses, as they conform more closely to our ever advancing technologies, will escape still further the control of art. Still more inimical to architecture will be those standardizations of thought and idea already widely established in our country; that assembly-line society which stamps men by the millions with mass attitudes and mass ecstasies. Our standards of judgment will be progressively formed by advertisement and the operations convenient to industry.

I shall not imagine for my future house a romantic owner, nor shall I defend my client's preferences as those foibles and aberrations usually referred to as "human nature." No, he shall be a modern owner, a post-modern owner, if such a thing is conceivable. Free from all sentimentality or fantasy or caprice, his vision, his tastes, his habits of thought shall be those most necessary to a collective-industrial scheme of life; the world shall, if it pleases him, appear as a system of casual sequences transformed each day by the cumulative miracles of science. Even so he will claim for himself some inner experiences, free from outward control, unprofaned by the collective conscience. That opportunity, when the universe is socialized, mechanized, and standardized, will yet be discoverable in the home. Though his house is the most precise product of modern processes there will be entrenched within it this ancient loyalty invulnerable against the siege of our machines. It will be the architect's task, as it is today, to comprehend that loyalty—to comprehend it more firmly than anyone else—and, undefeated by all the armaments of industry, to bring it out in its true and beautiful character.

CHAPTER TEN

love and little houses

IN the course of my researches I have accumulated some interesting data respecting the preferences of house owners. These may be useful to those philosophers, speculators like myself in the things of the spirit, who are curious to chart and account for the tides of popular taste.

I find, for example, that people are very fond of the dormer window. Surveying that wide fringe of new houses which since the war has encircled Greater Boston with a wreath of whiteness I estimate that there have been built here 743,128 dormer windows and that 134,321 additional dormer windows exist in embryo on the drafting boards of Boston architects.

I find that windows with shutters—green, orange, or Williamsburg blue—are even more popular. Before the end of the present year, if my careful statistics are to be trusted, the number of such windows in Greater Boston will reach the astounding total of 3,148,211, of which 2,128,001 will have shutters perforated with heart-shaped openings, 348,023 will have shutters perforated with openings in the shape of a pine tree, and the rest will have perforations in the shape of a crescent moon or scimitar.

As for garages annexed to houses, I have no precise figures, but it seems probable that the number of such additions designed in imitation of ye olde Mattachusetts wood-shedde will reach half a million.

Now there must be some explanation for preferences so universal—and it is evident that this explanation could not possibly be based upon rational or scientific grounds. No form of window could be less reasonable than a dormer window, none could outrage more violently the technological conscience. Everyone knows that a dormer window costs more to build than any other type of window; that it admits less light and air than any other; creates more difficulties in furnishing and decorating; encourages more dust and grime-filled corners; and affords the maximum opportunities for leaks and repairs. The shuttered window, to be sure, is somewhat more practical since it provides the chink through which one may aim an arrow at a prowling Indian, should one appear on the lawns of Wellesley Hills or Newton Upper Falls; and yet the money spent each year in Boston for shutters which are never closed, plus the cost of keeping last year's shutters bright with paint—green, orange, or Williamsburg blue—would, if invested with the Shawmut National Bank at 1¾%, provide annual scholarships for 743 students at the Pawtucket Genealogical Seminary.

People otherwise thrifty and practical who suffer such costs and inconveniences must do so from some inward compulsion not to be explained by ordinary methods of accounting and analysis. I believe that I have found this explanation. These preferences are preferences of the heart. They have their origins in love.

At this point, if I am to make myself understood, I must introduce a brief dissertation on the nature of love.

Love has, among its myriad facets, three which are especially pertinent to architecture. Love, in the first place, does not reason. People who love do not argue about the things they love or about themselves when they are in love. Analysis, experiment, deduction—these are for professors; and professors, as all the world knows, make the worst kind of lovers. Do not therefore look for logic in little houses. It is enough to know your own heart.

Love, in the second place, does not calculate. Ten million

novels have been written to describe the well-deserved fate of the lover who marries for social advancement or for money to pay his tailor. Will you, then, marry your house for money? Will your decisions rest on balances between value and cost— as if you were shopping in a department store? And when you have built your house will you live in it in mortal sin, year after miserable year, pretending that you love plywood, linoleum, and monk's cloth when all the time your real passion is for good old English oak and Kirmanshah? There is no hypocrisy so low as simulated love.

Love, finally, does not imitate. To build a flat roof and an unshadowed wall because you wish to be thought modern, to suffer a corner window in order to impress the neighbors, to keep up with the Joneses by means of tubular furniture and a Picasso: these are the unpardonable betrayals of love.

Love, then, does not argue, does not calculate, and does not imitate—or, if it does any of these, it is to that extent less love. People who build Cape Cod cottages, complete with dormer windows and wood-shedde garages, do so without argument or calculation; and if they imitate they do so, not to display a modish taste or a progressive mind, but instinctively as birds imitate when they build their nests, following love's perennial uniqueness.

Now this seems to me to be most relevant to the cause of architecture. We forget that it is not beauty which makes a thing lovable but love which makes a thing beautiful. Our houses, Georgian or modern, are only beautiful to those who love them. What then could be more heartening to a philosopher than the discovery that there is at least one kind of building that people truly love? I think it something of a miracle in these days that there are people who love buildings; and surely that circumstance is more important to our art than the fact that they love some particular kind of building. Love is not so constant a passion that we should fear this rivalry. Perhaps we are less than clever when we waste so much time in logic and exposition. It may be that there is a shorter road to the popularity of our new patterns.

I should like now to illumine that road with a little parable. I should like now to tell the true and instructive story of my friend Mrs. Quigley, of Potawatami, Massachusetts, who loved a dormer window and of what happened to her love on that fateful day when she met in the basement of a department store that cool and rakish seducer, that innocent-looking, gallant and designing fox, the electric automatic washing machine.

Mrs. Quigley's Colonial house was precisely like the 4,323 other Colonial houses of Potawatami; but then so was her baby precisely like the 4,323 other babies of Potawatami. Mrs. Quigley loved her Colonial house; loved the quaint roof lines and the widow's walk; loved the square cosy chimney and the rose-trellised doorway; the flowered wall paper and the chintzes, the bannister-back chairs, the grandfather clock and the gilt-framed portrait of Great-Aunt Amelia. But Mrs. Quigley was only human. The manly and confident form, the white and restful serenity, the sweet alluring promises of the washing machine were bewitching even to one who had lived intimately with a spinning wheel; and when that washing machine stood in Mrs. Quigley's laundry where once stood the dank wooden tubs, the dismal wringers, the pot-bellied stove where she had boiled her clothes, the platform on which she had stood to escape the soapy floor; when in the place of all these Mrs. Quigley saw the clean round obsequious automaton—washer, wringer, ironer, drier, sweet singer and companion all in one—well, at that moment Mrs. Quigley's love of the dormer window underwent a strange retro-gression. "I love you, Bendix," said Mrs. Quigley—and she gave a party for her friends in the laundry.

Mrs. Quigley's love for the washing machine was of a different quality from her love for the dormer window; but it was none the less love. It was like a hunter's love for his Enfield rifle; like a photographer's love for his Leica camera; a smoker's love for his Dunhill lighter. It was a love for perfection and elegance in technique, for competence in the thing to be done, in friend- liness and understanding and coöperative effort in the multiplex burdens which oppress our contemporary life. It was a love of the real and the present. It sprang not from remembrance but from the joy of being alive, of being a part of this wonderful new world of science and invention, of being free to enjoy it. It sprang from a delight in new powers, in new discovery and adventure, in new extensions of personality. It had nothing to do with quaintness and antimacassars.

The kitchen, as it happened, adjoined the laundry. It was a most romantic kitchen, full of marvelous smells, confusions, and the tried traditions of cookery; full of memories and the love of far-off things and things of the long ago. Yet that kitchen was the easy victim of the washing machine. Try as she might—and did anyone ever try very hard to hide a love?—Mrs. Quigley could not secrete her new love behind the laundry door. Brothers and conspirators to the washing machine, there soon stood in Mrs. Quigley's kitchen an electric refrigerator cool as a column from the Parthenon, an electric range as chastely melodic as a symphony by Haydn, a dish-washer and sink white and virginal as Mont Blanc, and all around the choiring cabinets in level files sang sweet hosannas of deliverance and praise.

Perhaps Mrs. Quigley really believed that she could confine the invasion of this mechanized world to her kitchen; it should stop short at the swinging door that led to the dining room. Mrs. Quigley would give only a piece of her heart to the washing machine and remain true, in a Cynarian kind of way, to the dormer window. Alas, how many wives attempt that double life, their hearts in two compartments, separated by that swinging door. How many, like the prudent lady in Boccaccio's story, burn two such candles, one to St. Michael, another to his dragon.

Are two loves at once really possible and, considering the nature of husbands, practicable? Efficiency, candor, simplicity, and sunlight in the kitchen, ye olde clutter in the parlor? Unfaithfulness is less detestable than pretending to be faithful—and more easily endured. The time came when the spirit of modernism boldly declared itself—and pushed through that swinging door.

Mrs. Quigley's dining room was formal, as befitted the high ritual of eating, and dignified in the extreme. A massive sideboard of oak stood at one side too heavy to be moved except by a steam crane and hungry for dust in its innumerable carvings. Opposite stood glass-doored reliquaries filled with priceless delicate spoil from Messrs. Plummer and Company, and surrounding the monumental dining table stood a brave fraternity of perilous chairs, high-backed, sculptured, lacquered with Chinese ornament. A mirror in a rococo frame glittered above the sideboard and reflected the portrait of Great-aunt Amelia which hung on the opposite wall; and from the ceiling hung the crystalline chandelier, of electric bulbs innumerable and of pendent cut glass, inviting soap and water every Friday morning.

Now, a sentiment for modernity can be less absolute in its preferences than many people suppose. It does not truly demand a machine to live in; and often, without inconsistence it will join grace and dignity to its cool efficiency. Mrs. Quigley—who, as my readers will have perceived, was a woman of good sense —did not think it necessary to move her dining table into the kitchen where it could be functionally surrounded by the smells of things being fried—nor did she turn her dining room into an icebox. Neither did she think of that room as "conspicuously wasteful" because it was used only three times a day or imagine the ceremonies of the table to be inconsistent with a liberated way of life or with the creed of democracy. Mrs. Quigley's dining room is as simple and as spacious as her kitchen but somewhat less antiseptic in appearance; her new furniture is light and unaffected and yet is not without elegance and wit; and the business of serving and of eating is provided for without the sacrifice of a decent formality. The spirit of our era is less uncongenial to good manners than our young architects sometimes imply in their designs.

And now before that spirit enters into and conquers Mrs. Quigley's living room and in the end takes possession of all of her house I must ask the indulgence of my readers for another brief digression. We know that profound changes in human thought and opinion are brought about only by crises. Without sudden tornadoes, floods, wars, crashes on the stock exchange, and unlooked-for encounters with new loves we would go on forever thinking the same thoughts, doing monotonously the same things, holding firmly to the same prejudices. Without a crisis we shall continue to the end of time, from Maine to the coast of California, our uniformity of taste and manners, seeking the same fashions in clothes and automobiles, drinking the same Coca-Colas, flocking to the same movies to laugh at the same jokes. When a crisis arrives we will look about us.

Consider then how great a crisis had shaken the soul of Mrs. Quigley when she entered her living room resolute that that room also, hitherto the very citadel and tabernacle of the Colonial style, should be made comfortable to the demands of her new and inexorable love.

Mrs. Quigley's living room was like her dining room, rich, elegant, and correct. At one end double glass doors led into the dining room; at the other end a pilastered mantelpiece supported a picture of the Bridge of Sighs. Over the wallpaper there were scattered little pictures of a mill with a water wheel alternating with pictures of a meetinghouse sheltered by a tree—232 water wheels, 231 meetinghouses—and the window curtains were splashed with passionate roses. On the floor was an oriental rug, manufactured in Newark. The furniture, precious and highly elegant, comprised a mahogany highboy, snooty and inutile, a gate-legged table, darkly treacherous, supporting tea things gay with China's richest dyes; two wing-back chairs, defying comfort, and a piano, jauntily draped with an embroidered doily, and an atmosphere overcharged with dusting, polishing, waxing, and extremely Sunday behavior.

Like the chambered nautilus, Mrs. Quigley cast aside her outworn shell. Mrs. Quigley discovered the present and took it to herself: not because she had been convinced by argument, not because she had persuasively calculated the costs and the rewards, not because she felt it the right thing to do, but because, being a woman of courage and conviction, and having only one life to live, she followed in architecture as in life her secret heart.

I wish that I could bring before my readers a clear picture of the house which Mrs. Quigley built in the little town of Potawatami. I consider it to be without exception one of the masterpieces of modern architecture: an estimate which will no doubt seem all the more remarkable when I add that Mrs. Quigley's house has not a single corner window or partition of transparent blocks, does not rest upon concrete cantilevers projecting over a waterfall, is not raised above the firm earth on slender columns of cast iron, was not entirely fabricated in a factory, and moreover is reasonably reticent in the use of plate glass.

Freedom, candor, and nature are the ingredients of Mrs. Quigley's house, developed not from strange new shapes publicized in the progressive magazines but from Mrs. Quigley's love: from her love of that newly discovered world which seemed to have been especially created for her by an obsequious science. Her house is not a mold into which her life is uncomfortably fitted, not an essay in form congruous to correct and tasteful standards, not a utility explained and justified by consideration of economy and expediency but a frame for her individual life, hospitable like its owner to the free scope of thought and personal preference, exulting like her in escape, its heart open to the sun. The spirit of modernity walks there, not as a guest honored with conventional courtesies, not as a rich relation who must be cajoled, not as a servant who must be as silent and invisible as is possible, but as Aladdin walked in his palace, conjurer, owner, and architect.

The sense of freedom, which is the most pervasive sentiment in Mrs. Quigley's house, has its origin, I think, in a new quality of space, somewhat hard to define but unmistakable to anyone who has visited her. My first impression was that of a space almost continuous throughout the house: of each room flowing into the others, so that each room acknowledged, so to speak, the presence of the other rooms around it. There were none of those rectangular boxes in which Mrs. Quigley had lived so long, those strict formalizations of axes, geometrical symmetries, studied compositions of wall and furniture; and everywhere the rooms seemed to be so casually bounded, so lightly separated from the out-of-doors—which penetrated the walls through terraces, porches, and walls of glass—that I imagined myself, not in one of those boxes of wood in which the people of New England are customarily crated, nor yet in one of those firm monuments in brick and Mansart roof by means of which the first families of Potawatami were wont to announce their immutability, but in a bright crystal through whose transparent walls there flowed the sweet air of New England's woods and meadows. Not that the spaces were unorganized: the rooms were defined, related, given form and sequence by walls and ceilings. I recognized the presence of architecture, of a conscious solicitude for relationship and proportion; but that architecture, partly because its forms were based upon functional considerations and partly because its rhythms were so intimate to the thought and feeling of its owner, seemed to be eloquent, even as it imposed its peculiar disciplines upon structure and space, of the beautiful freedom which it framed.

One of the sources of this eloquence was, I am sure, the subtle relationship which had been established between the spaces and the varying character of the walls which enclosed them. These walls were not continuous like the walls of a cave or a box but were more like a number of free-standing planes which seemed to arrest or direct the spaces with gentle pressures each in accordance with the nature of its materials and its form. Thus there were walls, or partitions, of stone masonry which by their stability and density gave a definite and static quality to that part of the spatial composition in which they stood; whereas walls of glass, often adjoining them, invited progressions of space through them, and screens of wood, bounding the rooms lightly, announced the presence of other rooms beyond their membrane-like boundaries. The family of Mrs. Quigley escaped in this way the confinements of closed rooms, except where these are set apart for personal use. They were at home in spaces merging into each other and organized, not only for the varying functions of family living, but organized also, not without subtlety, for changing perspectives and relationships.

I do not of course suggest that this principle of planning was the invention of Mrs. Quigley. It was, as every architect knows, the invention of Professor Mies van der Rohe and I know that Mrs. Quigley would be the last person in the world to wish to rob him of the acclaim which is so justly his. But the soul knows that which is its own and takes it to itself; and just as Mrs. Quigley took to herself without other promptings than those of love the white astral washing machine so she took to herself also, in a spiritual union less like imitation than marriage, Professor Mies van der Rohe.

This brings me to the second ingredient of Mrs. Quigley's house, an ingredient not less essential to its beauty than that sense of freedom which everywhere pervaded it. Mrs. Quigley's house was built with candor. It set forth without evasion or subterfuge the quality of her life and those sensibilities which had guided her life. Each part was adapted directly and without excess to the work which had to be done, the life which had to be lived; its surfaces, furnishings, arrangements were palpably dictated by their places in a scheme of living; and at the same time it was radiant with the joy which its owner found in its use and possession. It proclaimed Mrs. Quigley: her dislike of fussiness and pretense, the clear vision which had discovered a world, the courage with which she accepted its strange and exciting implications. Free of dissimulation and dust, of snobbishness and confusion, Mrs. Quigley's house was like a swimmer who, disdainful of furbelows and the flatteries of Fifth Avenue gives her lithe body without posturing or apology to the cool wind and the sea.

There is little ornament in Mrs. Quigley's house. She relied for color, warmth, and contrast upon the natural qualities of materials: on the rough and cool textures of stone masonry, on the light-absorbing planes of gray or white plaster, on shining glass, the friendly tones and patterns of wood. Where there are pictures, these are chosen, not because they were costly, curious, or fashionable but because of the happiness their presence gave their owner; and they were placed on the walls with solicitude for that general pattern of which they became elements. Where there were curtains these were recognizable as serviceable features tempering the light of windows, dividing at will the area of the larger rooms; and both curtains and rugs are quiet in color and in pattern so as to form backgrounds for the brighter tones of the furniture. As for the furniture itself, my readers may rest assured that Mrs. Quigley will have nothing in her house which is not used, nothing not fitted to comfort, convenience, and the well-being of family and guests, and yet she manages these things so adroitly that she has never found it essential to have chairs and sofas of bizarre or sensational patterns. There is no table built in the shape of a kidney bean, no sofa which parodies the dragon of Siegfried.

Mrs. Quigley will acknowledge, without being questioned, that her ideas of candor, of unconventional preferences, of a taste in interior design "guided but not tyrannized by necessity," * were all found by her in the published work of Mr. Le Corbusier and of those architects who are kindled by his clairvoyant and resourceful spirit.

Vasari said of the Villa Farnesina that it seemed to have been "born rather than built"—so intimate were its forms with the nature which surrounded it and entered into it. The phrase might have been applied, though with somewhat less grandiloquence, to Mrs. Quigley's house. The village of Potawatami offers less opportunities than Rome and the purse of Mrs. Quigley less than that of the Farnese for that subtle art through which the spirit of man can be extended outward from his house into wide areas of disciplined landscapes; and the building lots in Potawatami were laid out by a surveyor whose mind had been trained in that school where calico is carefully cut into measured yards. Nevertheless there were places near the edge of town which seemed to aim at Nature a somewhat less contemptuous glance; and by a judicious placing of her house so as to take every advantage of view, contours, prevailing winds, sunlight, and the planting out of neighbors Mrs. Quigley managed to give her house a unity with the earth upon which it stands, a relationship of structure and setting so happy that it could be said without hyperbole to give it a lyrical beauty not unlike that of a poem by Wordsworth.

* The phrase is that of Mr. Frederick Gutheim.

The sunlight flooded Mrs. Quigley's house through wide areas of glass; the gentle air of her garden entered it through its porches, loggias, and vine-shaded balconies; and the house reached out to the garden through unroofed terraces. There is an outdoor living room furnished with perfume-bearing plants and a flowered pool; there is a dining room in the form of a sheltered loggia; a green-embroidered roof for sun-bathing; and screened porches for sleeping. The materials of Mrs. Quigley's walls are those most congenial to that which environs her, the lines of her roofs and windows echo those of the landscapes around her; and on every side nature invades her house and is cloistered within it. And this friendliness to the out-of-doors which is truly more characteristic of present-day architecture than all the interminable fuss made about the rigors of logic was discovered by Mrs. Quigley in the work of Mr. Frank Lloyd Wright.

And now my readers must imagine Mrs. Quigley at home in her new house and entertaining her favorite guests: at her right the washing machine and Mr. Mies van der Rohe, at her left Mr. Le Corbusier and Mr. Wright. Her guests do not speak to each other, of course, but they speak to Mrs. Quigley; and when they do not speak Mrs. Quigley speaks to them, her heart full of thanksgiving and love.

CHAPTER ELEVEN

space and the garden

THAT which distinguishes modern architecture from all other forms of building is its acceptance, more or less complete, of the world in which we live. Other architectures practiced today are escape architectures: they affirm the beauty or dignity or good manners of some era which has passed away. Modern architecture looks at the present, seeking to discover and make known in visible form whatever may be worthy of expression in our own lives.

We have been told too often that Rome was magnificent, Amiens sublime, and Westover in the very best of Colonial taste. The reconstruction of these on scaffoldings of steel—the essential process of academic architecture—has grown somewhat tedious after a hundred thousand repetitions. That which will rekindle our imaginations and restore vitality to our art is some convincing assurance that splendor, dignity, and beauty are yet possible in this our existing day. I think that we shall have little use for architects, except as technicians, unless they can give us such assurances.

It is often said that modernity of expression arises from the use of modern materials and techniques. Such a definition mistakes the means for the end. Our new materials and processes often offer us new opportunities for the organization of space and for a simplicity and freedom not afforded by the older techniques; they free us also from that excess of romantic values which is apt to be inherent in traditional usages; but they are not in themselves essential to modern design. Although techniques are, assuredly, necessary elements in every culture, the designer must at all times be free to use them or neglect them. He is not compelled to exploit any particular technique.

We were once told that the use of the flying buttress was an essential of Gothic architecture. A distinguished professor—he was, I am afraid, a Harvard professor—defined Gothic as "an architecture of flying buttresses." In making this definition, he denied the word *Gothic* to all the cathedrals of England and to most of those of Germany and Italy. A similar aberration of judgment has defined modern architecture as an architecture of flat roofs, plate glass, and machine methods. Flat roofs are, to be sure, useful in effecting a flexibility of planning otherwise impossible; plate-glass windows admit a greater hospitality to the out-of-doors, to sunshine and trees, than do old-fashioned windows; and the use of machinery in building encourages that clarity and precision, that freedom from dust and sentiment, in which the modern mind delights. These things are, in short, useful media of expression, but they do not in any way prohibit the use of other media which may lie at the artist's hand. Architecture is idea, not concrete or steel. *Architecture,* said Walt Whitman, *is what buildings do to you.*

I have tried once more to make clear my conception of modern architecture in order that I may make clear my conception of a modern garden. Since men, from the beginning of recorded history, and no doubt long before, have striven to reshape both shelter and the environment of shelter in accordance with an inward need—since these have always been, not the consequences of biological necessity merely, but also at all times materials for expression—I see no reason to suppose that modern man will not desire to build, not only his house, but equally his garden in accordance with promptings thus universal in nature. I must confess that I am somewhat surprised to be told again and again that an impulse so old and confirmed will be frustrated by the difficulty of using new techniques and materials in our gardens or because Nature has failed to break down those climatic barriers which localize plant materials or to hasten that slow evolution by which new plants are developed.

Certainly the garden architects who created Caprarola and Vaux-le-Vicomte and Stowe did not demand of Nature that she should throw away her ancient palette of foliage, hill, and stream, to seek out for them new inventions. The invention was theirs, I think, not Nature's. When they looked into the heart of their time and made it visible—now in magnificent settings for Renaissance pageantry, now in the Cartesian discipline which reflected eighteenth-century France, and now in the lush sentiment with which Jean Jacques Rousseau suffused the landscapes of England—they yet placed no rigorous strain upon the bounty of Nature. Neither did they demand of architects as a prerequisite for expression a new vocabulary of structural forms and materials or new processes of manufacture and assembly.

I am impatient with those garden architects who attempt to create a new form of garden by no other means than the introduction of novel constructions or unusual plant forms. I find somewhat boring, after the first surprise, those tubular metal seats "designed for mass construction," those gazebos on iron stilts, those intricately formed beds and boxes outlined in concrete, and all those accessories in paving, furniture, and lighting intended as unmistakable assertions of modernity. One may, of course, obtain a certain congruity between house and garden by carrying out the garden accessories in materials identical to those used in the house. But this congruity cannot have any lasting or convincing character if the adaptation of the garden ends here. It takes more than a lily to make a Chinese lady.

I am equally out of sympathy with those architects who propose the abandonment of all attempts at garden form in the landscape setting of the modern house. The much quoted remark of Professor Henry-Russell Hitchcock echoes this feeling: "the important principle is the preservation of all possible values previously in existence in the landscape setting." The garden architect, it appears, is to add only the simplest and most practical provision for specific human needs. That keynote was echoed by Mr. Richard Neutra who says that the essential characteristic of the modern house is its intimacy with the out-of-doors, a "generous opening to health agents and a biologically minded appreciation of the soil in which all life is rooted." That is, of course, a characteristic of the modern house; but such intimacy-is an attribute which both gives and takes. The house, which holds out its hand to Nature, may expect that Nature should recognize its presence.

Certainly this extreme solicitude for nature seems more persuasive in the words of philosophers than in the practice of garden architects. A meadow with a house could not be the same as a meadow without a house; the values of the meadow are certainly changed by this intrusion even though the house conform in the strictest fashion to biological necessity. Art instantly alters the pattern of its environment. Cataracts, cliffs, and forest vistas assume a tamer aspect through a contact with humanity; trees crowd more sweetly into a shade when they enfold a fragment of human culture; nor is there any element of the knowable universe which does not assume a new quality when measured against the tenancy of man. Certainly a harmony between the modern house and its site is more evident when the site, like the house, has escaped both romance and an oppressive formality; but a deep or persuasive unity cannot be attained when one and not the other has submitted to a conscious control of form. Therefore I do not despair of gardens which are, like houses, *designed*. Around our new architecture, which will be increasingly intellectualized, a discipline will still be imposed upon plants, contours, and accessories; indeed I think that this will be made more rather than less stringent. Some organic relation between house and garden is imperative and this common organism must be conditioned not merely upon the visible world but upon the energies of the human spirit—a spirit which, fortunately, is not conformable to every aspect of the nonhuman world.

We must therefore continue our search for some basis of formalization if we are to create a garden for the modern house. Perhaps we can discover this basis within the house: some principle of order, or disorder, of its surroundings. One such principle at least has been suggested: that very provocative principle which is called *functionalism*. Whatever aesthetic meanings are discoverable in the modern house these were developed, it is believed, from a useful disposition of space and structure; may we not then discover analogous meanings, or create them, from the useful features of the site? A garden is a useful place: a place in which to rest, to entertain, to exercise, to play. Perhaps then the useful elements of the garden, like the useful elements of the house, can be made the source of contemplative as well as practical delights.

Necessity first charted the form that gardens took. The necessity for protection against marauding beasts brought the enclosing wall; the necessity for irrigation brought watercourses into the garden scheme; the necessity for giving certain kinds of plants the environments under which they thrive brought arbors and shaded areas. Out of these simple adaptations grew the main elements which figure in garden designs even today. As we look over the garden architect's wide vocabulary of ideas we find scarcely one that has not a homely paternity. Arbors and orchards, groves and hedges, orangeries, aviaries and dovecotes, gateways, walls, and stairs: each lovely ornament the garden wears dropped in her lap from some (pragmatic) head. We can, therefore, readily persuade ourselves that the modern gardener will find ample precedent for beginning his work with those new facilities which are addressed to the uses of contemporary life, confident in the knowledge that many a noble lineage sprung from as rude an ancestry. If the inherited forms which exist "for their own sake" unjustified by practical purpose and which clutter up the site with a tiresome fussiness must give way to utilitarian forms —to the rigid mechanical forms of tennis court and swimming pool, to concrete terraces, those "convenient outdoor living-spaces," to the drying yard and the garage, to regimented vegetables and roses grown like gooseberries—history nevertheless sanctions a faith that these may in time become sources of a discreet and carefully cultivated delight.

The theory is unassailable, and yet it does not promote a present delight in gardens. The fact is plain: we don't like those utilitarian forms. Philosophers may if they will await the slow metamorphosis of these into things of beauty; we in the meantime are apt to take refuge in unfunctional roses and the un-metaphysical gazebo.

From that vantage point let's examine this functionalism somewhat more curiously. This arbor, this wall, this water-course which we admire were perhaps not so admirable when years ago they were first shaped by necessity. If they have now, as they did then, the "sweet ornament which truth doth give" they yet received, before we called them beautiful, many reshapings which certainly were not exclusively utilitarian in nature. These practical constructions, in brief, attained their present loveliness by successive adaptations to a spiritual need, quite as exigent and as universal as our need for truth. Their development *proceeded from function* by means of changes which were as often as not the consequences of wholly irrational preferences.

Practical facilities then must be considered as means, not as ends, in garden design. Our gardens, like our houses, may indeed be conditioned upon use. They may be conditioned also upon

topography and techniques, and they may take into account the
need of men for play and for illusion; but if they are to attain
any enduring command of our imaginations, they must also be
conditioned upon qualities which have their origin, not in this
material world but in that inward experience which transcends
sensual reality. They must conform to our vision of Nature and
of man's place in Nature, to our need for peace and completeness in that world, to our own faith in a dignity and purpose
in human life. There are no processes of rationalization which
are likely to eradicate from men the desire to translate into their
environment these sovereign needs. The shape and arrangement
of the site, no less than the constructed forms of the house, will,
if subject to our control, proclaim these ancient aspirations. The
modern man, like his forbears, will remake nature in his own
image.

We have misunderstood the modern house if we have not discovered in it some hint of this universal quality. The modern
house is not merely a protest; it is also an adventure. The liberating spirit which invades this machine is creating an ideal of
form not less strenuous than that which is overcome. This free
disposition of spaces, lightly confined by thin contours, which
answer so intimately the pressures and directions of our society,
is as surely subjected to an intellectual discipline as was the
classicism which it displaces. These rooms that throw open their
walls to admit through wide areas of glass the light and freedom
of the out-of-doors are as rigorously conditioned upon a search
for expression. If roofs are made flat and floors carried on metal
columns and not on masonry, if walls are displaced by thin
membranes of wood or plaster hung like curtains on a metallic
framework, if surfaces inside and out are clear of ornament and
shadow, this is not to be explained as merely boredom with the
antique attitudes, nor as caprice intent on "something different";
still less as the necessary operation of a scientific law. These are

not merely the expressions of science, of efficiency, of hygiene; they are the elements of a new expression.

I am inclined to believe that this new expression is most clearly exhibited in the new quality of space and in the new command of space: a space free as in no other architecture from the tyranny of structure. In our new houses structure exists not to confine space but to model it, to direct its flow, to define the volumes into which it is only lightly divided. It is these volumes which are the important elements of our design; and we are as free to arrange them as a sculptor is free to evoke from inert stone his patterns of solid shapes. Our new arrangements of space are less evidently the consequence of geometric principles; they rely less upon balance, proportion, symmetrical rhythms; their separation from the outward cosmic space is less definite; but they escape, nevertheless, purely functional adaptations. From their inexhaustible variety in shape and relationship, and from the consequent freedom in the relations of distances, the ordering of intervals, the harmony or contrast of measured or dissonant volumes, there has been created a new material of expression whose range and resourcefulness we have until now scarcely guessed at.

Gardens, like houses, are built of space. Gardens are fragments of space set aside by the planes of terraces and walls and disciplined foliage. Until now we have defined too nicely the differences between that space which is roofed and within the house and that which is left outside and around the house. We did not see, until the architect threw down his walls, that the space of house and that of garden are parts of a single organism: that the secret of unity lies in a unity of spatial sequences. The new vision has dissolved the ancient boundary between architecture and landscape architecture. The garden flows into and over the house: through loggias and courts and wide areas of clear glass, and over roofs and sunrooms and canopied terraces. The house reaches out into the garden with walls and terraced enclosures that continue its rhythms and share its grace. The concordant factor is the new quality given to space.

The time will surely come when the garden architect will wish to awaken and intensify by his art a consciousness of a garden space at one with that of the house: of the house which is, or should be, only a sequestered part of the garden. Not that space will be his only material of expression: not that gardens are to be built of airy nothings wrapped in cellophane. I would admit to them, in due proportion and relationship, every flower and tree known to gardener, every ornament sculptured or constructed, and every quiet or active pattern of water, provided only that these were consistent with his central intention. But at this moment I am concerned with a principle of unification. Just as in the Renaissance garden this principle is found in the monumental character of the château, whose solidity and whose static geometry are repeated in the firm masses of balustraded terraces, steps and clipped foliage, so it may happen that the relation and balance of volumes in the modern house will be transmitted to the garden and reëstablish there the ancient unity of house and garden.

I am the more persuaded that such a unity is possible when I consider the importance of space as an aesthetic material in the great traditions of architecture. If the theme of our art is indeed some meaning discovered in the world, if the authority of architecture does indeed arise from its power to reveal the ethereal values, what other medium is more apposite to this intention than the enclosed spaces which are molded immediately by the uses and preferences of mankind? Architecture has always been developed about such spaces. It would be impossible, for example, to imagine the Georgian society in any other setting than in rooms shaped into prim, geometric forms and balanced decorously along enfilades. We cannot conceive of the seventeenth century except in the oval saloons which melt into each other under sumptuously modeled vaults or along the glamorous progressions of grand stairways. No other medium has received with such candor the imprint of every way of life: the Romanesque space, somber and inert under the cavelike vaults; the Gothic space, nervous and energetic under membranes of thin stone and amethyst; the Victorian space, fussy and self-conscious and broken into romantic episodes. Not in every instance has the garden echoed the spatial order of the house but when this has happened the splendor of the garden has been immeasurably enhanced by that unity of intention.

Our new space proclaims as eloquently the evolving scheme of our lives, the new patterns of idea and manners, the changed tempo, the wider horizons. Into these new orderings of space there shall be translated the grace and order which the architect has discovered beneath the infinite complexities, the speed, the vast dimensions, and the harsh mechanizations of our world. That which the house tells us, the garden must reaffirm.

CHAPTER TWELVE

fundamentals

I T is probable that the first buildings were created with as little conscious intent as were the nests of birds. They were the spontaneous consequences of man's need for protection against the elements and against animals stronger and better armored than he. Woven of branches in the fork of a tree or hollowed by rude tools out of the floor of the forest the primitive house was from the beginning a utility—a shield and outer garment, immediate and practical—attaining this its essential character before the builder was aware of himself as craftsman and maker of patterns.

At what moment then was the house thus fashioned shaped also by that need for expression which lifted the science of building into the art of architecture? In the earliest records of human life that science is already inseparable from those processes by which man impressed his spirit upon all things made by him—from that ardor for color, carving, and rhythmical disposition which saturates the primitive world. The making of shelter, like the making of weapons and idols, of marriages, wars, feasts, and burials, is already an occasion for symbol-making, already an element in that language which preceded the invention of language.

This dual nature of architecture, utility and humanity, established it may be before man had assumed a conscious direction of the processes of building, was not changed by the develop-

ment of civilizations. The forms of shelter, remaining conformable to needs which were biological in character, were yet made
eloquent of man's desire to understand and expand his life. Not
in the name of taste or academic sanction but as a part of those
methods by which wood and stone were assembled, shaped, and
arranged for a physical existence, these forms were given some
hint of those meanings which we are forever seeking in the
world. They were, as they are today, one of the means by which
our environment is brought into harmony with ourselves and by
which our environment, in turn, is made to sustain and illustrate
our civilized lives.

It was in that way that the heap of stones raised over a hero's
body became the pyramid. The shapeless tumulus grew slowly
into geometrical crystal, attained proportion, definition of plane
and profile, elegance of surface, exhibiting through these media-
tions Egypt's new awareness of a scheme in the universe. An
object set in space, actual, material, and permanent, flinging
the sun across the desert from its polished walls, the pyramid
consoled Egypt with the certitude of a life after death—and yet
remained a heap of stones protecting a hero's body. Apparatus
and abstract sculpture, language and ornament of a civilization,
the pyramid defines architecture.

When in the course of time architecture expanded its themes
it expanded with these the range of its expression. Architecture
embraced in its changing patterns the new and ever more complex requirements of successive cultures; the temple, the palace, the fortress, and the market took their places beside the
dwelling and the tomb; and at the same time architecture developed new relationships of form whose deepening significance
conformed to new vision and experience. If formal values appear
to depend upon practical values that is because they were, before
the advent of an architecture divorced from life, integral the
one to the other.

The temple in Egypt grew out of the dwelling, as the pyramid had grown out of the tomb, by functional adaptations into which new meanings were progressively fused. The divine communion, growing ever more elaborate in symbol and ceremony, demanded a theater which with each rebuilding became greater in scale and more sumptuous in ornament, but beyond that need lay the not less imperious need to translate into visible forms a pattern, newly discovered, in human life. Into his incomparable sequences of space and structure the architect of the temple built the rituals of worship—and built also a significance which transcends ritual and creed. The ordered progressions of sculpture-lined avenues, of majestic gates, of peristyle-embroidered courts, of many-aisled halls and mystery-shrouded sanctuary could not have held a people spellbound for twenty centuries had they not found there a consoling promise of a unity and completeness lying beneath the fragmentary appearances of the world.

In Greece as in Egypt architecture continued to widen its serviceable forms and with these to widen the range of its expression. In Greece, where religion became inseparable from the communal spirit, where the great mysteries were not apart from the popular life, the temple welded the hard and subtle city with the radiant faith which came out of the forest and the sea. The Acropolis, bright with the spoils of devotion, as evidently celebrates the splendor of Athens. So the Greek theater, which takes a population into its arms, is filled with a spirit of civic unfoldment and destiny; the peristyled dwelling is as luminous of the loyalties and withdrawal of the family; and even the market place invites in its portico-surrounded spaces an awareness of participation and joint possession. Such buildings could not have been impassive setting and convenience merely; they were active to shape and build; they created the citizen who had created them. Well into the Hellenistic Age the Greek architect continued to inform his hardening formulas with that inward authority.

That we should seek to recapture the spirit of this architecture by the imitation of its shapes and ordinances, disentangling these from the culture to which they were integral, is no doubt inevitable in an era accustomed to analysis and experiment. The time comes in every progression of architecture when we will strive by measurement and formula to seize the beauty we have discovered in antique buildings and to re-create this beauty by instruments of precision without reference to the experience in which it was originally framed; when we will value architectures "for their own sake" unassociated with the time and circumstance which occasioned them. At such times the totality of architecture as a phenomenon embracing both utility and expression will be overcome by an architecture of ritual. Cut off from the roots which reach into social activity and feeling, architecture becomes a formalism.

Greek architecture after Alexander submitted gradually to such an impoverishment. In Antioch, Ephesus, and Pergamum, where the Aegean fire was slowly smothered under eastern luxuries, a vocabulary of codified forms came between the architect and the idea to be expressed. These followed Apollo and Aphrodite to Rome and raised there temples as perfunctory as the religion to which they ministered. Under the Republic architecture existed in Rome as little more than a material of luxury, a means of bringing Rome into the circle of the Hellenic civilizations. Even Augustus seems to have valued architecture chiefly as a "visible manifestation and guarantee of the grandeur of the State." His ideal was that of correctness, of conformity to the civilized standard, of brick overcome by marble.

To discover the futility of such an architecture we have only to compare these earlier Roman buildings with the majestic and true affirmations of the Roman genius in the Golden Age of

Hadrian and Trajan. The Pantheon, the Ulpian Forum, the great thermae were invented, not copied; and because those who conceived and built them were solicitous of purpose in the general and contemporary scheme of Roman life, because they were kindled by the grandeur and promise of that world-order which was Rome, because they believed in it, approved it, took it to themselves, Roman architecture was made accessible to the Roman spirit which finds there a genuine and moving expression. The imperial idea, which had eluded the scholarship and piety of Augustus, is the very substance of this new architecture, as much a part of the collective faith as were the form of the government, the military triumphs, and the games at the circus and amphitheater.

That the authority which such buildings exercise over us can be made to inform replicas raised in our industrial cities is a folly which must now be tedious even to those who profit most from it. The structures we have copied from Rome participate neither in our life nor in the life of Rome. Aliens one and all—the Columbia Library, the Pennsylvania Station, the National Gallery of Art—they stand aside, spectators of our strange confusions, silent commentators on our impertinent occupations. Without belonging to us, without confirming that which we believe about ourselves, they wear in our streets the pale death masks of a culture which for good or evil has forever passed away.

The fallacy of the imitative process lies not in the scholarship of architecture but in the substitution of scholarship for the immediate vision, or, more precisely, in the attempt to guide our vision with codes and precedents. Not the intentions of the classical masterpieces but rather their outward and formal elements are presented to us as universal and eternal, so that the relation of these to the practical or emotional interests of the ancients appears as fortuitous as their relation to our own interests. The very methods by which the materials and conventions of the Greek and Roman architectures—I mean of course columns, arches, vaults, ornaments—are made accessible to the American practitioner are those most likely to confirm a divorce between these architectures and a present reality. We know the Parthenon in documents, in plaster casts, in innumerable appliqués against the sides of our buildings; we know it as museum piece and specimen; it no longer stands on the Acropolis.

Such theologies of architecture are not without their seductions. There is an adventure, as well as a discipline, in the subtleties of form unfolded in the pages of Vignola which ought not to be denied our students, and still less ought we to deny them the musical harmonies of the Doric peristyle or the majestic silences under the Roman dome. Such experiences are nourishment to the creative force, to which a genuine scholarship is never an impairment. Our learning is only dangerous when we mistake it for a process of design. We may even at times make a discreet display of our scholarship without, I think, inviting disaster to the cause of modernism. I should admit a portico now and then to the scenic architecture of our streets in much the same spirit as I might admit a Latin quotation to my English text. There would be fewer misunderstandings among architects if, like authors, they could frame their transcriptions in quotation marks.

I am more tolerant in these matters now that our architecture has escaped the trap set for it by the dialecticians of the Classical and Gothic revivals. I am by no means indifferent to the beauty of stylistic reproductions; I understand how they can be loved. If only, like Cleopatra, they would set a bourn how far to be beloved!

The trouble lies not in our reproductions of past architectures but in the fashion which has given them so wide a command over the public taste. The limitations they lay upon the perception and feeling of our people are such as almost to prohibit an apprehension of the more genuine qualities of architecture. There is a public, of no mean proportions, which can imagine no higher excellence in our houses than decorative charm and the recreated "atmosphere" of a vanished time. To have so steeped oneself in the Georgian culture as to be able to think and imagine in Georgian terms; to acquire by study and habit a command of the Georgian way of building; to enrich that way of building with inventions—this is to be an architect. The practice would be innocent, as millinery is innocent, if it did not make millinery of all our suburbs. Our historical playthings are highly paid for when they render mute all the deeper harmonies of our art.

We have not understood even Georgian architecture if we think of it as a screen of ornament which may be lightly transferred, like an embroidered coat, from one wearer to another. That somewhat facile style had its definite source in an order of thought and feeling; the secret of its harmony lies not in the surface characteristics which we measure and reproduce—in the prim correctness, elegance, and good sense which makes it so appealing as fashion and make-believe—but in the eighteenth-century rationalism of which these are the apposite stamp. The Georgian architects, unlike our architects, lived intimately with their world. Their apprehension of that world did not depend upon analysis or aesthetic speculation but arose directly from an identification of their art with the life about them. The architects of Bedford Square and St. Martin's in the Fields, of King's Chapel and Independence Hall, drew their designs not out of a romantic sentiment but out of a mode of belief. If their art was aristocratic that was because aristocracy was the religion of their time; if it was bound in by etiquette that was because etiquette was then a process of living; and the reticent taste they gave their houses was an element in a morality somewhat more absolute than that of the Ten Commandments. An ardor and faith in the general art of Georgian life entered into the art of architecture, inseparable then from that whole. Ardor and faith, not arch and column, are the sources of its beauty.

Recently we have taken refuge from Georgian architecture in a luxuriance of inventions. We have ever increasing treasuries of new shapes, new materials, new relationships of space and structure, new principles of planning. Out of these, new modes of expression have appeared, born in the experimental essays of those daring spirits who, confronting the new uses and the new temper of our day, have attempted to draw from these a new art of building.

All honor to these the pioneers in a new realm of art; but we must not mistake invention for architecture. A foundation has been laid from which a new progress is possible; but we must not mistake progress for fulfillment. No architecture has been created. An architecture is a crystallization, a completion. An architecture comprises an established vocabulary of shapes, defined by acceptance and convention, together with a code of principles, confirmed by practice, for the organization of these shapes. The movements of our new art are as yet too many and too devious to permit such a harmony of utterance among its many voices.

Our experiments and our theories lead in many directions, into many confusions as yet unreconciled. We have searched, for example, for an aesthetic specific to steel construction and that search has engendered many surprising shapes and relationships, but we must not assume that these are necessarily consistent with those shapes and relations which conform to the doctrine of functionalism. There are speculative painters—cubists, Dadaists, constructivists—who extend their influence and their enigmatic achievements into architecture and there are those who, rejecting all aesthetic responsibility, believing beauty to be the automatic consequence or by-product of structural truth, create as if by a tyranny of natural law the Dorian forms which are

bread to those surfeited with sweets. There are also men of
genius who draw unprecedented shapes from the secret recesses
of their souls; men of less genius who find in the flexibility and
freedom of our new construction illimitable avenues of fantasy
and advertisement; and all the while our technologies continue
their exultant march, pouring out the challenging harvest of our
machines (not less inventive than our architects), and our evolving culture demands each day new audacities in the forms of
shelter.

We have before our eyes an architecture which is struggling
for life and growth. We shall understand that architecture only
if we apprehend it as life and growth; as a ferment of invention
and experiment, as an architecture on its way to a distant end
both in serviceability and satisfying expression. Such an architecture, whatever the wit and resourcefulness of its practitioners,
cannot be, like Georgian architecture, ready-made for our comfort and delight. No one should touch it who fears adventure
and participation, who will not wait for fruition.

What force then is driving this architecture towards its inevitable triumph? What is the secret of its rising authority?
What is the principle which beneath all its multiplicity of appearances compels these to an ultimate conciliation and unity?

The art of architecture, whatever the genesis of its appearances
and ideas, arrives at its developed character through social use
and selection. That was true of Egypt, Greece, and Rome, of
Venice, Paris, and Georgian London; and it is not less true of
this our present civilization. Those principles of form which survive and those patterns of space and structure, of color, texture,
light, and ornament, which spring from genius and find their
way into general use are those which fit the patterns of social
need and acceptance. Architecture is an art which arrives at its
destiny through collective practice and through the silent arbitra-
ment of that communal mind which without partiality or pity

selects, rejects, or compromises. In the thought and feeling of our time lies the key to our architecture. Not the ego, but the universal soul, is its fountainhead.

I am not unmindful of the beauty with which our contemporary architects have consoled the world or of the insight of those modern philosophers who lay open the roots of architectural excellence. I know that good design is not a spontaneous growth; that architecture is the creation of men whose keener sensibility to patterns of structure and space set them apart from other men. I know that architects need the guidance of theory, nor do I imagine that there are not ideas to be expressed which are other than those of a collective whole. Individual character and sentiment, surprise and symbol, wit and salient commentary are as congenial to modern architecture as to any other.

Nevertheless it must be obvious that architecture, which except in rare instances celebrates the life of men in associations, which takes as its persistent themes family, church, government, and the city, is of all the arts that least illumined by individual thought and feeling. Architecture could not be, like poetry or music, an introspective art. The spiritual values which architecture exhibits are those of the collective life; its ideas and passions are the general ideas and passions of mankind; its patterns are relevant to individuals chiefly as these participate in the patterns of society. Not gratitude, fear, or friendship are its concerns; still less the storms and secret sessions of the soul; but the grandeur, strength, and promise of the state, of the communal whole, of the communal religion.

There are intimate architectures, gay architectures, architectures of perversities and of escape, and yet these form as a rule branches from the stem of a collective architecture without changing its essential form and direction of growth. There are few of these, even when they seem most curious, wanton, or abstract, which do not draw their lives from a social soil or which could have attained any importance apart from the general life in which they occur. In architecture genius and theory are only other names for social love and understanding.

Whatever therefore may be an architect's principle and tradition, however subtle his skill and invention, he must be first of all medium and instrument of a present society, the true author and appraiser of whatever architecture may in our time have lasting force and meaning. An architect must know that society and the mode of his knowing must be neither scientific nor mystical. An architect must know our civilization as he knows his home, by living in it, sharing it, believing in it, and his knowledge must be so intimate and so pervasive that he cannot lay stone upon stone without the silent channelings of the world around him. He will reëstablish the unity of architecture as social utility and social expression, not through his learning or through his philosophy but through his way of working.

That architect is modern who, forgetful of self-expression and self-advertisement, develops his constructed forms out of the work to be done, the techniques to be employed, the idea to be expressed. That architecture is modern which, addressed to serviceability in a modern world, penetrates to that pageantry, health, and grandeur which lie beneath its outward confusions and dissonances.

It is of great moment that we should discover that beauty and guard it in our art.

part two

ON THE ARCHITECTURE
OF CITIES

CHAPTER THIRTEEN

the invisible city

PERHAPS because I was born and brought up in the country I have always wanted to live near the heart of a great city. Even now I look forward to the day when I can live again in New York: in a little flat, say, at the corner of Broadway and Forty-second Street. I should like to be clothed again in the strength and space of that city; to taste again the diversity of its fashions and humors; to feel about me the encompassment and drift of its opinion. I am not alone in New York even when I am alone. The city furnishes and fortifies my mind.

I once owned a farm near Westport, Connecticut, and for twelve years I tried valiantly to simulate that compassion for rusticity which was and still is fashionable. I was not successful. I could not after the first careless rapture dissemble my boredom with a cottage which was as quaint as a daisy chain at a Vassar commencement and as full of Ye Spirit of Ye Olden Tyme as an eggnog at Christmas. It was all very well so long as I had the fun of adding things on; but when I had added on a loggia, a terrace, a garage, an outside stairway, a gazebo, and all the money I could borrow my week-ends became something to be got through with. Every recollection of my "little place in the country" is filled with a definite vexation and ennui. My memory flies from it like a bird from its cage to those familiar symbols of urbanism which each Monday morning greeted my return to New York: the houses gathering ever more closely around me across the Bronx, the iron bridges over the Harlem River, the long tunnel expectant of the day's adventure, the sudden light-filled space of the Grand Central Station.

The literature of the world is filled with a poets' conspiracy against the city: with advertisements of the city's clamors and indecencies, with the illusion of the country's solace. Only God, we are reminded, can make a tree. As if He had no part in the making of poems and cities!

I am not of course speaking of holidays in the country or of traveling in the country. These are altogether different experiences from that of *living* in the country. Of course I take pleasure in meadows and woods, in mountains and in the gentle forms of New England villages, nor have I forgotten the taste of strawberries fresh from the vine. I am not speaking of recreation or of play, essential ingredients in every life, nor of reverie and the contemplation of sunsets, but of the notion that a rural environment is more congenial to human happiness than the environment of a city. I am thinking of that fantasy of feeling which projects a paramount virtue and health on the country way of life and especially I am thinking of that strange inconsistency of our minds which in spite of poetic sensibilities and discomforts innumerable holds us in the city. My friends in New York talk constantly of escape and yet do not escape. If they had to live there they wouldn't exchange the tip of the Woolworth Building for all that part of the continent which—doubtless through no fault of its own—lies westward of the Hudson River. There is a paradox here which ought to be resolved.

We say that we are imprisoned in cities by economic necessity. A casuistry, surely. There is nothing in the business of making a living, whether it be by way of manufacturing or merchandising or professional service, which absolutely demands a civic environment. Our enterprises grow to larger proportions amid huge concentrations of populations and yet taken as a whole they breed no richer or more numerous rewards than they would if population and place of work were both scattered over the countryside. We could break up our cities without serious consequence to our economy.

Leonardo, in 1486, laid at the feet of Ludovico Sforza a practical plan for dispersing the city of Milan into ten satellite towns so that the people "should not be packed together like goats and pollute the air for one another." Four hundred years later Ebenezer Howard offered London the same program; and today the British Ministry of Town and Country Planning is again flirting at no small expense with that seductive phantom. If we pay little attention to these physicians of our society it is because we do not wish to do so.

The city's pleasures, then? We are held here by crowds and neon lights, by the excitement and comedy of streets and shop windows, by theaters, spectator sports and places of recreation, by the arts which flourish only amid brick and asphalt landscapes?

These are the distant magnets for country-bred youth but they do not explain those acres of our interminable cities in which such pleasures exist in the merest shreds. The pale colorations woven into the tedious fabrics of Queens and the Bronx would seem to afford a dull recompense for mountain vistas and the voices of forest streams; and even if the delights which lie along the spine of Manhattan be considered sufficient to anchor a few thousand there we ought not to overlook the millions of New Yorkers who taste these delights infrequently or not at all. In Chicago there are tens of thousands who have never ventured within the enrapturing atmosphere of the Loop.

We are held in the city neither by pleasure nor by economic necessity but by a hunger which transcends both practical and sensuous experience, a hunger seldom revealed by appearances, seldom acknowledged in our consciousness. We are held in the city by our need of a collective life; by our need of belonging and sharing; by our need of that direction and frame which our individual lives gain from a larger life lived together.

There are city habits and city thoughts, city moralities and loyalties, city harmonies of valuations which surround us in cities with an authority and system which, whatever may be the turmoil in which they exist, are yet friendly to the human spirit and essential to its well-being. Beneath the visible city laid out in patterns of streets and houses there lies an invisible city laid out in patterns of idea and behavior which channels the citizen with silent persistent pressures and, beneath the confusion, noise, and struggle of the material and visible city, makes itself known and reconciles us to all of these.

We have lived in that invisible city a very long time and are patterned more comfortably than we suppose to its congenial mold. It was in the invisible city that we grew over centuries into what we are today, shaped less by forest, wind, and soil than by the social relationships and activities which are city-engendered. Our human nature was created, not as some imagine in treetops and caves, but in that invisible city. It was there that we learned the art of living together, developed the shield of values and relationships which protect us, least armored of animals, from the hostile powers that array us, and it was there that we came to know the destiny which on earth we must share together. In the invisible city, frail crystallization of idea and habit of thought, we learned, circumscribed by forest, river, and the near horizon, to meet the recurrent crises of birth, adolescence, and death, of flood and famine and the malice of our gods. There we learned to organize ourselves with language, conference, magic, education, and law; to use tools, fire, animals, and seed; to possess property and women; to trade and manufacture; and out of all these to build that structure of meanings which reconciled our new-discovered spirit not merely to the nonhuman world which surrounds us but to the growing complexities of our economies and the tyrannies of our swift technologies.

Under the mechanizations and the new freedoms with which science has transformed the material and actual city, under steel, electricity, and machine, under subway, hospital, and grand hotel, under democracy, progressive education, and assembly-line manufacture lie the firm strata of experience gathered across the centuries in the invisible city. Mound above mound, a thousand Troys laid on Troy, these lift us above the arid plain of biological and economic existence. The roots of our minds reach deeply into these deposits and draw from them the law of our present vision and behavior. We are not always aware of that law so light is its accustomed authority, so nice is our conformity to its channelings; nor do we always understand, wrapped in the business of living, how these give steadfastness and direction to our lives.

Every creature on this earth finds happiness in that setting which gives scope to his peculiar energies. Tigers are happy in the jungle, birds in the shade-bestowing trees, and men in the free air of cities. Each living thing attained its present attributes by adjustments long continued between itself and the world which encircled it. Each has its home having been fashioned by his home. Creature and environment are parts of a whole. Tigers, birds, and men do not always know that they are happy; but take them out of their familiar elements and they soon know what it is to be unhappy.

Our poets are too ready to give the city to the devil. The city, I think, was the tool with which God made man. Perhaps it is the tool with which He is making man.

Almost from the beginnings of human history the invisible city has been the theme of the social art of architecture. The musi-

cian, the dancer, the poet were the channels through which the
experience and emotion of individuals were made known but
the architect celebrated the intangible fabric of communal feeling discovered by him beneath street and wall, beneath family,
ambition, and the market, beneath the tumult of politics and war
—discovered by him and by him advertised in his many-voiced
art.

There is a mode of that art having as its materials not buildings
or gardens or public places merely, but the totalities of cities: a
mode of architecture—sometimes anonymous, sometimes guided
by genius—sometimes swift in process, sometimes operative over
slow centuries—which sets forth in the language of form that civic
consciousness without which cities are only biological conveniences; which seizes upon that consciousness and holds it
before us in a thousand different interpretations, each universal
in substance and yet specific to time and circumstance. The practitioner of that architecture is the collective soul, silent for a
moment beneath our present turbulence of circumstance, but
certain of renewal and regained authority. Our necessity paves a
channel for that inevitable progress. Our hunger prepares the
table which shall nourish it.

We are too apt nowadays to think of architecture as a minister of individual comfort and delight, and even when we remember that architecture may be an element in civic patterns it exists
in our minds as decoration or ceremonial background. The design of cities has become a matter of traffic highways and housing projects—with here and there a splash of peristyle and ordered
space to give dignity to a city hall. The idea of form in cities,
of cities which exhibit in their aggregates of shelter, space, and
tree an ideal and pattern of life, of cities which are works of art:
this idea seems to be lost under the present urgencies of our
mechanizations. In the great traditions of architecture this idea
was not, as it is today, thus alien to our minds.

Architecture did not impose itself upon the practical activities of a city, was not an intruder into social or economic life, was not inconsistent with politics, war or individual ambition, but marched with all of these holding before all the shining symbols which revealed the direction and unity of the general life.

An invisible Athens existed beneath the visible Athens and was the deep source of its splendor. The Athenians were well aware of their city as commercial utility and political instrument, but their imaginations were not, happily, limited to that awareness. Themistocles planned the city with a regard for profit and empire not less strict than was Burnham's solicitude for the railroads of Chicago. The roads to Athenian supremacy were the trade routes which led to Egypt and the Black Sea and the great harbor of the Piraeus was laid out with the intent to keep open these freedom-freighted avenues. The quays were wide, straight, and well protected, the warehouses and arsenals were ordered and convenient for maritime trade, the exchanges for corn, wool, metals, dyes, and slaves were designed in accordance with the rigid and functional science developed in the technological schools of Miletus. The plan of the Piraeus, so far as it has been revealed under the foundations of the modern city, seems to have followed a practical and systematic geometry not unlike that which Le Corbusier proposed for modern Paris: the traffic regulated, the quarters clearly bounded, the public works set apart from the homes of the people. The art of civic design— that art which Aristotle called a "sociological architecture"—was a useful art, appropriate and at home under the life-filled porticoes of the crowded agorae.

That art nevertheless was not limited by the technologies of enterprise. It was not the architecture of commerce—of the Piraeus whose arms embraced the sea-borne traffic of a hundred nations—nor the architecture of politics, nor yet the architecture of their homes, threaded with narrow and tortuous streets, which best served the Athenian people, but the shining temples built out of loyalties and memories, out of great deeds accomplished together, out of gratitudes never to be forgotten in the collective heart. This was the city the Persians could not destroy, the invisible city, proud, exultant, and eternal, which the people had guarded behind the wooden walls of Salamis. Symbol and sentinel of that city the Acropolis stood above the clash of party and of class, a harmony crowning a harmony, the white crest of a wave which had gathered strength across centuries. The Acropolis was not a political document or a civic decoration or an abstraction of art—still less a "cultural center," pale refuge such as we build for our besieged civilization—but a spiritual reality which kindled the collective life and yet was intimate also to the life of every Athenian.

I am sure that the Romans, whose lives were lived under stately porticoes and amid the pomp of great temples found in that background an ever present dignity which must have followed them even into the poverty and confusions of the crowded, many-storied *insulae.* The wide forums and the glittering thermae did not arise merely from the vanity of emperors and the corruption of the people. These were the songs in which the Roman soul made itself known above the cries of the circus and the clash of civil swords. The Gothic cathedrals were, in part at least, prayers of thanksgiving for a joy discovered in the revival of cities, and the *piazze* into which Venice poured her compressed splendor are jubilant with that new enfranchisement. These are not each an ornament added to a city but summations of a city's spirit to which houses and streets, walls, canals, and the domes of public buildings are the harmonious counterparts. Florence, Padua, Cordoba; the Paris of Richelieu, the Philadelphia of Franklin: each of these might have been the work of a single architect so consistent is the ordinance and expression of their streets and structures. With what persistence have they held their characters over the years in spite of political crisis and economic change! Because the men who lived in these cities lived also within the city's pattern of idea, from which no citizen could imagine himself apart, the pattern in which they clothed themselves became, even without their conscious consent, the mirror which revealed the city's anonymous heart. In that mirror the citizen recognized his own dignity and his faith. The architecture of the city—a term which included all of the city's structures and ordered space—confirmed that which men believed about themselves.

All things—even the suns—are subject to deformations. Trees are gnarled and twisted by the sea winds, green fields turn to dust under drought and sun, and peace-loving men become savages amid the frenzies of war. Through long progressions the million species of the earth reach each its characteristic form and yet none is invulnerable to accident. A sudden crisis may arrest any progress—a violent alteration in wind or sun, an invasion of new enemies, a storm too rough for accustomed measures of security—and distortion, blight, and adventitious growth may overcome the healthiest organism.

So it was with the city under the fierce impact of the Industrial Revolutions and of that explosive mercantilism which at the end of the eighteenth century scattered the European peoples over the earth. Cities, new and old, grew rapidly to unprecedented dimensions and as they grew shattered that humanity of texture and expression which had once been impressed upon them by collective thought and feeling long continued. No longer do our cities exhibit in their outward aspects that framework of social purpose, that cement of manners, conventions, and moralities, that *tradition* built by slow change and patient compromise which once gave character and beauty to the city's life.

The symbol and chief actor in this disintegration was the factory—the factory and its accomplice, the railroad, together with the thousand other children of iron and steam. We did not guess when we admitted the factory to our cities that it would destroy their patterns; destroy them utterly and with that destruction provoke the questionings and discontents which color our present judgments of cities. Servile and seemingly innocent utilities, born of windmill and mountain stream, growing slowly in the green forests beside their white waterfalls, their many windows caressed by sunshine and fresh winds, there was little in the first factories that was prescient of Birmingham and Chicago. No one was aware of crisis. Across the countryside, silently, unnoticed, factory and city began their unequal duel.

Nevertheless it was inevitable that the two should meet on closer ground. People must work where they live: the factory must invade the city, or the city come to the factory. The railroad and the steam engine were prompt to respond to that necessity; these united city and factory; united them but not as the elements of an art are united in a pattern, not as new functions are united by slow development to a growing organism, but as aliens forced together by outside pressure, as a foreign body is thrust into living tissue. The factory came into the city not as architecture but as machine. Unlike the temple and the theater, the house and the market place, the factory was built, not out of love and the commerce of society but out of calculation and economic necessities. A consequence, not of feeling but of ingenuity, a device by which men—and children—lent themselves to machines and machines to men, the factory was little else than pulley and wheel grown to vast proportions.

We know how that growth, once the factory was firmly planted within the city, eclipsed in speed and consequence all other growth in the long history of mankind. Within a single century pulley and wheel gathered the city within their giant shadows and gave the city a new law. Pulley and wheel raised new values for the city to live by; refashioned the city's manners, speech, and faith; recoined the city's time; remade in its own image the city's streets and squares. The people of the city must then arrange their lives in accordance with its uncongenial necessities; government must listen to its decrees; religion rewrite her mythologies to condone its tyrannies; and social custom, family life, recreation and the arts, the ambitions of men and their standards of right and wrong, must be made conformable to these mechanical rhythms, to these uniformities of process and product. The cathedral, once generator and guardian of cities, had cherished and consoled all who lived at its side. The palace, also a generator of cities, ennobled the citizens with an ordinance and art of living; the distant trading posts bound together with common enterprise and shared destiny those who gathered around them; and even the fortress inspired in those who must live beneath its walls a loyalty from which they drew a communal strength. The factory merely used the city. As if in response to some blind biological law the city transformed itself from home and commonwealth into storehouse and machine.

The giant lizards could not survive a sudden change of climate. It may be that man now confronts that peril also. Could that be one of the secret causes of the giant wars which now convulse the earth?

Please do not misunderstand me. I am not for imitations of Venice and Athens set down in Cleveland and San Francisco. Our cities are the homes of our great industries and they must take the way of industry. I am for mechanized cities and for every technological improvement in cities; nor would I hide these under cloaks of romance or academic decorums. Neither do I believe that we can restore the old and beautiful patterns of society by inviting our civic populations to enter shining new houses laid out for them by architects confident of their art to transform the universe. Our architecture, and especially the architecture of our cities, will be created by our society to whose mood and necessities the architect is instrument. I am for no Utopia.

Nevertheless I have faith in the power of man to shape his environment in accordance with his inward needs and I know that that reshaping is most essential for human happiness. Beneath these wheels and pulleys, these endless turnings and meaningless propulsions, there still lies that invisible city in which we must live or perish. That city has desperate need of architecture: of an architecture peculiar to itself, unlike any other architecture, and yet as constant as any other in its affirmation of purpose and dignity.

Sometimes when I am in Rockefeller Center, where skyscrapers, music halls, gardens, and shops innumerable crowd into an islanded harmony I imagine that I feel the promise of that new renaissance of our art. A city rises about me; I am in a theater prepared for me as if by ancient usage and rehearsal. At such times I like to believe that architecture may indeed reassume its forgotten importance as outward frame and envelope of a communal life, being shaped once more by the commerce of a society that is civilized, polite, and urbane.

Civilized, polite, and urbane—each word rooted in a word that means *the city*.

CHAPTER FOURTEEN

on form in cities

A RECENT book on city planning, written by an authority in that field, begins with a definition. City planning, we are told, is a *sociological-economical-technological-psychological-ecological science*. City planning is an application of scientific ways and means to the social habits of city dwellers, to their ways of making a living, to the streets, bridges, and subways which facilitate their movements throughout the city, and to the ordering and reshaping of those geographical features which environ the people in a city, such as rivers and harbors, hills and ravines, the cold of winter, and in summer the excessive heat of the eye of heaven—all of which are the materials and media of a comprehensive practice, or group of practices, of which the city planner is master.

In a footnote on one of the last pages in his book the author adds a bit of practical advice to architects. Since architects are not armed by nature or by experience for a task so obviously integral to social and economic valuations as city planning, nor have they as a rule the resourcefulness and diplomatic skill which are essential for the practice of that political art, and since planning has become a profession distinct from architecture, having principles and observances of which architects are by a law of nature innocent, architects would do well to withdraw altogether from the field of city planning—and the footnote ends with the suggestion that, vis-à-vis the planner, the architect's attitude ought to be one of humility.

I must confess that I entertain some prejudice in this matter, a prejudice encouraged, I am afraid, by my long sustained interest in the history of architecture. There came into my mind as I pondered this little homily a procession, not lacking in color, of architects engaged in city planning—Christopher Wren laying his *Plan of London* at the feet of King Charles, Gabriel receiving his prize for the Place de la Concorde, Héré de Corny pacing the bright new sequences of Nancy—and I could not resist a certain sadness at the thought of the architectural talent thus wasted on uncongenial themes, the great renowns which are now seen to be undeserved, and the pomp and pageantry of a stream so long continued and now doomed to extinction between the bogs and quicksands of the ecological sciences and the perilous sea of politics.

Certainly there was no one until quite recently who could have predicted this untimely end of the architect-planner, so ancient and aristocratic was the tradition of architecture in city planning, so firmly were its conventions, its modes of operation, and its philosophy guarded in that field. With what confidence only thirty years ago the architects of the *Plan of Washington* framed their parade of palaces, their heroic abstractions of vista and monument! With what condescension they acknowledged the presence of the population, audience to their sculptural symphonies; with what impatience they noted the troublesome intrusions of economists; and even when at times they admitted to their company the shy, necessary engineer it was only to hide him instantly behind discreet draperies of pediment and peristyle. For centuries the architect had in this way carried into the organization of street and plaza the habits of thought and vision which had shaped cathedral and palace; for centuries his materials had been monumental structures and organized space, axis, vista, and sequence, climax, balance, proportion, and rhythmic disposition, and the correct authority of Rome. With these he had built enclaves for civic life indistinguishable except in breadth and scale from those which he built for a private clientele. The two arts, architecture and city planning, were in practice one.

Yet there were in motion, even as Burnham and Olmsted laid out the vast geometry of Washington, two currents, separate and in some ways opposite, which were to shatter this unity with sudden impacts. These had gathered force slowly over more than a century. Their invasions of city planning, however explosive to architecture and to city planning, were yet prepared by movements long operative below the placid surface upon which that aristocratic art was accustomed to bask.

The first of these currents had its origin in the ascendancy of economics among the speculative sciences of the nineteenth century; the second grew out of the new social philosophies engendered by the Industrial Revolutions. A new industrial system, wasteful and cruel, was allowed to evolve itself out of the "free play of an enlightened egotism"; magnificent new technologies were used to make that system the more barren in social progress; and maladjustments acute, sudden, and devastating inevitably appeared in the fabric of society. Nowhere were these more terrible in their consequences than in the great cities which everywhere poured their populations, increasing as frantically as the broomsticks of the Sorcerer's Apprentice, into ever widening miles of civic dishevelment. The impotence of classic architecture to bring order into these vast complexes could not be long ignored, and the hope that social health might be restored by science was wholly congenial to the temper of a people who had put their trust so completely in that form of thought and analysis. The time was bound to come, moreover, when men should discover principles of civic reconstruction in those imposing structures of theory which confidently predicted the reign of reason and philosophical system in the living organisms of cities. The eclipse of architecture ought not to have been surprising.

Baron Haussmann is said to be the first city planner to announce a secondary role for architecture in the design of cities.
If he was not the first to conceive the city as a great machine for
production and consumption, he was at any rate the first to
translate that principle into practice. Certainly there were few
architects in that staff of specialists which formed his tool for
the rebuilding of Paris. He relied upon economists, politicians,
physicians, engineers—in a word, upon scientists—to bring the
queen city of the Renaissance into conformity with an industrial
age. The bases of his projects were not architectonic principles
but the requirements of traffic, the promotion of industry, the
conditions of public health. A science of planning replaced the
inherited art of civic design.

It is true that Haussmann made Paris magnificent with many
showy buildings, for he was not ignorant of architecture, but
these buildings were introduced as incidents merely in a pattern
of streets. They gave no law to the city. His gorgeous constructions were ornaments pinned here and there on the breast of
Paris and, like ornaments, were useful to give continuity or
emphasis to the pattern of streets. They were subordinated not
in relative scale merely but in their influence. No longer do they
project their principles of order into the civic elements which
surround them: plazas, streets, and vistas no longer echo their
proportions or continue their rhythms. When the Emperor decreed that his own splendor should be confirmed by splendid
monuments conspicuously placed, it was enough if these were
given an axial relationship to a street. The Opera, for example,
looks as if it had got in the way of a boulevard which otherwise
would have gone on to the edge of the earth.

From that time on the sovereignty of architecture in city planning was progressively challenged: not the sovereignty of architecture alone, but of the architectural principle. The authors of
the *Plan of Chicago* made a great to-do over mighty ensembles

of public buildings but their real solicitude was for the railroads. *The Regional Plan of New York* flattered that city with many a fine proposal for monumental symmetries, but we know how adventitious these appeared beside more exigent schemes for harbor reconstruction and industrial redistribution. The economist and his cousin, the civil engineer, were the true authors of these ambitious efforts for civic order. Economist and engineer are arbiters in the great number of civic improvements actually undertaken in our time. The architectural legend has reached its final chapter in New York City where factual-minded administrators, impatient of idea, measure city planning by the acreage of concrete pavement laid on escape routes leading to the country. In that city the very limited objectives of planners include, to be sure, some architectural tidbits; but the idea of civic form, of that comprehensive structure and balance which is the essence of the *architectural idea*, is by official decree taboo.

It is not surprising then that a new profession should come into being and stake out for itself a province which seemed to have escaped the authority of architecture; nor is it surprising that those who seized that province should defend it against the more orthodox pretensions of architects. A wide shield of professional observances and mystifications, distinct from those of architecture, at once surrounded the planner; a new language was invented for a new theology; and by means of the familiar well-tried artifices of organization, by annual conventions held, officers elected, by-laws enacted, papers read, and dues collected, the profession of *city planner* made known its ambitions and its perilous autonomy.

The city planner, thus defined, is a strangely different creature from his architect ancestor. Whereas the traditions of city planning were integral to neoclassic precedent, to academic usages, to theories of form made visible in perspective and water color, the stock in trade of the newly coined planner is composed of statistics, diagrams, surveys, and charted data. The new planner is a maker of maps, enigmatically colored, of documents and reports full of strange new transcendentalisms; and he will plot you a curve at the drop of a hat. Being of a compassionate nature, he tolerates architects so long as these know with becoming meekness their place in the shining scheme of his new world.

Now it is doubtful that this new profession, if such it be, can hold any serious threat to architecture provided that it remain accessible to the architectural idea. Architecture is an art not confined to buildings; it exists wherever men seek for expression through constructed form; and we know that the form-giving principle which architects developed in the design of buildings is operative on many a field which has escaped the boundaries of our profession. So long as planners exercised their new art on street systems and railroads, on water fronts and bridges, on the distribution of industries and of industrial facilities, there was created only a new branch of engineering which, whatever its name, could exist side by side with architecture. The architect —I use the term here in its narrower professional sense—has shown himself only too ready to abandon to engineers the new structural techniques engendered by steel; why not, then, the engineering of cities? The gigantic children of steel which live in our cities as if they had wandered there from another planet are not inaccessible to architecture, whatever may be the profession which nursed them. They do not necessarily destroy the architecture of cities. The Eiffel Tower has no quarrel with the Louvre; the huge *Missouri*, the Golden Crescent under her guns, acknowledges the serene sovereignty of Sancta Sophia; and the rough intrusions of the Brooklyn Bridge leave unruffled the gentle City Hall of New York. These rise above our streets on a scale consistent with their new energies and, subject to their own laws, are also the themes of a new architecture.

Engineering always tends to become architecture. The monsters which owe their forms to calculation and the operation of mechanical laws cannot long remain monstrous; with each rebuilding they submit silently to the persistent demands of the human spirit. Hell holds no fabric more hideous than that of the Williamsburg Bridge, which nevertheless contained within itself the lithe elegance of the Whitestone Bridge; under the clumsy *parapluies de fer* of the *Halles Centrales* lay the shining apparition of the Crystal Palace; and those glacier-like shapes of concrete which impound the waters of the Tennessee River, are they not stepchildren of the Pyramids and foster-parented by architecture?

Architecture surpasses engineering in one respect only: it takes into account not only the surface phenomena of human cultures but includes a harmony of these with the secrets of their occurrences. The need for such harmony lies too deep in our hearts to be long denied by engineers. Sooner or later architecture takes command of every structure raised by man if only to resolve those deep misgivings which engineering creates: to reaffirm the insufficiency of material devices to sustain the happiness of mankind.

Now it happens that the new art of city planning is by no means bounded within the sphere of engineering. It escapes both engineering and the economic objectives to which engineering is addressed. Even as the city was being transformed in the consciousness of those who are called, somewhat rudely, "physical planners" into a mechanism for manufacture and merchandising there were other planners, no less fertile of theory, who conceived the material of their art to be not industry and commerce and the facilities which serviced these nor yet that "economic man" who was to be made happy by producing and consuming, but rather that society, that aggregation of human beings who with all their inheritances of social habit and cultural tradition of conflicting loyalties and inapposite folkways, had become through the blind operation of economic law imprisoned in these unpitying machines. It was evident that the undirected growth of our cities had produced not physical chaos merely but social chaos; and the daring thought was ultimately inescapable that by giving direction to that growth chaos might be overcome. There should be a *social science of planning* having as its objectives the establishment of patterns of behavior among men.

Man cannot live except in a society. Since we cannot abandon our cities nor yet delay the onward march of invention, we must create in our cities a society tempered to withstand the attritions and subversions of modern industry. If we are to endure things so monstrous as mass production and the assembly line we must contrive some new armor against them. We see how our new technologies of production challenge our familiar ways of life, our time-honored institutions, our most cherished superstitions, and we know that these must be reconstructed if our civilization is to be continued. Why not then search out the guides to whatever new social crystallizations are possible and try to discover the means for setting in motion the currents of feeling and thought which may assist these? These guides and these means will at least be as certain as those of economics and as worthy to be called a science.

These considerations, formulated early in the nineteenth century, have prompted an art of city planning addressed to that social health without which economic prosperity is of little consequence. I know of no better illustration of this kind of planning than slum clearance and the construction of government-sponsored housing for that part of our civic population tactfully called by politicians the "lower income group." Here, if anywhere, is an arrant interference with the operation of economic law, an interference which deliberately prevents the free determination of rents by the law of supply and demand and as clearly nullifies the ancient appanage of the poor to live and die in want and misery. When housing projects are further developed so as to encourage the growth of *neighborhoods,* when the nature and distribution of institutions—the school, the church, the shopping center—are among the materials of planning, and when the spiritual life of the people is sustained by recreational areas, parks, and playgrounds made accessible and patterned for their use; well, you have then the beginnings of an art of sociological planning.

It is that art, and not the practical science of the municipal engineer, which most definitely appears to prohibit a critical role for architecture in the planning of cities; nor is it surprising that those who are concerned with the invisible structure of society and with the hunger of populations should exclude from their practice all relevance to an art which to their impatient eyes is concerned only with the outward clothing and pomp of cities. The tradition which architecture established in city planning—the art of contained space and vista, of dome and portico, of antique symmetries and Parisian sophistications—has quite evidently proved impotent to stay those cruel winds, raised by the uncharted course of our vast and mechanized industries, which social reformers hope to conjure or rechannel; and it is unlikely that the aesthetics of steel and contemporary function will prove a more serviceable instrument.

Now it must be admitted that if the art—or science or philosophy—of city planning is indeed addressed to a total reconstruction of society, this could scarcely be considered a mission prescriptive also to architects, or indeed one in which architects could be expected to participate on any important scale. If architecture is properly understood as an art concerned chiefly with structural techniques and aesthetic satisfactions, its processes and principles might reasonably take a secondary place when measured against the stern realities of social reform. If indeed city planners are bent upon Utopia or revolution, in the manner proposed for example by Karl Marx, or if they have in mind the development of a race of philosopher-administrators, in the manner proposed by Plato, then clearly they have reached a stratosphere of theory and of self-confidence which, although often penetrated by architects, is one which we would gladly resign in practice to their less cabined ambition.

Are not these hypotheses based upon misconceptions both of city planning and of architecture?

Whatever may be the scope of the new city planning in those literary and philosophic spheres into which its flights are so many and so volatile it must be in practice concerned with material circumstance. In practice city planning is making and doing, not dreaming. City planning is a technology, a procedure of science applied to the form and content of cities, a technology concerned with such realities as the control and flow of traffic in our streets; and even when it is concerned with social facilities such as the distribution and nature of housing, schools, and recreational areas, its concern must be in practice with physical actualities. However intimately this technology may rest upon economic and social principles, the formulation of such principles must remain, except in rare instances, prescriptive to scholars and philosophers rather than to practitioners.

The city planner, like the architect, is often kindled by an awareness of social objective but he must nevertheless set a boundary to the province in which he functions. There is a frame beyond which he must recognize, not in his theory merely but in his active labors, the authority of other men: of the economist, the lawyer, the sociologist, the scientist of politics. To embrace all of these in the profession of planning—whatever currency and meaning *planning* may have outside that profession—is to inflate the city planner to so superhuman a status as to place him, willy-nilly, among the spectral citizens of Utopia.

I do not suggest that the city planner should return to neo-classic architecture or to neoclassic thought. The city planner has rightly acknowledged the impact of modern thought in the world. The city planner has rightly renounced the mode of design established by Gabriel, by L'Enfant, by Burnham. The city planner builds his art on function and serviceability, on realism and opportunity; his design is practical, direct, free from cant and oppressive formalism; his practice is illumined by social relevance. There is a modern art of city planning.

If there is a modern city planning there is also a modern architecture. Architecture, like city planning, has keenly felt the changes of a world transformed by science. Architects, no less than planners, have been prompted by the study and experience of science to renounce their Greek and Roman toys. With equal resolution architects have set about the task of adjusting their thought and vision to the civilization now in process so that these might parallel the thought and vision of the sciences of society.

What is the idea which illumines that new architecture—that architecture whose very substance is social serviceability, whose one intention is to assist the balance and stability of the social fabric? Is it not the idea of *planning*, of planning not only to secure the comfort of individuals but to lift and sustain the happiness of populations? Is not architecture also a sociological-economical-technological-psychological-ecological science?

Nothing could be more misleading, then, or more damaging to the cause of planning than that description of architecture, not without currency among economists, as an art of "physical planning"—a term intended to distinguish sharply the tangible and practical patterns of architects from the patterns of idea which occasion them. The architect need not trouble himself then with the social objectives of his constructions? It is enough if he is given a program which will lend itself to a material realization? And if architecture embraces not only the practical technologies of steel and the forms of shelter but also academic usages, the meanings with which history has overlaid our constructions, and a conscious effort to express in the forms of buildings the temper of a society—well, these are to be understood as merely the elements of a private Heaven which could in the design of cities be conveniently sacrificed?

Architecture, not less than planning, is a social art. The architect is and must indeed remain the master builder, the man of practical skill who creates the important materials of cities; and yet he is something more than an avenue through which technologies rain a blind influence upon dwellers in cities. His structures not only act upon civilization but, what is more important, they do so in a manner consciously determined by their builders. The architect not only uses technologies but controls them; addresses them to social objectives as clearly revealed as those of the planner; addresses them, indeed, to objectives indistinguishable from those of the planner.

Whatever dissonances may exist between the traditions of architecture and this new and crescent art, there can be no fundamental or lasting dissidence between that art and the new architecture. If each of these embraces an area of human interest and a mode of operation peculiar to itself and not included in that of the other these divergencies are yet of less importance than those interests which bind them together. Each is inseparable except in rare instances from the collective life, the smallest unit of which is the family, the largest the population of a city. The materials of each art, if not the same, are yet alike in character since they comprise, first, those aspects of human existence which invite structural adaptations, and second, the material substances capable of such adaptations. They are integral also—architecture no less than city planning—with both the social and the physical milieu in which they exist and gain their vitality and usefulness from that integration. Identical in origin, these arts attained individuality as the consequence of a growing diversification of social activities, and yet in intention and character they continue an unequivocal and—until recently —acknowledged unity; nor is any high achievement possible in either art except as it flows from a philosophy mutually acknowledged.

Why not, then, honor the city planner with the title *architect* —the title which he was proud to bear down to that yesterday when he became suddenly aware of professional jealousy and advertisement? Let's call him *architect-of-cities,* surely the name most descriptive of the planner's profession and of its relation to the profession from which it sprung. *Planner* should be reserved for those economists who delight to claim that title; *city planner* for those social reformers to whom planning is a mysticism.

I would have the architect-of-cities believe that the social sciences are relevant to his art in a way not essentially different from their relevancy to architecture, nor should he imagine that in any deep sense his art is framed in a different way by society, climate, tradition, or the market. The architect-of-cities will have techniques, procedures, valuations, and political relationships peculiar to himself; he will have also his own salesmanship, his own high language and graphic devices; but even here I think an overemphasis is possible. Too much hocus-pocus is an open invitation to the charlatan.

It will be said by some that the arts of city planning and architecture, although alike in their materials and methods, are divergent in one fundamental objective and that this divergence prohibits an invasion of city planning by the spirit of architecture. The modern city, it is thought, can no longer be conceived as it was in other times as a medium of expression—that is to say, as a work of art capable of receiving the imprint of the civic soul. Urban beauty, being made impossible in a city created by a machine technology, is believed to be a thing of the past; the city builder builds in effect a great machine to which the idea of expression is necessarily alien—or if not alien then dependent upon an idiocratic functionalism unrelated to architecture. Our modern streets are, like railroads, lanes for rapid transit; our squares and plazas are stations for the relief of congestion; our cities are designed for a "synthesis of activities rationalized for production"; and if in the city thus mechanized there exists a communal awareness which might demand a visible celebration—in the city where radio and newsprint take the place of assembly, where political action and the commerce of society require neither locality nor architectural frame, where art hides her head in galleries and even entertainment, public observances, and sport are mechanized and mass produced—our new inventions contain within themselves and by their own virtue attain without the aid of art that technological grandeur which is the modern equivalent of beauty.

The theory ignores man's immemorial hunger for a reconciliation between his environment and his dreams. If the harmonious patterns of the antique cities have been shattered by our epochal revolutions there is yet operative that same necessity which raised them at such infinite cost of genius and love. We may be sure that this necessity will not be forever denied. Beneath the utilitarian appearances of our cities there still rests that sempiternal will which almost from the beginnings of history gave humane form and character to cities wherever these appeared: that beautiful necessity of which Florence and Renaissance Paris, Venice and the Rome of Bernini, Georgian Bath and the Philadelphia of Franklin are image and consequence.

It is most urgent that we recognize and make way for that regenerating force. Our cities are shaping us into little simulacrums of themselves. Our cities act upon us and they act in ways not always apprehended by those practical-minded folk who think in terms of land valuation and traffic control. This materialism which environs us invades our thought; this mean enframement is resonant in our manners and our speech; this iron theater prompts an iron comedy. We suppress the form-giving impulse at the peril of our civilization; and there are few undertakings more exigent, none more far-reaching, than that of recapturing in the visible and felt aspects of cities that harmony with the universal thought and aspirations of men which makes them active to sustain, not our comfort merely or our security merely, but the dignity and worthwhileness of human life.

Of course I know that the forms of our new cities cannot be like the old; that we must search for new values and new principles, a new and specific aesthetic, a beauty in unison with our technologies. The spirit of our times has given us already a diverse palette of civic forms: the crystals of steel and glass, as yet undisciplined, which rise out of the centers of our cities; our immense bridges; the swift unfoldings and progressions of our new highways; the play of green areas against areas of brick and asphalt; our miraculous control of artificial light; and the majestic profiles of our wide horizons. To these I would add, and without an excess of humility, those million structures in each city which are called buildings, the character and disposition of which appear to be also among the materials and the foundations of the art of city planning. Out of all these and out of change and developments unforeseen, and with forces as yet anonymous and contradictory, we must create new cities.

Architecture—not as an art of shelter only but as idea—is the bridge over which the spiritual forces participate in the design of cities and by that participation gain an ascendency in the city's life. To say that this ascendency is less important than technological service—and the conscious redirection of economic and social life, assuming that to be possible—or to say that this is less worthy of the devotion of resolute and resourceful men is to give added life to that disease which is destroying our civilization.

We must not think of city planning as a technology merely or as a complex of technologies. Although city planning rises out of scientific thought, although it is reasoned, documented, fitted to the commonplaces of everyday living, yet it takes possession of us as vision and desire. It is at once the consequence of the physical energy and invention of our era and of that religious prompting, called democracy, which is slowly giving these direction and meaning. Our science and our faith meet here. Upon such foundations were built the great traditions of the architecture of cities.

CHAPTER FIFTEEN

the political art of planning

AMONG the amiable sayings of the celebrated cliché expert, Dr. Arbuthnot, is one which deserves at this moment a brief commentary—all the more so because it is one certain to be quoted wherever three architects are gathered together in a circle. "It is important," said Dr. Arbuthnot, "that planning should not be mixed up with politics."

Dr. Arbuthnot was himself earnestly if somewhat vicariously engaged in planning. He was one of the five eminently respectable citizens who together formed the planning board of his city and who met twice each year to make many interesting suggestions. It was through Dr. Arbuthnot's influence that a Master Plan for the city was made. It was he who persuaded the Board to engage as planner a young man, just graduated from Yale, who for a very modest fee introduced all the newest ideas of his professors. The Plan, exquisitely colored, was displayed for several weeks in the office of His Honor, the Mayor.

Heaven only knows how many Master Plans are buried in the Library of Planning at Harvard. They are of every size and shape: from the great solemn plans, sumptuously dressed in leather and gold, which are ranged along the floor, through the long rows of middle-shelved plans, bound in bourgeois cloth and fattened with statistics, to the thousands of eager little plans, paper bound, which line the cornice like *amorini* above a rococo altar. It's hard not to be a philosopher here in this necropolis of plans, "each in his narrow cell forever laid," and to meditate

the fate which decreed so brief a span to so many bright beginnings. Born in hope and pride, nurtured by the very best of
intentions, each basked for a moment in luxury and honeyed
words, and died of starvation. They had this in common also:
they did not get mixed up in politics.

Now it will not be denied that the making of Master Plans,
even should this reach the proportions of an industry, can
scarcely comprise the sum and substance of the art of planning
cities. Master Plans embody as a rule some hope for a future
translation into space and stone and tree. They are *espaliers*
intended to give form and healthful growth to the vagabond
vine of the city. No doubt many of their authors, like the sculptors of Reims, find a proud satisfaction in remembering their
Virgins forever hidden behind parapets; and yet it must be that
in the long run even the most pietistic of planners must recognize a certain futility, however sublime, in his exertions. He will
then blame the insensitive heart of our times.

Standing in the Library of Planning—which has become of
late one of my favorite haunts—I have wondered if there might
not be some means by which so much ingenuity and high faith
might be brought to a wider usefulness. I know that the times
are insensitive; and yet it may be that there is some ministration—prenatal or in the nursery and hitherto neglected by their
parents—which, if provided, might encourage in these problem-
children a growth and transmutation. Could that ministration
include, the erudite Arbuthnot to the contrary notwithstanding,
a larger dose of political sense? Perhaps planning *ought* to be
mixed up with politics.

Politics is an art which depends upon some knowledge, intuitive or otherwise, of those means by which things are accomplished in the life of communities. The means by which planning may be made real comprise not ideas and techniques only
but men, institutions, and laws. All of these, then, might well

be included among the materials and processes of planning—and some experience in these matters, by the way, might be included also in the education of planners. Whatever planning may be in theory, in practice it is a political art.

"In proposing his plans," writes a learned authority, "the town planner should take into consideration the possibilities for their achievement." The author, I think, will not be reproached for an excess of audacity.

In all of its great traditions the art of planning was integral with the practice of government, or at any rate an adjunct to that practice. Baron Haussmann, for example, nonpareil of planners, can scarcely be imagined disentangled from the regime of the Second Empire, so closely were his achievements knit to that prestigious contraption. The Baron made as great a use of men and of the machinery of government as of paper and pencil. Committees, senates and constitutions, finance, law and human necessities were the prime components of his art. Paris was his pie and he sliced it not with his crayon but with the more caustic edge of a gold napoleon. He could flatter an emperor and he knew also how to bribe an alderman and bully a land-owner. John Nash, architect and prince of British planners, also knew a thing or two about men and parliaments. Being English, he by-passed these rather than go through them; nevertheless, Regent Street, which he bent around churches and around ducal mansions, became, as every Londoner knows, "the finest street in the world." And for the patron saint of planners I give you Nero, Emperor of Rome. Nero's method of slum clearance was impetuous but very thorough. Standing today in a Sahara of paper plans I share across the centuries the joy that must have been his as the impatient flames ate their way into acres of vile tenements and opened to the sun the dark and diseased streets of Rome. On a clean page of gray ash the calm emperor then drew the broad, magnificent line of the Sacred Way, compan-

ioned it with ordered and porticoed streets, laid out at its end
the garden that was a fragment of Paradise, and set there the
Golden House, *astra colossus et crescunt*. A planner with so
majestic a will could scarcely have deserved the character which
history has given him. It was some real estate man who invented
that story about the fiddle.

I know a quiet professor who has nonchalantly erased Philadelphia. I know a lawyer, law-abiding as a rule, who has cut
broad, ruthless boulevards through the heart of St. Louis and
lifted from their beds the Missouri and Mississippi Rivers. They
did these things, I regret to say, only in their dreams. Repressed
by an uncongenial politic, their noble rage is sublimated in
Master Plans.

The feats of planning which illumine most brilliantly the pages
of the historic architectures were elements in political absolu-
tisms. The intention of the art of planning was clearly to affirm
and celebrate the principle of absolutism; its practice was integral
to the practice of that peculiar form of political art, congenial
always to the monumental project. The Golden House and
Garnier's Opéra, gorgeous flowers of imperial policy, were, with
the complex of streets and squares around them, the instruments
of that policy. Nero, as I remember it, was not embarrassed by
a hostile majority in the Ways and Means Committee, and the
Baron's dictatorial talents were not, as Mr. Robert Moses somewhat wistfully informs us, "subject to the accident of vote."

I do not suggest, therefore, that we are in need of a Nero
or a Haussmann, refreshing as these might be, and I am aware
also of the incompetence of plaza, boulevard, and palace to
capture and exhibit the spirit of an industrial democracy. It
should be understood that I am not pleading for the beautiful
antique patterns, still less for the methods, technical or political,
by which these were arrived at, but only for the vision and purpose and realism which were built into them.

It is a great pity that the term *city planner* has come to have so nebulous a meaning nowadays. If I had my way, so imperative a title should never be given to the makers of Utopias; nor should it be given, on the other hand, to that very vocal person, the "planning expert," child of the scientific spirit, who opposes to the generous antique tradition bleak wildernesses of data, tabulation, and diagram—and solemnly describes these to earnest Garden Clubs and innocent Chambers of Commerce as city planning. And those squirrel-like folk who inhabit the municipal planning agencies and lay up such store of data and digits: how does it happen that they are classified by the Civil Service as city planners, junior and senior, first, second, and third class? Of course I know that surveys and reports, statistics and maps, are necessary instruments of planning, but these, like the data and calculations of engineers, might be kept for the discreet and understanding eye of professionals. Most harmful to the cause of planning is that air of satisfied accomplishment with which these are paraded before the public. Propaganda for planning? That is a vicious propaganda which encourages a pride in means —and leaves ends to the coming generation.

People invent too many words nowadays: I have already suggested the term *architect-of-cities* to distinguish that city planner who both conceives and executes his plans from the dreamer-reformer, on the one hand, and the juggler of techniques on the other. I have called the art of city planning, which is not the same thing as its scientific basis, the *architecture-of-cities*. That is a sound tradition which entrusted city planning to architects, and its basic reasonableness should not be obscured by the growing dependence of city-planning practice upon new technologies. I do not suggest that a competence in the planning and construction of buildings should be a prerequisite for the practice of city planning. I do not suggest that every architect can plan a city. What I have in mind is not so much the colorations of architectural practices as that quality of thought and action, that way of working, which habitually translates patterns of ideas into patterns of performance and for that purpose uses not techniques merely but men and institutions. I mean the kind of thought and action which creates skyscrapers, cathedrals, and the giant power stations of the TVA and lifted these above the plane of material necessity. Architecture also is a political art.

An eminent critic has classified planners as "creative" and "executive." That classification has been long implied in the commentaries of critics and is one of the causes of that dreamlike character which informs our most ambitious planning projects: the *Plan of Chicago*, for example, and the recent *Royal Academy Plan for London*. The creative planner is the creator of phantoms; the executive planner is that fabulous person who will give these reality. I have never met that sculptor who could design a Venus "in the mind's eye" with the expectation that a collaborator would free her from the marble block; and he would be a strange architect who would expect contractors and workmen to capture his thought in steel and stone except under his own strict supervision. Among the architects-of-cities there should be only two categories: master and apprentice, both of whom should be mindful of the truth, so often demonstrated in the arts, that imagining and making are, in practice, parts of a single process.

By city planning (since I must use the accepted term) I mean that art which is concerned with the form and disposition of the physical elements of cities. The principle that social health can be promoted by healthful environment sustains this art in our time together with the need, confirmed by the centuries, of form and order in that environment. Whereas imperial planning maintained the power and authority of the state, and medieval planning the power and authority of the guild, modern planning, like modern architecture, is addressed to the happiness of populations. That theme implies not merely social research, precedent and parallel to physical change, not merely scientific processes applied to street patterns, land use, and traffic, but beyond these a social ideal clearly conceived and resolutely fought for.

What is needed to give consequence and direction to our art of planning is a political process more definite, understood, and resourceful than any which now obtains. That process must be consonant with the spirit and habits of our culture—of that brave, romantic culture we call democracy. We must discover such a process and use it.

What reasons are there for supposing that an art of city planning, in the sense herein implied, can be successfully practiced in American cities?

Consider, first of all, the present achievements of this art. I will mention two: the Metropolitan Park System of Boston and the Lake Front Development of Chicago. For the first of these Charles Eliot and Charles Francis Adams invented a political instrument "whereby forty municipalities obtained the power and means to do for all what no one could do for himself." As for the second, was not Professor Merriam, a member of the city council, "active in obtaining official support"?

This idea of civic playgrounds designed in the popular taste, open to all the people, is one of the fecund ideas attributed to Louis Napoleon. As a political expedient it left little to be desired since it menaced no landed interests, made use of areas which at the time had no apparent usefulness, and was incontrovertible proof of the Emperor's solicitude for his people— a sentiment underlined by the assignment of the royal parks, Boulogne, Vincennes, Monceau, to popular use. Everyone understands a park; and it is no misprizement of our landscape architects to say that they encountered political difficulties less formidable than those encountered by persons who sponsored projects more disturbing to economic complacency.

That is true in part of those who conceived and carried to completion our parkways, radial highways, and bridges—which I shall also claim as examples of the city planner's art. Everybody wants to go somewhere: a desire to which our politicians, prompted by the manufacturers of automobiles and Portland cement, have been exceptionally sensitive. We have also "civic centers," a notion which seems oddly outmoded at this moment, and waterfront developments, partly developed; but for a political art, comprehensive, persistent, and effective, the shining example is that of the advocates of public housing. The housers knew what they wanted. Their art rested almost from the beginning upon political adjustments, local and national, and, favored by circumstance, was practiced with an adroitness which might well be compared (in means, of course, and not in objectives) with that superlative political adroitness which has maintained, year after year, the governmental purchase of silver or the geostatic immobility of the tariff on Newfoundland cod. The home, with its environment, is certain to be the central theme of planning in our time and there could be no clearer proof of this than the controversies which housing policies provoke. Everybody is in favor of the express highway along the Hudson which raises real estate values at each of its ends and abbreviates so admirably the space between Wall Street and Westchester County; but divergent in the extreme are our estimates of the Queensboro and Harlem housing projects which, if multiplied, might make express highways unnecessary.

Said a banker to me recently—and when a banker speaks of planning let no dog bark—"These housing schemes seem to have a socialistic tinge." Socialistic is a *political* epithet.

We have thus, already established, a political art of planning. This growing habit of political action is at once the cause and the consequence of a growing number of political agencies which have been useful instruments of planning and which promise a wider usefulness. These, in turn, rest upon new bases, made progressively firm, of law, precedent, and usage.

Not long ago these agencies were uniformly unofficial in character. They were associations, societies, charitable foundations, chiefly engaged in research or propaganda. Today there are to these added many bureaus, committees, or boards fitted, somewhat uncertainly, to be sure, into the structure of government or fluttering about its edges "in an advisory capacity." Tomorrow these will be dressed in authority—as in some instances they are today.

It must be admitted that those very empiric persons who control the machinery of government in our cities show no very ardent desire to divide their hegemony with planning boards, and these boards in turn rarely offer to grasp such a hegemony either by force or guile. We know with what furious efficiency planning boards sometimes operate within their walls, creating programs vaster and more vast, arming these with the formidable profits of social and economic research; and yet how atrophied are these on the threshold of political performance.

An agency having no other function than the accumulation of the instruments of planning, with no power to use them other than for the formulation of advice uniformly ignored, might, it seems to me, be given a name less equivocal than that of "planning board." If I had my way, that name should be applied only to agencies so integral with a municipal administration as to stand or fall with that administration. The responsibility of such planning boards to the people should be immediate and acknowledged. That "guarantee of political independence" of which these boards are so solicitous, that philosophic remoteness from the purblind herd, robs them of dignity and prohibits more than a precarious usefulness.

I am referring, of course, to the policy-making members of planning boards and especially to the chief executive officer (in those rare instances where he can be found). I should think that a planning agency might include a considerable number of "career planners"—like the career diplomats in the State Department—who would carry on from year to year the routine business of planning and would build up that funded body of knowledge and experience which might form the common, ever renewed tools of planning. Nearly every bureau of government has such men who owe their appointments and promotions to the accepted methods of the Civil Service. I do not suggest that technological problems and the day-to-day difficulties of administration should be resolved by popular vote, nor do I take lightly the work of those engineers, statisticians, budget-makers, and investigators who sustain the functioning of cities. There are people, however, who mistake air conditioning for architecture; and there are people, not inexperienced in the education of planners, who mistake traffic surveys for civic design.

As for the policy-making planners, the architects-of-cities, these should be as directly responsible to public opinions as are mayor and aldermen. Their policies should originate in election pledges and should endure the searching absurdities of campaign oratory. They should give and take blows; and they should now and then be spattered with mud. One year Republican and the next year Democratic, the policies of the planning board should, if I had my way, attain that lack of continuity which, however costly in practical terms, is the certain evidence of vitality in the democratic process; and if it should happen that the people of a city preferred bad planning to good, then, God bless them, they should have it.

Many people believe that the National Resources Planning Board died when a petulant Senate refused its annual appropriation. On the contrary, it was then that the NRPB came to life. From that time forth, the programs of this agency will live in politics—to win and lose elections, to make and unmake the careers of Senators—and in the end the NRPB in some form or other will be reconstructed. No doubt it will be given another name.

This formulation of political instruments of planning, however hesitant, sustains a faith in an architecture of cities; but there is, besides this formulation—and the many successes of our planners in practice—a deeper and more persuasive witness of that faith. I mean those currents in the public mind which almost daily are becoming more favorable to planning. In this, the final court of appeal, there is a growing comprehension of its purposes and its promise, and, what is more important, a growing discontent with that outrageous calumny which our present cities offer a proud democracy. These are necessarily formative influences in the politics of our day—and in the end will not be denied.

We need not despair of an architecture-of-cities. We need not despair of a principle of form as consonant with our industrial democracy as was the neoclassical principle with the eighteenth century. We have already discovered and practiced some elements of that new architecture; we have created and strengthened the political tools which are necessary for its continued practice; and in all of this we are sustained by a public opinion increasingly enlightened.

The colors are ground. The canvas is taut. The brushes lie ready on the tabouret. We await the master.

CHAPTER SIXTEEN

what a young planner ought to know

SEVERAL years ago, being troubled in conscience, I examined somewhat more curiously than usual the curriculum in regional and city planning which was being given at Harvard —nominally under my direction. I discovered many strange practices and conventions; but these seemed less arresting to me, after twenty-five years of university life, than the singular fact that no two instructors in planning had the same notion of what ought to be taught. The architects on the Faculty of Architecture taught architecture, the art historians taught art history, and the landscape architects taught the gentle art of improving nature: each had his circumscribed fund of knowledge, his codified body of doctrine. The planner's province was the universe, amid whose illimitable stretches of space and time he appeared to have no other guide than his estimable intentions and his vagrant intuitions.

Unaware of my audacity, I set out to bring some definition and order into this unplanned cosmos. I began by asking advice. I asked the chairman of each of the seven score departments into which Harvard is divided (we live here in separate cells like doves in their dovecote) to tell me what courses of study were, in his judgment, indispensable to the education of a planner. "What is it," I asked, "that a young planner ought to know?" I had in mind not so much the knowledge which pertains to a planner's trade—the tools by which he makes a living—as that range and depth of understanding which makes a planner truly serviceable to the forward march of humanity.

One hundred and twenty courses of study were described by at least one of my colleagues as essential to this end; seventy-five others as "desirable."

Now there are three things about this fishing expedition which seem to me remarkable. First, the range and variety of the game which came to my net. Almost every intellectual discipline—excepting, as I remember it, the discipline of architecture—was included. The *Politics* of Aristotle and the *Divine City* of St. Augustine, for example, were offered to the student of planning in the same table d'hôte which included the *Sanitation of Water Supply* and the *Statistical Analysis of Municipal Budgets*. For soup, a bowl of *The Cultural History of the Age of Elizabeth;* for fish, *Theories of Social Consciousness;* and for sweets, *New Trends in Education at Chicago*. No profession, I think, was ever complimented by so wide an appraisement of its necessities.

Yet the range and variety of this program of studies—the synthetic program which would have implemented the advice of all the chairmen of departments—astounded me less than its extraordinary length—a length unusual even for fauna as hardy as students of planning. Thirty-three years would be required by this program for the general education of a planner—I mean by this the cultural disciplines which properly precede, or at least accompany, professional courses—so that, including these vocational courses (and of course the necessary period of apprenticeship in the field) a student would be ready to begin his professional career at about the age of seventy years.

The variety was indeed wide, the vista long and formidable; and yet these characteristics of this composite curriculum impressed me less, when I came to understand the true nature of planning, than still another and less easily recognized characteristic. I mean its wisdom.

Who is this planner? this man who is to guide, to rebuild, to reorder this world? who is to recognize and evaluate the deficiencies of our economy? to shield and encourage the healthful growth of society? prepare the way for the perfect life? This virtuoso in foreknowledge, this deputy-God dispensing thunderbolt and sunshine? what discipline is too severe when measured against the fateful decisions that he must make? At what risk shall we place a single province of learning beyond his ken? He will build his ignorance into the fabric of the universe.

Plato prescribed thirty-five years of education for the planner. Only at the completion of that long curriculum was he to be flung into the world to make his living; and only if he survived fifteen years longer in the world, unaided by special privilege, was he admitted into the sacred circle of planning.

This education was not out of scale with the responsibility which Plato gave to planners. Once admitted to that circle, they were philosopher-kings: planners untrammeled by money, wife, child, or Congress, ruling by the serene uncontroverted power of wisdom over businessmen, farmers, soldiers, private property, and the CIO. In Plato, as in Lucretius, the planner views as from a mountaintop the clash of legions on the plain below and, like the gods above the field of Troy, charts the course and the victory.

When Plato and the Harvard Faculty are in agreement there would seem to be little more to be said. We may give our attention now to some of the details. I do not intend to catalogue all of the one hundred and twenty courses of study prescribed for the planner; but I think it will be interesting to consider some of the more pertinent among them.

Take, for example, *history*. I sometimes find among planners a certain rudeness towards history. They turn their backs upon that somewhat threadbare muse or, if they notice her, they do so with no other intent than to call attention to the poor lady's inconsistencies and frustrations.

Now, history offers the planner some gifts which are very essential to his art. Cities are not static things ready like wood or stone to be reshaped by the hand of a giant sculptor. Cities are things *in process*—things that are going places—and have a momentum engendered by events which lie very deep in time. How can we hope to know that momentum and estimate its direction and its power, being ignorant of these events?

Planners, who live in time no less vividly than in space, must think of time as a continuous flow. This breeze which cools our garden today was yesterday above the snow-wastes of Greenland and tomorrow may be among Caribbean palms. These problems of change and of becoming which seem most specific to our day have had in truth a long continuance. They are but little disguised by our mechanizations and our new manners.

Ten courses in history were recommended. These are not too numerous or too arduous to create that sense of continuity, that awareness of past crises and conflicts, of the march of 'peoples and empires, of the impact of great renowns and ideas, which ought to furnish the mind of a planner and illumine his forward path.

Nevertheless the study of history seemed to my colleagues less essential than the study of the *social sciences:* I mean, of course, sociology and economics. These are, I suppose, only deductions from history; and people who are in a hurry may be expected to take the deductions and let the history go. Planners, who are always in a hurry, are sometimes unaware even of the deductions. I am continuously surprised by the number of people who plan the happiness of mankind without taking more than a momentary glance at the structure or the movements of the society which environs them. There is no field where men argue

so romantically and from premises so scant, or where they seen
less hesitant to follow their convictions into action. Of course
know that our society is in need of reconstruction; but I coul
wish that some of our planning officials were more adequatel
armed for that somewhat exacting undertaking.

A knowledge of what men are rather than a vision of wha
they ought to be would save the planner the labor of man
Utopias. Shall we, for example, give the city order not knowin
whether or not the citizens may not be made happy by disorder
How do we know that neighborhood centers will encourage th
good life? What kind of class consciousness is this which is pro
moted by housing projects for the lower income group? An
those divergent and uprooted cultures which have been brough
by accident into our industrial cities—these conflicting folkways
moralities, standards of conduct; how are these to be fitted int
the general code proclaimed from Washington?

Our planning practices are crowded with rules of thumb, con
ventions, clichés, a priori assumptions which rest chiefly upor
habit and the deductions of do-gooders, too seldom supportec
by objective studies or experiments in the field. We must buile
a basis of realism under that meringue.

Some of my friends on the faculty advised my planners to seek
that basis in the study of *politics:* politics being, I take it, a kind
of sociology translated into action. The materials of the planner
are, as I have more than once explained, not only the ideas of
populations, not only the use and distribution of wealth, nor
yet the physical substances merely which these create, but also
the machinery of government and the men who run that machinery. The planner must be at home amid constitutions, cabinets, legislatures, and laws. He must know how ordinances
originate, how they are enacted, how enforced, and how evaded.
No doubt the making of Master Plans is a pleasant vocation;
and yet there is nothing, I think, which could so revive my faith

in planning as to learn that some upright, irreproachable planner had neglected his Master Plan in order to buy half a dozen congressmen.

History, sociology, economics, politics—these are the more important of the social sciences which the planner must command; but they are not less essential than a knowledge and a sustained experience of the physical sciences. These were contrived for the express use of planners. The world, in majestic flight through space, obsequiously offers to the planner her vast and variegated surfaces of land and sea, of mountain, prairie, island, forest, and river, strewn with the multiplex inventions of man. These the obliging geographer and geologist have in part catalogued and described; these the biologist and the anthropologist have made into functions of human life. Here is the planner's oyster, dressed and made ready for the table.

The planner must know the physical world not as a traveler might know it but as it is known to those who have unlocked the laws which govern it and which bind together the pageantry of the universe. His keys will be mathematics, laboratory techniques, statistical methodology, and the languages. He will examine the nature of matter and of living force, of light, heat, sound, and the new kinds of rays; he will know the secrets of magnetism, metallurgy, and mechanics, of rainfall and forestry. He will acquaint himself with the species of animals, plants, and men; with the diversities of populations and cultures; with the laws of respiration and of the circulation of the blood; with the spectrum; the theory of neuroses; the effects of aspirin and dynamite; the peculiar behavior of uranium; nor should the nature of any one of the substances out of which the world is fashioned be considered alien to his catholic art.

Such knowledge is not to be valued by the planner "for its own sake" but rather for the sake of those technologies which rest upon it. These are the inexhaustible material of the planner's art: the multiform applications of science to human life. Plato did not, as I remember it, include such disciplines—certain evidence of our present progress. It is certain that here in Cambridge at least the planner's role is considered an active one: he is not merely to observe and comment, but to practice. Therefore he has need of tools. These tools are technologies.

In our time coal and steam, electricity and the waves of the ether, have made over the world. The conquest of power, the speed and facility of communications, the volume and unlimited variety of our production, have created a new nature. That new nature, a nature in process, is as much the material of the planner as are forest and hill, plain and valley, and the society of men. The internal-combustion engine and the dynamo are circumstances in our environment as firm and as consequential as are tree and meadow. The railroad is an agency of commerce as palpable as are river and sea lane; and the newly charted highways of the air, invisible and unsubstantial, will soon as definitely channel and determine the activities of man. The printing press, the camera, the radio which hourly hurls its tornadoes of sound across the land; these and the thousand other mechanisms of our day surround us, mold us, and challenge the planner.

We do not realize how suddenly this machine took us into its colossal arms or how incalculable are the vast anonymous energies which shaped it and are each day shaping it. Only yesterday we lived with meadow and forest, our quiet cities only a little set apart from the green realm of nature. Suddenly, like an apparition, appeared a metallic universe. James Watt, obscure engineer and maker of mathematical instruments, tinkered at Glasgow with a steam condenser—and our cities were presently ringed with the black stacks of giant factories. Michael Faraday, in the quiet laboratory he had entered as a humble assistant, recorded a new relationship between magnetism and the electric current—and in our cities day was extended through the night.

Wilbur and Orville Wright lifted their frail contraption of wire and cloth above the sands of Kitty Hawk—and across the earth the continents draw together.

These were the forerunners: outposts of a great army. Today, in the absence of such solitary inventors, technical progress moves forward in echelon, the collaborative work of thousands of men, each master of some fragment of our funded experience. Our inventors are organized, disciplined, equipped with costly and elaborate instruments, and sponsored by universities and great corporations. Behind the walls of innumerable laboratories there is constantly expanded the intricate engine upon which rests our civilization.

What planner shall comprehend that giant Frankenstein? What specialist in prevision shall plot the road that he will take tomorrow? What charts, diagrams, statistical analyses shall measure his speed, stepped up each day, or his power, such as men have never imagined? And what strong hand shall stay his swift triumphant feet?

Thirty courses in the technologies are noted on my list—not too many, I think—and among these are included not only the technologies of engineering but of commerce and of social functioning. These also are applications of science. Not the methods and principles which govern manufacture, transportation, agriculture, and the construction of skyscrapers but the methods and principles which govern, or ought to govern, education and advertisement, public health and medicine, law enforcement and the prevention of crime, the organization of force on land, at sea, and in the air, and the structure and administration of banking, industrial management, and labor.

I could extend the catalogue; but I shall lay only one more claim upon the patience of my reader. I shall mention, with instant apology to the earnest planner for troubling his attention with a subject which Plato himself thought trivial, only one more of the groupings into which my list—more by usage than by logic—seems to divide itself. That grouping is art.

I am not of course thinking of art in the general sense of making and doing—as, for example, the art of city planning or the art of politics—but rather in the more specific sense of making and doing in that manner which transcends utility and has as its objective the interpretation and illumination of life. Such art includes music, sculpture, letters, the theater, the dance and, when these rise above the shallow level of the market, the crafts and the new arts of the machine.

With some hesitation I remind planners that there is, or at any rate was, a province of planning not accessible to those sciences upon which they build their confident practice. I have seen recently Utopias—and shining ones at that—which were conceived in terms somewhat lower than those of civilized living. The town functions; traffic moves; there is light, air, and proper exposure in the buildings; but all of this is without grace or dignity in the civic pattern. There is no *architecture*—a term which implies, not good construction merely, but proportion and balance in the general scheme, form and sequence in shelter, street, and open space, and in the whole the eloquent meanings of the collective life. I could wish that our planners, losing none of their resolute science, were yet solicitous for the companionship of a tradition so beautiful and so consoling.

I offer the suggestion with all due modesty. In the meantime the student of city planning—having completed his one hundred and twenty courses of study; having added to these the disciplines specific to planning; having served ten years of apprenticeship in the field; and having arrived at the age of seventy-five—is at last ready to begin his professional career.

Even now he will need one more store of human knowledge: I mean philosophy. Philosophy, interpreter and comforter amid the world's confusions; guardian, shield, and companion to man

throughout his long upward journey; master planner and architect—divine philosophy must now sit beside the planner's hearth
and console him for the world's indifference. We must be careful
lest he should meet that enrapturing goddess at some earlier
point in his education.

CHAPTER SEVENTEEN

the true and sad story of greater boston

DURING the early years of the nineteenth century the philanthropic society known as Tammany Hall, solicitous to provide on Manhattan Island accommodations for a population at least equal to that of China—and incidentally to enjoy the maximum number of lucrative paving contracts—extended the city northward in innumerable straight and wide thoroughfares. In Boston, where the government was strict and upright, no such extravagance was entertained for a moment. Here we were scrupulous to continue our streets, as these led outward from the growing city, in the tight, wayward, and venerable style established by our ancestors and their cows. In Boston no penny of public money was wasted either in unnecessary paving or in the acquisition of land not essential for the flow of horse-motored traffic.

Today the crooked government of New York has taken its gains and departed; but the crooked streets of Boston—still paved, I am sure, with the very best of intentions—remain, exacting their diuturnal toll from her strict and upright citizens.

The moral is plain. Honesty is not always the best policy.* Honesty, to be the best policy, must be seasoned with clairvoyance. Something more is needed in civic affairs than economy in administration, commendable as that may be. I have been surprised more than once in reading the history of cities to dis-

---

* A principle which, it is only fair to add, has been at length recognized by Boston's politicians with a zeal which must in part condone their former probity.

cover the evil which honorable men have wrought and the good which we owe to scoundrels. When neither takes thought of the future the one may as readily as the other hit upon the just course of action.

What is important in streets is not their width and length and degree of curvature, nor the ways in which they are paved and lighted and policed, nor yet their costs either in construction or in maintenance, but the places to which they lead, the kind of people they bind together or keep apart, the currents of activity and interchange which they assist or retard; and these are the important considerations in the design of every element, tangible or intangible, in a civic pattern. An immediate convenience in the location of an airport, for example, would scarcely be worth while if such a location prohibited a later expansion to provide for a growth in foreign trade; and the construction of a new skyscraper, even if crowned with the cupola of the Invalides, might in the long run, through the congestion it provoked in our streets, prove to be an expensive luxury in spite of the astral relief it might afford our civic budget—all the more so if its aggressive bulk were to shatter the beauty, developed over long years, of the city's silhouette.

In all these matters the prime consideration must be the consequence upon the life of the people—the way in which immediate action directs future growth, promotes or discourages a future unity, facilitates or embarrasses a future prosperity—and the prime faculty in administration must be that clairvoyance which raises these consequences in the mind's eye. Cities are never static. When you touch a city you must know its dynamic nature. You must be conscious of a growth and a becoming never ended, of something that is on its way, of something crowded with potentialities of change and surprise.

Clairvoyance is an aristocratic quality, congenial only to great minds, seldom discriminating the conscience of an alderman.

Themistocles, alone among the Greeks, possessed in any large measure that crowning intelligence; Augustus alone among the Romans; and in later times Saint Benedict, William the Conqueror, and Thomas Jefferson. Perhaps Governor Winthrop also who, writing from Salem to the merchant-adventurers of the Massachusetts Bay Company, asking them to send him tools, seed, firearms, rum, and beads, added this postscript: "Pray send also a Frenchman that he may lay out a town." The town was Boston.

The merchant-adventurers did not send a Frenchman. The first streets of Boston, as everyone knows, were made to follow Indian trails and the new paths which led from landing places to the common land. Nevertheless, Boston was planned. The planner was the anonymous and aristocratic spirit of English society and enterprise. There existed in the minds of those who built this city, and in the minds of all of those who raised English cities along the edges of distant seas, a city concept so established by familiar custom and habit of thought, by an ingrown and subconscious clairvoyance, that they could scarcely imagine a city in another pattern. The men of Boston would seek out that pattern without other guidance than the communal habit which they had brought with them. The seed which was planted here contained a tree as peculiar to itself as oak to acorn; its course of growth was as predestined; and whatever might be the accidents of soil and weather, of politics and commerce, which might bend the tree this way or that, no one who encountered it could doubt its provenance or its quality. If at this day you walk in the old streets of Boston you will come upon splinters of a city which might be Bristol or Chelsea.

Because the growth of Boston was thus guided by the silent pressures of an unseen artist it assumed in its general aspect the unity and coherence of a work of art. It possessed, as a whole, an architecture which clearly announced its character. A beauti-

ful town, as it stood after two centuries of growth, rising tier
above tier from the black wharves and frail masts that fringed
the harbor to the dome of the new State House: from the warehouses and the workshops of millers, coopers, and bolters, the
manufactures devoted to gin distilling and the printing of books,
the bright-colored alehouses, dramshops, and taverns to the higher
ribbon of retail shops packed with dry and household goods,
with English millinery and French fashions, with wine, grocer-
ies, and tobacco; and still higher to the houses of the people,
ascending the hills on the sides of which long rows of wooden
tenements sustained mansions rivaling in splendor even those of
Philadelphia; and a hundred white spires rose like slender flowers out of the gray roofs.

There was at that moment a pattern of urban life—awaiting
the shattering impact of the Industrial Revolution—of which the
pattern of the city was true and moving counterpart. Invisible
firm planes divided the people as they divided the town into
functional strata which nevertheless rested one above another
in such a way as to confirm a general sense of civic unity and
participation. There were paupers, the underprivileged, the unfortunate spilled up by the sea, suffering the immemorial con-
tumely of their betters; there were tradesmen and artisans, God-
fearing and thrifty in their way of life, at home in plain wooden
houses; and there were merchant grandees who filled their fine
houses with furniture from England, with plate on the sideboard
and stamped paper on the walls. Boston business men planned
broad enterprises of manufacture, transport, and merchandising;
Boston lawyers, doctors, and schoolmasters practiced each the
peculiar mysteries of his craft; Boston preachers held up to
packed congregations the awful iniquities which beset the prim-
rose path. Boston gentlemen dined, gambled, gossiped, and
were honorably carried to their graves behind generous and
expensive corteges, and Boston gentlewomen had negro coach-

men to drive them to church and to afternoon assemblies.

Such stratifications there were; and yet there lay between them the cement which bound them into a social whole. No doubt our vision is colored by time and by our present anarchies and yet all that we know about the early history of Boston—and indeed of all eighteenth-century towns in America —seems to assure us of a pattern of living which was definite, known, and accepted. There was a feeling of belonging, of being a part of a common enterprise, which pervaded all of society and overlay all consciousness of class. The people, whatever their rank, faced the wilderness together and together reached out into the sea for the trade upon which all depended. The confusions of the world came to them more faintly than to us, distracted incessantly by new fashions of thought poured in from every outpost of the earth, and a common enterprise, a common wealth, fixed the vision of the citizens and knitted their sympathies. Merchants, I think, make the best citizens; and every Bostonian, whatever his appropriate craft and mode of life, was at heart a merchant.

One language, one law, one conscience, one architecture; one standard of interchange and companionship; one fund of experience, forest-made or brought from across the seas: these were the threads which bound the people together as they went about their business, met each other, worked together, quarreled, celebrated, and worshiped—bound them together, not as faggots are bound, but rather as tapestries are bound, a hundred strands, a hundred dyes, tied into a harmony.

The fate of Boston was not different from that of other cities, English, European, and American. Coal and the railroad brought the factory to the city; new mechanizations followed in ever accelerated tempo, disrupting continuously the settled rhythms of living; capital accumulated and filled the minds of Boston's business men—less citizens now than men of the New World—with visions of western enterprise; the Poles, the Germans, the Italians, bringing with them their customs, languages, moralities, invested on all sides the invisible walls which had framed and guarded the city's tradition; and the city grew suddenly and swiftly to its vast dimensions.

That growth was no longer guided by the unseen pressures of a civic pattern known and acknowledged by those who built. The eighteenth-century spirit which sought decorum, balance, self-control fought valiantly in Boston—and was overwhelmed. Moving outward in wide concentric circles from the crescent of her bay Boston poured through the gates of her besieging hills with the prodigal energy and carelessness of consequence of lava flowing from a volcano. Wide areas of marshland were reached and built over, the shallow watercourses were filled with a tangled profusion of warehouse, factory, and the iron deserts of the railroads, the ranged hills clothed with square miles of the three-decker wooden tenements unique to the Boston civilization, and at the center of the city the narrow streets were shadowed by a clutter of high buildings, less audacious than those of New York, but as little disciplined. Boston spread over her uneven site like a great carpet, ragged at the edges, rent by jagged rivers, ravaged by wide areas of blight, confounding in limitless miles of dishevelment institution, home, and places of work. Only when, faced with the growing competition of the Western towns, the outward surge of the city came momentarily to an end did Boston find time to look at herself.

Planning is one of the sweet uses of adversity. People plan when they see that something in their affairs is going wrong. When all is going well they will leave the event to God. Never did England plan so valiantly as under her rain of bombs; never did America plan more ardently than when her factories were silent and her bread lines long. There was no need to plan Boston when her crowded port was a self-sufficient distributing point for the foreign goods consumed by a continent; no need to plan Boston when the expanding West provided an unlimited market for her calicoes and her rubber shoes; when the exploitation of an empire opened a million channels for her venture capital; when the starving land of Eire packed her slums with an inexhaustible supply of that commodity called labor. Only when her port began to grow empty of shipping, her market decreasing daily, her frightened capital running for shelter to error-proof trusteeships, her people deserting the congestion of her streets for the salubrious air of distant suburbs, did Boston begin once again to plan.

To plan? How can we plan when there is no longer a common understanding of what is excellent in planning or any tradition of principle and procedure which might guide a practitioner of that art? when there no longer exists beneath this wilderness of brick and asphalt—inconceivable as a work of art, incomprehensible as consequence and goal of science—that habit and purpose in communal life, that *invisible city* firm and distinct enough to impress itself upon its visible home? when, in a word, we have neither will nor tool for planning? But we can write prescriptions.

What, then, shall we prescribe? An express highway, of course; better yet, a system of express highways. Everyone understands a highway; indeed these are for most of us the sum and substance of city planning. Is not the most renowned hero of that art he who provided New York with those magnificent escape routes which bring Wall Street so much nearer to Westchester County and Oyster Bay? For Boston, then, a system of concrete roads leading in (and out) from all edges of the greater city, following the shores of her watercourses and her parkways, burrowing under her harbor, roofing her streets wherever these are ill adapted to their swifter currents.

Now I am for express highways and I have no doubt but what a system of such thoroughfares, spread over the metropolitan area like a great spider web, would be not only a practical advantage in the life of the city but also an element of civic form. Haussmann in that way gave form to Paris. But that kind of form is always more apparent on paper than in substance and would be even less tangible in Boston than it is in Paris. Haussmann's boulevards were not until recently mechanized nor did they carry traffic so swiftly as to assist, as our highways do, the dispersal of the city. The street, when people walk in it, is a unifying element in society; the express highway slices the city, disintegrates its society; and indeed I can think of nothing else, unless it be the subway, which so encourages the mechanization of city life. A planner who puts his faith in highways is brother to that architect who would remedy the maladjustments of family life and put an end to divorce with electricity and air-conditioning—and cousin to that do-gooder who would overcome the evils of the slums with modern plumbing and ventilated stairways.

We pay dearly for traffic highways when these destroy the peace of our beautiful rivers and parks. Perhaps we should not expect an engineer to understand the social relevance of a park or to grasp the role that a system of parks and parkways might play as an element of form in cities. I am sure that Charles Eliot, who laid over Boston her green mantle of parks, solace and common possession of all her people, understood that role and that is why I think of him as the foremost among American city planners. Nothing can destroy a parkway more thoroughly than an express highway. The lake-front park of Chicago and New York's Riverside Park—once the most beautiful of all our parks—are ravaged now by plagues of automobiles more ruinous than locusts; and we may be thankful in Boston if our planners leave us a fragment of the Charles still unlined with asphalt.

After highways—or systems of highways—the favorite physic of our planners is political reconstruction. Equally at ease amid structures of idea and material realities our planners constantly devise for us ways and means by which Boston may disentangle herself from that casual, irrational net of political subdivision and usage, of conflicting authority and responsibility, in which the city seems to be enmeshed. And certainly we have here in Boston great faith in the curative virtue of political change—which, nevertheless, we fear more than anything on earth.

In the course of her growth Boston engulfed a score or more of towns, embedded thenceforth in the greater city as plums are embedded in a pudding. Cambridge, Quincy, Brookline: each has still its physiognomy, its way of life, its economic and social interests. Each defends itself against Boston, builds for itself privilege, tradition, and legal armaments: like lost battalions besieged behind the enemy's lines. Each renounces in whole or in part a responsibility for those evils which beset the city's heart. Each welcomes, with varying warmth, those who would escape from these evils into the illusory security and semirural peace of a suburb. A "Greater Boston" is created half by expansion and half by accretion: a cellular city cut into fragments by ineradicable barriers. These barriers separate the interdependent functions of the city. They confine the central city, no expansion of which is possible through the firm ring of surrounding communities. Boston, downtown Boston, drained of her wealthiest citizens and burdened with the growing costs of facilities which these still enjoy, has no means of redressing her unbalanced accounts, nor any avenue left open for new adventure.

Now it may be that Boston, like London, is "too big to be regarded as a single unit." Before we invite the residents of Milton, Cambridge, and Newton to place themselves under the jurisdiction of Boston's central government—to embrace with patriotic joy the proud martyrdoms of new taxes and unrighteous government—we might ask if Boston is not fortunate in having established through a phenomenon of growth not unlike that of nature a community grouping which London is seeking to recover through the artificialities of parliamentary procedures. I am by no means sure that citizenship in any one of the sixty-two self-governing communities which together make up the Metropolitan Region of Boston does in itself prohibit a true and active citizenship also in a Greater Boston, and an individuality of character in such communities might actually encourage a unity of character in the larger community to which each might be integral.

It may be then that we ought actually to encourage this separatism—if such it can be called—of Boston. The pattern of the greater city might be conceived as a mosaic in which each element, fitted together with all the other elements to form a whole, might yet retain its endemic form and color. We could make use of parkways, highways, and watercourses to confirm the boundaries of such communities and we might anchor them by commercial and cultural centers; and if we carried our principle to its obvious end we should reëstablish as separate communities those once independent towns—Roxbury, Dorchester, Charlestown—which one by one have been annexed to the central core of Boston. I should go so far as to invite these enslaved cities (and East Boston, South Boston, the West End and, if this be not blasphemy, the Back Bay) to secede from Boston and to join in independent comradeship their carefree encircling sisters. Thus, by making the heart of Boston dependent, not upon a part of her people but upon all those who are nourished by it, there might be excited in all of these a more immediate sense of a responsibility shared together. Political adjustments would be made speedily once that habit of mind were created. It is unlikely that without that habit any machinery for coöperative effort will bring about a genuine collective order.

The greater part of those who write prescriptions for Boston turn, after these first solicitudes for traffic reform and for political reorganization, to those industrial maladjustments which they discover in the city, finding in them the deepest cause of our civic unrest. An economic regeneration is then prescribed and becomes the third and often the most essential part of a program of planning.

Many of the people of Boston are aware of a decline, relative to other cities, in the city's business. We are less prosperous than Detroit and Los Angeles, less prosperous even than Philadelphia, and it is not difficult to find the causes of this change in our circumstances. A plentiful and daring capital, a generous proportion of skilled labor, an advantageous geographical position, and a lack in its special fields of truly able competitors placed Boston only thirty years ago among the first American cities both in the value of its manufactures and the number of men employed in manufacture. Timid capital, a lowered proportion of skilled labor, changes in economic geography, and an abundance of aggressive competitors have now placed Boston in a position less favorable for continued prosperity than at least eight other great cities.

We are invited to be courageous, inventive, adventuresome, and less inclined to protect our children from themselves. We are advised to claim a larger share of federal disbursements (always less than our contributions) and to prepare a shelf of public works ready for execution at the drop of a hat. We must revamp our system, or systems, of taxation and assessment, so clearly unjust, irrational, and antiquated; rebuild our harbor, extend and multiply our airports; advertise more widely the climate of New England, and constantly remind the nation that no educational institutions are quite so good as those of Boston. Nor should Boston retreat from enterprise. That habit of industrial specialization which has long characterized this city, that mode of operation which results in quality production, that hospitality to idea and invention, that imaginative promotion which the world has associated with Yankee trade: these must remain the sure foundations of future wealth as they-were of past prosperity.

Brave words and well pronounced! All that we need now is someone to show us how these things can be done.

No doubt our paramount resource is our tradition; but I do not need to remind my readers that our tradition embraces something more than comfortable living and successful business. When people remember New England they are not apt to remember first our ingenuity in making and selling, important as these are. People remember first that which New England has done to build the structure of the Republic and to guarantee the liberties of the American people. They remember that flowering of letters which first gave distinction to the American culture, they remember the birth of those principles and practices which gave us free and liberal systems of education, they remember the ethical convictions which destroyed slavery and defended religious freedom. It is not surprising then that there are planners in Boston who attempt a solution of those social maladjustments which, although not unique to Boston, are yet of all our distempers the most inimical to civic health. Not all the gangsters live in Chicago, not every racial and class hatred is confined to Los Angeles, nor are chaos and uncertainty in the patterns of society unique to Detroit. In all the world no slums are more horrible than those of Boston, no blighted areas more wide and mean.

Programs of slum clearance are indeed among the proposals of Boston's planners, but it must be admitted that they are offered, and received, with a somewhat tremulous enthusiasm. Our liberalism does not prohibit a certain chilliness to ideas which prejudice, however remotely, a 4¼ per cent return on our investments, or which are tinged with the horrendous dyes of socialism. I wish that I could have found in those eighty modest proposals * for the rebuilding of Boston which once occupied my long summer

* The Boston Contest, sponsored by Boston University. The author was one of the judges.

a deeper interest in the way the people of Boston live, in those elements in their environment which determine in so large a measure their ideas and their behavior, and in whatever social forces are operative here for good or evil. These matters seldom lend themselves to diagrammatic analysis and pictorial represen- tations as arresting as those for traffic networks—nor do they fit so neatly into imaginations shaped by the automobile.

We must not believe that the imagination of Boston is shaped by the automobile. Everyone knows that Boston, which is a state of mind, is most truly expressed, not in the confusions and frus- trations of her traffic lanes, not in the strange pattern and quaint procedures of her politics, nor yet in the uncertainties of her com- merce and her finances, but in her institutions. That is why I think it a great pity that the buildings of these institutions—public library, museum of art, university, orchestral hall—do not count more in the visible pattern of the city. The monuments scattered along Huntington Avenue should have been brought together so that they could have supported each other, not necessarily around Copley Square, not necessarily in conformity to any principle of academic order, but in such a way as to give centrality and splen- dor to the Boston idea. They would be good neighbors in spite of their diverse costumes and they should take each other by the hand, to crown the city with a coronet of architecture. There is a Boston style. Boston selects her ornaments in many strange bazaars but makes them all Boston by the way she wears them.

Our planners are right to include among their plans such group- ings of our institutions, not only at the city's heart, but on those scattered sites called "neighborhood centers." Our institutions are not precious remote shrines of culture but are living things active to build and to unite. They should not be isolated, like the Museum of Fine Arts, on a site so distant and leisurely that we must go in search of them as one goes in search of buried treasure, nor should they be pressed against mean neighbors nor, like

Symphony Hall, placed so near the street that they must forever hold their feet in a gutter. Nevertheless, we must remember that such groupings have force only when they are participants in and symbols of deeper and less visible unities. It is unlikely that buildings could do more than invite such a unity. Planners, like architects, are sometimes too confident of their art.

These, then, are the many prescriptions, not without good sense and true patriotism, of Boston's planners, astonished at their own moderation, incredulous of the stubborn strict horizon of the town. Yet the secret of Boston's indifference is not so far to seek. Our planners have only to turn to that earlier Boston, standing at the threshold of the nineteenth century, facing with a communal soul first the sea and then the continent, to find precisely that element which Boston now lacks and which, being lacking, now prohibits a vision of the stars.

In all planning, the essential consideration is that fabric of thought and feeling which underlies the visible forms of cities. There must be included in that fabric a certain way of apprehending the city and of the citizen's part in it. If we could imagine a new Boston, a Boston which is not an accident but guided in its future development by that communal soul, a Boston which shall be a work of art, a piece of architecture built around civic life as a house is built around a family and of ourselves as the architect; if we could think of the city as frame and channel for all those patterns of social conduct, of business enterprise, of politics, education, recreation which environ us; and if we could think of ourselves as the responsible authors of all of these; well, then, we might begin to plan.

CHAPTER EIGHTEEN

second thoughts on the skyscraper

THERE is an aristocracy among buildings as among men. Like man buildings gain importance when their ancestry is known and recorded; like men they may derive a vicarious dignity from distant authors of their existences. The light from Amiens shines like a nimbus behind even the crudest of neo-Gothic cathedrals; the meanest courthouse remembers Rome; and around the iron dome which crowns the American Çapitol we feel the silent renown of that older dome which is the crown of London.

The skyscraper has no pride of ancestry. A *nouveau riche,* if ever there was one, it rose from sudden obscure beginnings and surprised the city without other authority than its own acquisitive will. No bishop confirmed it, no heraldry emblazoned it, no academy crowned it with laurel, no democracy invited it. Ignorant of polite usages, the skyscraper pushed into the disdainful company of the ancient architectures, turning into toys their quaint palaces and temples, stealing the sky from behind their fragile spires, shattering into anarchy the decent patterns of their cities.

During the first decades of the twentieth century skyscrapers rose in our American cities like weeds at the sudden advent of spring. A great wave of speculation swept the land buoyed by an uncritical confidence in the serviceability of steel and of the mechanics of steel, of faith in the heroic destiny of modern industry—and when the wave had passed, the hearts of our cities were found ensnared in giant brambles of steel towers. In part untenanted and in part made seedy by neglect, these towers stand today in the midst of the blight which they imposed upon their neighborhoods, monuments to a dangerous prosperity and to a pride which, like that of Beauvais, mistook great height for civic grandeur.

The drama was made possible not by economic circumstance alone but equally by that great advance in the science of building which accompanied our prosperity. I shall not pause here to disentangle cause and effect: I note merely that the skyscraper is an engineer's idea no less than the idea of the banker. It is not, like the temple and the cathedral, the product of social effort long sustained, or, like the dwelling, the intimate loved companion of men. It is a contrivance, a machine, the product of ingenuity and calculations.

Two inventions, the elevator and standardized steel construction, both arising from the new technologies of iron and electricity, formed the materials out of which was built this the newest toy of our architects. We must understand these inventions if we are to understand the skyscraper.

By means of the elevator, operating in a shaft hundreds of feet in height, a building is transformed into an extension of a street. It becomes a vertical thoroughfare: a thoroughfare which draws a selected traffic from the street and returns it to the street. Around this thoroughfare we must imagine a steel cage: a cage endlessly divided by thin partitions into uniform compartments. A scaffolding composed of a thousand cells is raised around a cluster of elevator shafts. That is a skyscraper.

Here is a traffic lane, privately controlled, which supplements the street and differs from it chiefly in the character and the degree of its mechanizations. As the street progresses towards the city's center it stems upward in vertical branches ever more closely spaced; its currents flow into these; it becomes a tree. The branches of the tree are skyscrapers.

A street system, hitherto laid out on a plane, thus attains a three-dimensional character, and the city also is made sculptural. The street is no longer merely a canal, walled by low buildings, opening into other canals; it is seen to reach upward along its length into vast stratifications, into shelf after shelf of activity and interest; and the city rises with it into mounting complexities of space and structure. The lower end of Manhattan Island is a mountain made of thin air. Through and around the base of this mountain men move as they do in Paris, right and left across a table; but over their heads reach the intricate veins which fill hollow cliffs with enterprise.

These veins are mechanized. A central core of elevator shafts, sometimes as many as fifty in one building, raises and lowers a stream of men smoothly, precisely, and without effort. The currents here are rapid, much more rapid than in the street, and yet they are more controlled. People move here, or are moved, without fatigue. They arrive at their destinations with a mechanical certainty. Three hundred places of business may open on that superhighway, the highway that is a machine.

Surrounding this machine is the steel cage which forms the second principle of its organization. Skyscrapers are, in effect, great skeletons, built of light rigid elements held together by rivets or by welding. The energy of their structures is not that of stone laid on stone, of solid arches pushing against each other: the structure presses only against the ground, its internal forces being inert. The interaction of weight and arrested force which is essential to the apprehension of stone architecture cannot be made accessible to the imagination here where no such interaction exists other than in the theory of engineers. We understand the building, if we understand it rightly, as a frame which, being clothed with thin membranes of masonry, may be made to define and shape a fragment of space; but that space, unlike the space within stone walls and under a masonry vault, is cellular and lightly contained.

That which astonishes us about this space is not its nature but its vast dimensions. From so simple an expedient there grew structures so sudden, so many—and so overpowering. We see that these are merely boxes, that the substance inside their thin containing walls is air, that this air is divided into a monotony of useful offices; and yet there is in their immensity, in the scale they oppose to our normal habitations, something inhuman, something terrifying, challenging our control, a growth and a becoming uncatalogued in our experience.

We ought not to reproach our architects too severely if their art was at first impotent to discover in skyscrapers a form immediately favorable to the human spirit; if the tried expedients of their art failed at once to civilize these giants, to give them manners and polite forms, to clothe them in poetry. We should be astonished rather that our architects should have made such an attempt.

It was also natural that this attempt should first have been directed towards the disguise of the new technologies. Architects had been too long occupied with brick and stone—with plans and patterns conformable to the laws of brick and stone—to apprehend suddenly this new basis of expression or even to be aware of it. Steel played in their designs the role which the unconscious plays in human psychology. They used steel as a convenience to stretch a Renaissance palace into the clouds; very slowly the metal armature forced its way through the chiseled envelope, demanding a part in its form and expression.

The structure of the skyscraper, unlike anything hitherto experienced in architecture, offended by its monotony. Cathedrals had lifted their walls as high in the air but they had done so in order to canopy majestic halls. The weight of their vast abutments proclaimed the energy which captured and held great fragments of undivided space and the towers which rose around these spaces were apprehended as things ponderable, cohesive, and solid. The skyscraper affords no such dignity of scale, still less a comparable dignity of use. It offered the designer only its uniform fabric, its bulk, and its artless story.

There were, indeed, only two ways in which architects could have given architectural form to the skyscraper. They could, on the one hand, have acknowledged its unique and perverse character—its cellular structure and thin walls, its relatively constant form, its mechanical ethereality, its commonplace function—and they could have tried to discover and make known even within the limits of this cold theme some human relationships which might have given it interest and meaning. Louis Sullivan followed with some success that brave and exacting principle. On the other hand there were those who despaired of such a discovery and who, not without some charge on the imagination of the public, dissembled this stubborn utilitarianism under forms ready-illumined by history.

The fact is that almost all American architects did lay such a burden upon our imaginations, nor was that burden for a time at least uncongenial to the temper of American enterprise. The skyscraper assumed its thousand and one costumes gaily, innocently, supported by the vast naïveté of industrial corporations intent on the exhibition of their bigness. In a holiday spirit the colossal frameworks which rose almost overnight from the rocky bed of New York were encrusted one by one with the debris of the ancient civilizations; the libraries of architects yielded each day new discoveries, apt and rapturous spoil for the new art of "exterior decoration"; and the campaniles of Italy and the cathedral towers of France were made to pierce the Manhattan sky with a hundred new felicities of form.

The masquerade was not long-lived and even before the Great

Depression brought to a sudden end the building spree which followed the first World War the skyscraper had begun a rationalization of its appearances. The functional theory, pronounced in Chicago, was not without its effect and the public mind, incredible as that may seem, began to be cloyed with romance. People continued to admire the Alpine face which Wall Street turned towards Hoboken, but they were bored with historical detail. It was sufficient presently that the top of a skyscraper should be crowned with a necklace of columns; the shaft below might be wholly unvarnished with ornament.

Skyscrapers then assumed briefly the form of stone temples raised above the street at the tops of great honeycombs of steel. A bank in Broad Street, of innumerable cells and forty stories high, could be endorsed, so to speak, with the Temple of Apollo Palatinus; and in Chicago the great metallic box which holds, strata above strata, the million machines of a metropolitan newspaper could be resolved as it neared the sky into a new edition of the *Tour de beurre*. As if a brick were laid upon a birdcage; as if a radio should put forth leaves, ambitious to be a rose.

These are, seen in the light of those excesses which preceded them, progressions towards a revived sanity. There can be no doubt but what, had the building boom lasted a few years longer, the skyscraper would have turned still further towards its common-sense beginnings. There is a skyscraper in Philadelphia which clearly presages that trend; and in New York there developed just before the Depression a skyscraper style which displayed each day more clearly the true image of its recalcitrant character.

The skyscraper is undergoing also a moral regeneration. It is astonishing how many iniquities our critics have uncovered beneath its seemingly innocent façades. There is something inordinate about a contrivance which places a thousand people on a piece of land which formerly accommodated only a hundred: clearly an antisocial creation of big business. No one was ever known to love a landlord—how avid then for rent must he be who thus piled story upon story! It is also convenient to have a landlord whom we can blame for our own want of prescience. If skyscrapers are built too close together we must not reproach the public who failed to discipline them until it was too late. If they shatter the traditional pattern of land values around them it will not do to ask who established the rules of the game.

It is hard to explain, when we look backward, our failure to devise in advance some regulatory statutes for skyscrapers—that they should be more widely spaced than low buildings would appear to be too obvious a principle to demand long argument—but the mind of man is curiously inflexible when faced with the habits of buildings, and the right of men to do as they please with their own property is very fundamental in a laissez-faire economy. Our imaginations, besides, were stirred in those days by visions of towered cities—Babylonian we called them, as we stood "on the threshold of new wonders" and drew oracular pictures of giant ziggurats crowned with temple and amphitheater.

It was not until 1916 that New York worked out the first zoning law which placed an invisible envelope around nascent skyscrapers through which they could not be extended. The effect was immediate and far-reaching, not only upon the appearances of skyscrapers but upon their behavior. It was then that skyscrapers began to reassume that rationality which had been denied them since their Chicago youth. Not only did they rely more upon form and less upon the development of surfaces but they admitted in both form and surface a more certain relevance to their purpose. They were becoming good citizens, and we hear less and less of their immorality.

This change had something to do with the lessening value of the skyscraper as advertisement. People who deplore the untimely end of the Chicago primitives—and what friend of architecture does not?—are apt to overlook the skyscraper's very evident role as a channel of publicity. The Woolworth Tower made instantaneous and convincing this wide, if unorthodox, usefulness; thenceforth the great corporations built steel towers on conspicuous sites in order to call attention to their own importance. The medieval church had set them an example, imitated none too shyly by Louis XIV. Neither of these measured the success of their constructions in strictly financial terms; they were satisfied, as were often the builders of skyscrapers, with a certain prestige value difficult for us to appraise.

The ethics of advertisement lies somewhat beyond the scope of this book, but it may be taken for granted that logic, especially logic in construction, will not have a wide publicity value outside of a community of philosophers. A reticent quality would seem also to be out of place in structures built for the purpose of attracting attention unless of course the quality to be advertised is good taste or decorum or integrity—as in the house of a tailor or a banker—where these also must be insisted upon. It is a nice boundary where expression ends and advertisement begins. It would be interesting to know how many new accounts were attracted to the Guaranty Trust Company by the massive probity of Medician stones held in place by secret scaffoldings of iron. We have been, I think, somewhat too squeamish in these matters. The spiritual content of skyscrapers is not as a rule such as to prohibit an evident mercantilism in their façades, and it may be that advertisement, as an evidence of character, is not wholly inconsistent with the creed of functionalism.

European critics, aloof in that antique balcony from which they view the American scene, often wonder at the aberrations which surrounded the skyscraper with so much sentiment and false pride and blinded us so long, not to its true nature merely but to its latent possibilities of expression. One explanation, I think, lies in our conception of the city. Cities had always been built of stone. The towers which rose out of Venice, of Florence, of Chartres, were stone towers and through stone proclaimed their harmony with the stone city. The cage of steel was alien to that harmony. We could not yet imagine a city of steel.

This is of course only another way of saying that our arts of expression had lagged behind the more eager advance of our structural techniques. In that respect we differed from Europe not in kind but in degree. France, where the technologies of steel were first developed, used these to astonish Paris with the Eiffel Tower; America put them to work in the Woolworth Building.

Steel has set us free to create in buildings every shape and combination of shape which may be demanded by the complex movements of our civilization. The old materials—brick, stone, and wood—bound our buildings to convention and to geometry. Until our time the techniques of stone construction, confirming the laws of the academy, disciplined the forms of buildings within strict boundaries and imposed upon them a conformity to masterpieces completed, framed, set solidly upon the earth. The new materials release us—not always happily—from that constraint. The forms which buildings may now assume are limited only by practical resource and the daring of our imaginations.

We need not be surprised then by the caprices of our architects. We should be surprised rather by their sobriety. These walls of glass, these interlacing spirals, floating walls, and penetrating cubes of air: are these not the inevitable children of steel? Dull indeed must be that mind which, working by calculation merely, would wish to leave unexplored an aesthetic so diverse and entertaining.

Nevertheless we must be careful not to mistake such diversity for architecture. An architect may play with the new forms engendered by steel in much the same way that architects play with the columns and arches of Rome and yet kindle no spark of that fire which translates building into architecture. Not invention, but the use made of invention, is the measure of an architect. Confronted with the thousand surprises which await us in steel and in the industries which depend upon steel, we must not make surprise our standard of excellence.

Our essential problem is that of making steel construction and the infinite shapes and arrangements which it provokes into a language of form. I do not assume that the deepest human experiences can be translated into a skyscraper, and yet skyscrapers could be made eloquent of much that is true and beautiful in our civilization. Our giant industries are not wholly built out of profit and accumulation; the promise they embody of wider happiness and new powers could be, I think, a thrilling theme for our social art. They who built our great ocean steamships have shown us how steel, in part at least, might exhibit that theme.

We must imagine a city of steel. Not the skyscraper alone but all of the city is to be of steel. The streets are of steel and are threaded with the steel subways which receive and carry the mechanized traffic of the skyscrapers. The houses of the people; their theaters, shops, and schools; their hospitals and their cathedrals; all share the lightness, freedom, and grace of steel. There, where all conform to the laws of steel, the skyscraper will be at home.

Already we have built a piece of that city; I mean of course Rockefeller Center. Here the skyscrapers are in part at least reconciled to the city; they rise out of the city as naturally as some great phenomenon of nature. They rise out of street and plaza, out of shops, theaters, music halls, clubs, broadcasting studios, restaurants, and banks, out of hanging gardens and a vast underground city, and even as they possess the sky affirm their kinship with all of these. The skyscrapers of Rockefeller Center do not ask a patent from the past; nor are we apt to be curious of ancestry in buildings so clearly relevant to the future.

That relevance, I think, is most evident at night. By day the skyscrapers of Rockefeller Center cling uncertainly to that monumental quality, solid, inert, and static which they inherited from stone construction. In their forms are strange unwilling recollections of the cathedral tower: lithic envelope, ascending line, planes set back towards the center as they rise, and cavernous doorway encrusted with colored sculptures. Only at night when the surfaces of stone become dark curtains pierced with a million squares of light does this monumentality disappear and the huge cages, aglow above the roofs of the dark city, proclaim their integrity to our present and genuine culture—a culture not congenial to monuments.

That relevance confers a strange grandeur on these unromantic buildings, announcing in the night their true character, so apposite to our way of life and to the terms of their manufacture. They persuade us of a new splendor and power which is coming into the world. We acknowledge, not without pleasure, their harmony with the thought and practice of our time.

CHAPTER NINETEEN

art and our schools

IN one of those aphorisms with which Bertrand Russell illumines the path of philosophy, he describes the basic impulses of men as two in number. These, the prime generators of our thought and activity, are *the possessive impulse* and *the creative impulse*. The mind, he tells us, is a battlefield upon which these struggle for sovereignty.

The possessive impulse, that which is concerned with acquisition, is the source of disharmony and conflict among men. From the possessive impulse arises the undisclosed poverty of our lives, outwardly rich and starved within. The creative impulse, that which is concerned with making and doing, is the source of freedom and health. The creative impulse is that which by giving direction and meaning to our activities transfigures life into an art.

This postulate of Bertrand Russell is no doubt somewhat too religious for human nature's daily fare; and yet it is one which promises a certain usefulness for those who are responsible for education. These definitions, however abstract, are yet pertinent to that crisis in valuations which now confronts the teacher—and with the teacher, the nation. What education is genuine? What is the true measure of its value? And if that true measure is the expansion of life and its enrichment, why have we given in our schools and universities so narrow a guidance to the creative impulse? Why is it that the arts, which are the typical manifestations of the creative impulse, form so meager and so neglected an element in the educational process?

The explanation lies outside of school and university. Our ideal and our system in education are fashioned not by teachers but by that society which teachers serve. Education is conceived as a means of habituating children to the ways of the world in which they are to live, the deficiencies of that world being accepted as not less necessary than its virtues. Our children are fitted into the pattern of the social cosmos which surrounds them; are made to share its rituals and opinions, to obey its laws and taboos, to accept the legends and folk tales which rationalize and illustrate it. That has been from the beginnings of history the accepted role of education.

When therefore the school and the university seem primarily concerned with those disciplines which help their students to get on in the world—when the processes of education appear chiefly to encourage the possessive impulse—we have as teachers played that role which is assigned to us by society. Whether he lives in the white villages of New England or on the red Arizona range, in the crowded streets of Chicago or in the cotton fields of Mississippi, the American child breathes with the American air the ambition to acquire and hold his share of the good things of the earth. Our society confirms by temper and example that universal imperative. Our religion disturbs, without redirecting, the possessive impulse, to which romantic love affords only a brief interlude and our machine-made leisure only desultory anodynes. Education, which has escaped all aristocratic and ecclesiastic control—and sometimes, I think, the direction of scholarship and the learned traditions—does not walk apart from the general march of our time.

Now it must be admitted that the free play of the possessive impulse, sometimes called *private enterprise,* is, or at any rate has been, essential to our present economy. If, as Mr. Russell tells us, the possessive impulse is the source of conflict and dis-harmony among men it would seem to be also the source, or one of the sources, of our economic well-being. It may be that conflict and disharmony are essential precedents to that well-being. Nor can it be said that conflict and disharmony have atrophied the creative impulse. The multiplex children of the creative impulse cover our land with hurricanes of invention and gadget. From our million workshops and furnaces, from laboratory, arsenal, and farm, there flows a fertility of production, prodigal and incessant, like that of nature.

Like that of nature; and yet not like that of nature. Nature, to whose realm man is paradox and intruder; nature, who pours out her inexhaustible invention of plant and animal, of mountain, sea, and sunset, without taking note of the presence of man yet builds for him a mansion more nobly planned than that which he builds for himself. If we perceive in the nonhuman world that same impulse to create and possess which guides our human lives we perceive also that these impulses exist there as circumstances which are incidentals to far wider progressions. If we cannot guess the purpose of nature's infinite fecundity we can yet feel the grandeur with which she surrounds us. Whatever may be the movement and active energy of each living thing, however fierce the struggle of each to possess and use its sphere, each is fitted into the majestic scheme of the universe.

In our society we are unaware either of a general pattern and progression to which our passion for accumulation and manufacture might be addressed or of a larger purpose which might impose a harmony upon these. We have invented for ourselves a way of life, peculiar to our age alone, which encourages to the utmost the creative impulse only to make it the tool of the possessive impulse; a way of life which corrupts and distorts the creative impulse so that, while it is active to make and multiply, its range is limited to economic—and biological—servitude. Our industries and our commerce, and the political and social concepts which sustain them, occupy our hearts; idea, fashion, and language are made conformable to the practices of production and consumption; idea, fashion, and language are limited to the range of our engines.

There has come into being in our time a functionalism of thought so pervasive and so confident as to bring into contempt all that does not pertain to the strict business of living. We are impatient of meanings and general principle; impatient of form, tradition, and intellectual speculation; impatient even of order; and we erase from our lives the observances and ornaments, the ceremony, interest, and circumstance, which these engendered and which once illumined and interpreted the frame of our living. We are fitted into a great machine and perform there each his appointed task with the impersonality of pulleys and levers; and our cellular lives, mass produced like our faith and our preferences, are dull, regimented, and barren.

We must at all costs escape this tyranny which we have laid upon ourselves. We must open a new channel for the creative impulse, source of freedom and health, a channel through which it may enter into and nourish the general life. We must make that impulse operative, not only for the promotion of prosperity and security, but for the building of a civilization.

Now it must be obvious that we cannot by an act of the will or by some process of imitation or make-believe recover those arts of life, peculiar to departed eras of history, which have been discredited by the progressive revelations of science or by the evolution of political and social idea. We cannot return to an aristocratic regime; or to an age of faith; or to that "picturesque and dutiful order which rested on the authority of the family." We must, for good or evil, live among our industries. We must live in a democratic, perhaps socialistic, state; and it may be that we must live also in a world in which the valuations of the Asian cultures are to be as determinant as those of Western Europe. If we are to create a civilization it must be upon the premises which obtain in our time. We must discover the sources of our art in the world which envelops us. We must build with whatever patterns of behavior, moralities, and ways of apprehending life may exist in that world; and the ideal which guides our building must be faith in the perfectibility of these patterns, in the virtue which the human spirit possesses to remold and purify them.

I do not know where such discoveries are to be made, such rebuilding undertaken, if not in our schools and universities. If we could inspire in our pupils, or even in a number of them, a craving for some purpose in work beyond individual adventure, a desire for some pattern in their lives and in the collective life beyond that essential to security and prosperity, a habit of creating set free from material circumstance; if, in a word, we could give our students that way of working which has always characterized those who built, not machines, but human cultures; then we should have made a beginning towards the healing of the social ills which afflict our time. There is in our age, as in all others, a leaven, a power of self-healing, to encourage which is a service as prescriptive to the teacher as that more immediate service which assists our students in the practical conduct of life. Our teachers have not, of course, neglected that service; but it may be that there are methods of teaching which, if developed and practiced, might make their sacrifices more effective against the corrosive influences of our world.

It may be that the teaching of art, or at any rate the teaching of the artist's way of working, may be a more useful weapon in this our eternal warfare than we have hitherto believed. Among all the educational disciplines which time and experience have placed in our hands the teaching of art is that most likely to encourage the creative impulse apart from that passion for pos-

session which has so hardened and narrowed the spiritual out-
look of our land. The practice of the arts, even of those arts which
are called practical or utilitarian, has in it the power of freeing
the practitioner, if only for a moment, from the oppressions of
circumstance. Music, painting, architecture, dancing, and the
making of poems are arts which impose upon those who serve
them generous ways of seeing, of believing, and of building.
They awaken the mind to selfless adventure. The arts, taught in
our schools, may be the most valid rehearsals for the drama of
living.

Consider for a moment how vast are the achievements which
have been the consequences of those movements of the mind
which are most characteristic of the arts. I sometimes think that
through the artist's way of working there was created the greater
part of all that is important in our civilization—and all that is
civilized in our lives. Through that way of working, for example,
we shaped all that fabric of convention, manners, and amenities
which sustains the commerce of our society; all that armature of
principle and usage, that constitution, law, and system of understandings which binds us together as a nation; and by that way
of working also were formed the structure and ornaments of our
religion, our free and stable channels of industry, and our organization of education. All of these and all else which confirms our
status as civilized beings are works of art: not works of art made
by lone men of genius but made rather by the millions of men
and women who had discovered in home and school and community a dignity and direction not revealed by those lanterns,
however glittering, which are turned in the direction of self-
promotion and self-prosperity.

I do not imply, of course, that the architects of our civilizations
were trained in schools of art. They were trained in schools of
life in which life was an art. University, home, church, market,
and government were elements in the curricula of that school

and in each of these there was confirmed by concept and practice, by habit of intercourse and collaboration, by valuations
assumed and known, the responsibility of men for the making
and operation of that complex of idea and conduct within which
the human drama is enacted. There was an art of thinking, an
art of morals, an art of language, an art of religion, an art of living together, and there was one art which embraced all of these.

The distinctive value of painting, music, and architecture, considered as educational processes, lies in the encouragement they
give to those forces which are addressed towards order and health
on this wider field. Essential to all these arts is the act of translating idea and impression into patterns—patterns of shapes, of
sounds, of movement—and by so doing give order and meaning
to experience. They teach, without moralizing or penalty, the
supreme utility of order in all things made or enacted. Their
important purpose is to assist the student to discover form in
life, not as decoration or amenity, but as a necessity to his being
and as a binding force in the structure of society. Through the
practice of the arts the student learns to search for and attain
form, seeking out accords and sequences, setting the parts in
relation to the whole and the whole in relation to idea and technique; and in doing this he learns the power of form to clothe
and animate not only his own thought merely but the thought
and feeling of his time.

The student who plans a house, working out in his mind the
shapes and relationships of living-room, kitchen, bedroom, garage, and garden, has learned more about correlation and ratio
than he who demonstrated by rote a thousand algebraic equa-
tions. The student who plays Pyramus before an audience of his
classmates and blinks at Thisbe through the fingers of Sweet
and Lovely Wall has learned more about coöperative enterprise
than is found in the most solemn page of Ferguson's *Introduction
to the Study of Elementary Sociology*. The student who makes a

cake, stirring into it sugar, flour, and white of egg, common sense, skill, and appetite, has learned more about science than he who commands a battery of test tubes and chemical symbols. The ingredients of a cake can be blended into a very pretty simulacrum of the good life.

Of course I know that the arts cannot form the whole of the disciplines of our schools, nor would I grant them so wide a tenancy; and yet I think that the way of knowing and of doing which the arts afford might be made basic in all that we teach. That way of knowing and doing should not be limited to the teaching of the arts, nor should it be reserved as it is today for periods of play or escape, nor should it be introduced as an appendage to the more arduous disciplines of science and language, but woven as a silver thread into every part of a student's education, coloring his expanding understandings of the world, informing with meaning his developing aptitudes. If I had my way it should be our typical and central process. Segregated no longer in those annexes called "arts and crafts" or timidly available as extracurricular activity to those who dare the scorn of their classmates, the artist's way of working should fill every inch of the schoolhouse with its transfiguring light.

We have grown too confident of our sciences and of the power of literary and factual knowledge to develop the hearts and minds of our students. Science, technologies, and knowledge are utilities, essential to a well-rounded and balanced life, essential no doubt to responsible citizenship and parenthood; but their importance as tools of education has been so exaggerated as to place in jeopardy the ultimate and true objectives of education. We measure our education as an instrument for success, or as one of those absurd keys which unlock the doors of the professions; it is quite possible that even when so measured our ways of teaching are sanctioned as much by habit and superstition as by sense. Even in the most utilitarian of occupations an imaginative command of form, a habit of seeing beyond utility, may be the deter-mining factor in utility itself.

I am not concerned here with aesthetic judgments, but with a manner of making and doing. The art which I have in mind is activity, not contemplation: a certain kind of activity, an activity characterized by a coördination of vision and skill and distin-guished by a search for interpretive values. In such art, the method and not the subject matter is the first consideration. Pictures or chairs: not the kind of art but the process of creat-ing is the essential thing. Of course pictures may, and sometimes do, express ideas inaccessible to chairs (even when these are made of plywood) and I have no doubt but what in the realm of art there are infinite degrees of expressive values; but in edu-cation we must consider the things that are made less important than the ways they are made and their relation to the one who makes them.

I want our students to experience, even at a very early age, the great masterpieces of painting, music, drama, and architec-ture, and yet I am somewhat skeptical of the value of those stud-ies which aim at "appreciation." The student who has known, not as precept and description merely, but as revelation the stately structures of truth and feeling raised by Dante and Bee-thoven, the beauty and grace of the Greek tradition, has appre-hended however dimly that order in the world which is inacces-sible to the senses and to which all human order must be echo and counterpart. He has been lifted if only for a moment above the dull earthen air of necessity. The phrase is Schopenhauer's and was used by him to define the redeeming nature of art.

Nevertheless there are few courses in art, divorced from the activities of art, which afford any such experience. I have seen great architectures presented as if architectures were species of fauna in a prehistoric wilderness. I have seen masterpieces of painting catalogued, annotated, analyzed as if they were bugs in a test tube: Goya, Constable, Raphael so veiled in mists of data and second-hand opinion as to be forever curtained from the student's mind. It is no part of the experience of art to learn the three manners of Vermeer, still less the fifty-seven manners of Picasso; and we know only too well the unconscious sadism of many who love Shakespeare. "My hard subject," a little girl once told me, "is not geography or arithmetic but the *Merchant of Venice.*"

The masterpieces of art are best known to those who have themselves attempted masterpieces; only they know the deepest joyousness of art, the peculiar and inestimable joyousness which is attained, not through contemplation, but through companionship. Those who have never touched a chisel or a brush, who have never danced or composed a sonnet, know very little about art; and our children, to each of whom is given at birth abundantly if not equally, the basic sensibilities and promptings of the artist, will leave our schools dulled in soul if they have not found there opportunities for the awakening and strengthening of these generous aptitudes. I should not take the art of childhood too seriously and yet I think that we cannot expect any really excellent art to spring from our soil until that soil is prepared by the practice of many thousands whose craft attains something less than greatness. Music, painting, and architecture are the more stately brothers of the homely arts and need to be cherished with these, not in cathedral and palace, still less in the museum, but in family, neighborhood, and school. These fuller expressions of the creative impulse never flourished in forcing beds apart from that common garden in which all art is rooted and I am sure that this isolation is one of the causes for their impoverishment here in America.

I have heard the arts defined as avenues for self-expression— or, to use a more fashionable term, self-realization. These are, of course, true definitions but they are much too narrow. Their currency arises from our excessive concern with the art of painting. Idea and feeling are as often collective as individual and as often demand a collective expression. For that reason the social arts, such as architecture and city planning, should have a place in our schools beside music and the arts of letters; and we should encourage also those manual arts in which a search for form may be made integral to contemporary use and manufacture. Machine technologies are likewise inseparable from modern production and should be invaluable in reëstablishing in our schools that sense of a unity between life and art which we know to be essential to social health.

Our schools should be laboratories for the demonstration of that unity. They are built too carefully for precept and formula; we must open them to activity and freedom. We must make them into workshops—into aggregations of workshops each shaped for exercise and practice. It will be no calamity if in that fulfillment we should suppress about half of the apparatus of the sciences, about two thirds of our textbooks. There should be workshops and studios not only for the plastic arts of painting and sculpture, but workshops for the making of music and for dancing; workshops where stories and poems are made; workshops for textiles, ceramics, and metalware; for photography, model-making, and the graphic arts; workshops for the designing of houses and of such products of industry as come within the range of the student's aptitudes. There should be workshops which prepare the student for the art of living together in families—that ridiculous name *domestic science* being forever anathema; workshops for the art of living together in communities—I mean, of course, the art of politics; and workshops for those applications of science which we call technologies—for these also must be made accessible to those who will use them as the agencies of art.

That which the school teaches the schoolhouse should also

teach. We have had enough of those tight brick boxes, hung with the tiresome relics of temples and palaces; those monuments which imprison pupil and teacher within the solemn ponderable romances of architects. Let's have low and rambling buildings laid out around green and white-walled courts, with sunny workshops opening through walls of glass; buildings adapted without affectation to the activity of work and play; buildings which nevertheless are full of grace and which take the children lovingly into their arms. Set these buildings in wide lawns; let them be free of exterior steps and basements; frame them in elm and evergreen. I sometimes think that the architects who build our schoolhouses know very little about children; their cruelty could not otherwise be so deliberate.

We see around us the corrupting winds which the war has awakened, the filth and disorder, the hatreds and brutalities it has engendered, the dissolution of the values by which the nation lived. We see that our children must rebuild our world and we know that we must prepare them for that rebuilding.

How then shall we teach them a way of building? persuade them of a noble purpose in their building? By training them for production and earning, for security, comfort, and enjoyment; arming them to wrench from life the fullest measure of power and applause?

William James said that education is without value unless it is the right kind of education. He said that our faith in education is much too naïve. We think of education as the salvation of democracy without being curious of its ways and its objectives.

Education is only good when it is anchored in some definite and true conception of the good life. For my part, I cannot imagine a good life unguided by art.

CHAPTER TWENTY

the gate into the desert

I HAVE in the top drawer of my desk a medal which for more than thirty-five years has been for me a source of renewal and pride. It was awarded to me, while I was still a student, as a recognition of promise, and of industry, in the professional study of architecture.

On the face of this medal is the form of a lady, lightly but discreetly clad. She is the Goddess of Beauty and holds in one hand the Parthenon and in the other a scroll bearing my name. At her feet lies an Ionic capital supporting a lamp; behind her Phidias, Michelangelo, and George B. Post, delicately limned, look politely into the distance; while all around, amid fanaticisms of laurel and oak leaf, there radiates the beautiful legend: *Awarded for Excellence in Design.*

The students in five schools of architecture competed for this medal: I was the representative of one of them. I remember that the subject of our program, "A Palace for the Governor-General of Algiers," was an exceptionally difficult one, not only because the African sky behind our elevations had to be rendered in twelve washes of ultramarine but because the style of architecture called for was that of the Moslem-Mediterranean, a style not then well developed—not even in Florida. We had besides to show the jury all four of our façades, a most annoying and unusual requirement—all the more so since there was no feature of any importance or interest suggested for the façade towards the desert.

I should like my readers to know how my instructor—who was also my critic—assisted me in the design of that façade and how in doing so he won for me my beautiful medal. I think that the story throws a clarifying light on our educational processes, and on the habits of mind which these engender.

"Why not," suggested Mr. C——, "assume a river on the desert side?"

"Assume a river, Sir?"

"Yes. And if you assume a river, what could be more logical than a water gate? And a water gate would be a most interesting feature."

We were judged in those days by the strict code and precedent of Parisian logic. Logic, as everyone knows, is a process of rational deduction from assumed premises. I assumed a river and deduced a water gate. It was altogether logical that I should have the prize.

I am frequently arrested by the subtle way in which ideas encountered in college follow me through life: how they walk a little way by my side, disappear into the forests which line my path and when I least expect them reappear and take me by the hand. It seems to me as I look backward that this water gate, which after all was only an idea, has accompanied me in that way and that the logic it represents has in some subconscious way shaped my life.

I have for example helped to build in Cambridge a school of architecture. Each year we invite young men to spend four or more years of study in our halls. We expose them to drafting rooms, studios, lecture halls, libraries, professors, and curricula of studies, assuring them admittance at the end of their term of discipline to a world that shall acknowledge and use their eager talent. We have built for them an enchanted gate beyond which lies the promise of a paradise wherein architects distill for a ready market a beauty serviceable to humanity.

We do not mean to deceive our students. The things we tell them are confirmed by proof and logical consequence from premises which ought surely to be true. Our enchanted gate *must* open upon that gentle river, tree lined and musical, margined with shaded cove and dotted with breeze-swept island, which we assumed to be there when we raised our high lintel and wrote upon it: *To the Stream of Creative Happiness.* We have long since forgotten that our gate leads into the Great American Desert.

In our hearts we know that throughout the nation the fine arts, with the single exception of music, are widely discredited. We know that modern painting is dismissed as a fraud practiced upon the public; that modern sculpture is considered an evidence of insanity, modern architecture the negation of every amenity, and the criticism of these a form of quackery; and even the arts of speaking and writing which fling their daily tornadoes of paper and sound across the wide range of the continent, even these are recognized as little more than avenues of entertainment and information. The arts are valued, when they are valued at all, as a means of filling idle time in the intervals of getting and spending. We know that these things are true—but we have assumed a river.

People like to think of the war just ended as something more than a competition for political power and economic resources, something more than a struggle for survival, more even than a prelude to international peace. To make the war endurable we gave it a higher meaning. We said that we were defending an *American way of life.* We were fighting for the four freedoms which assure that way of life; for freedom of worship and of speech, for freedom from want and from fear.

These are more than phrases coined by politicians. We were, and we still are, fighting for the four freedoms and they are worth fighting for. Yet these freedoms are less important to us than the uses we intend to make of them. They are of little significance except as opportunities. Freedoms are shields, not swords; armor, not action; means, not ends. When we are free we shall have only the privilege, the priceless privilege, of building if it so pleases us our own theater of life. Because we shall be free we may build in any manner we may wish to build. A theater, then, built without art?

I have heard convention chairmen and candidates for public office describe amid elevated language and applause the kind of America which is our heart's desire: that America built for comfortable and safe living, carried irresistibly forward on the proud full sail of her triumphant technologies. In that America there is no poverty, sickness, or oppression. No one is hungry or unsheltered. There are jobs for everyone and leisure for everyone to enjoy the good things of life. Labor and Capital, cooing doves, there unite to give us an abundance such as no nation yet has seen; Government, firm and wise, there plans a little but not too much; and with all social and economic conflicts resolved a population of happy, well-fed automatons outworks, outproduces, outinvents, outprospers, and outconsumes any people on the face of this earth.

Our traditional culture? Useless, impractical, highbrow. Our religion? Necessary as safety valve and material of oratory. Our arts? For those who like them.

And architecture? I sometimes think that our architects live in our desert as anchorites once lived in the wastes of the Sahara. Because America can dispense with architecture, because there is no place for architecture in the iron currents of our civilization, we have taken it with us to those little oases which are still watered by the diminishing springs of aristocratic tradition; there we guard it, precious inheritance and secret sacrament, against the erosive siege of an insensitive society; and there we live, behind walls of convention and precedent, amid mutual sympathies and admirations, unmindful of the obscurity with which the impatient sands slowly envelop us.

Beyond our shaking palisade we hear the clash of the armies which struggle for economic and political control; we see the chaos which terrible new inventions have brought into the world, the dreary standardizations, the mean fantasies; see also the disappearance of that shared tradition which once identified our art with the thought and experience of the nation; and we find solace in the rituals of our secret gods. Solemnly we debate the relative morality of classical columns and corner windows, the aesthetic satisfactions specific to Colonial brick or steel construction, the appropriateness of thatched roofs or giant cantilevers for the expression of domestic felicity. Because our esoteric culture is alienated from the general culture, because our art is not competent to express the emotions which occupy the hearts of the people, we have invented an art of expression which is expressive only to ourselves. The world hears behind our palisade the echoes of our shrill and unintelligible quarrels, advertising to mankind the importance of our aesthetic preferences—and the world gives its patronage to the engineer, the realtor, the speculative builder, and the *Ladies' Home Journal*.

Something has been gained now that we have exchanged the peristyle and the dome for flat roofs, unshadowed walls, and the materials of our mechanized production. Certainly this new diet has removed some encumbering fat from the frame of architecture and, not without sacrifice, directed the attention of practitioners to the immediacy of form and function. Nevertheless the habit of thought, taking our profession as a whole, is not greatly changed by new techniques of planning and construction. We have merely exchanged our old wonderland for a new. We have a new arsenal of aesthetic effects which yet seduce us with that same magic which was once the exclusive possession of the Ecole des Beaux-Arts. These have as a rule little consequence other than to afford us a new field for speculation and argument. We are still alone on our sheltered oasis where we find it more important, and more agreeable, to dispute the Doric versus the Gothic mode, to argue the creed of Le Corbusier versus the romance of Wright, the morality of machine versus handicraft, than to discuss the crises in labor and production which are shattering the bases of our profession. Often it happens that little Cape Cod Cottages excite us more than big atomic bombs and innocent Lally columns distress us more acutely than the collapse of that great prop of confidence which upheld the authority of the Supreme Court.

Not long ago the architect directed every process of plan and construction by which men created and controlled that part of their environment which was malleable to the human will. They invented, so far as this included man-made elements, the *mise en scène* of civilization. Not buildings merely were their handiwork, the dwellings and workshops, the temples, markets, and courts of justice, but also the streets and squares through which the life of the city moved, the gardens and parks in which the city breathed, the citadels and walls which guarded it, the furniture of its streets, the *décor* of its triumphs and fetes, and, not infrequently, the products of its crafts and industries. The themes of architecture comprised every useful or ornamental structure which might through arrangement and form be made to sustain the spirit of men.

See, now, how willingly we have submitted to invasion and seizure. We look with complacency on an ever narrowing province. It was actually a matter of pride among architects in the England of Prince Albert that the beautiful bridges built by Rennie and Telford for that uncivilized monster, the railroad, were not to be called *architecture;* these, like the Crystal Palace and the *Galerie* of Cottancin could not be decently clothed in the costumes which filled our jejune wardrobes. We were undisturbed when the making of gardens, parks, water fronts, and the recreational areas of cities were taken over by our romantic cousin, the landscape architect; interior space and ornament we ceded without regret to that merchant-architect, the interior decorator; and today the planning of towns, the most splendid among our ancient offices, is claimed by still a new profession, nebulous as yet but promising of suns, the profession of the city planner. Meanwhile with ever growing assurance contractors and realtors exercise their ancient privilege of pirating our ideas and techniques; corporations, governments, school boards, housing authorities, and churches set up their "architectural departments"; and magazines furnish house plans with each subscription. We know how during the great depression architects flocked to Washington like frightened sea birds before a storm to take refuge in the Great Mill set up there for the mass production of official art; and we shall long remember the recent disdain with which the mighty chiefs of state and army greeted our modest pretensions to a wartime usefulness.

This disintegration of our profession could not have occurred had the arts, and among them the art of architecture, remained integral to the culture of our times; if they had remained, as they were in the eighteenth century, necessary elements in the pattern of life: as necessary for example, as marriage, the processes of justice, or the ceremonies of worship.

Our impoverishment is a symptom, not a cause: a consequence of a malady which lies deep in the general structure of our civilization. It will not yield to the palliatives of aesthetic theory however convincing are these to the practitioners of the arts. Our arts wither wherever they appear unnourished by those spiritual values from which they have always drawn their strength, and our lamentations over their pale existences will trouble heaven as little as they disturb the implacable course of industrial enterprise. The American people, engrossed in the serious business of making money, will walk as they do now curiously through our galleries and, however deeply felt and competent of technique are the pictures we hang there, return at once to their ledgers. Art gave them a momentary escape and that is all they ask of art.

Our modern architecture hangs in such a gallery and is as remote from family and market. Those who look at our buildings do so in a mood undistinguishable from that in which they look at a Picasso. We address our designs to a "cultivated taste"; they are things one must learn about in a book; and like the painter and the sculptor we defend our theory against the indifference of the world, our shield being our contempt for the opinion of the world. We forget how pale is our art cut off from the out-of-doors and the sun.

Architecture alone among the arts has the power·to escape that gallery and, by escaping, leave open the door to the arts of painting and sculpture. The way of escape lies in the integration of architecture with the practical services and necessities of our civilization. The way of escape lies in the participation of architecture in the life of the people, not in their moments of exaltation or of curious inquiry or of holiday making, but in the daily humdrum currents of society. We must make the art of architecture so closely knit to the technologies of our day, and so intimately a part of the industry of building and of the way of life in family, school, and community, as to make it an inseparable element in each of these. We must arrive at expression, and at beauty, not as things evolved from our theories and precedents, but as a very part of those practices by which materials are assembled, shaped, and arranged for shelter and use.

If we are to give form to these materials—and form, I take it, is the final crown of architecture—we must forget our theories of form in order that we may first give ourselves to the practical methods of building and of planning as these have been developed by our time. Our form must have its genesis not in our thought but in the thing to be done; our expression must be the consequence of that idea which generated the program of building. Our form lies in the task. It is there for us to discover and make known.

Because architecture has this power to identify itself with the realities of our culture, architecture alone among the arts can speak to the people in unison with their everyday experience and by so doing become a part of that experience. Being thus shared architecture may reassume that virtue which it once possessed to capture and exhibit those wider values which are inherent in both the intimate and general forms of shelter. Architecture may become again a reality; for when our art rests upon the methods of our time, when it again celebrates our time, holding before the people the dignity and value of our time, we may be sure that the people will again take it to themselves. There is this hunger; there is this fertility below these arid appearances; the land awaits this husbandry.

Now I do not suggest that a change in our teaching, either in method or in temper, could bring about such a reorientation of architecture, but I do believe that our schools of architecture could be, and ought to be, effective agencies for that reorientation. We must not permit architecture to exist in the compartmentalized minds of our students as on the one hand a vocational interest and on the other as a humanity, but as vocational interest and humanity inseparably fused. We should envisage the task before them not as one concerned with aesthetic values merely or with technological service merely but as a ministry through which these are blended into the pattern of human society. Our students are not to grow flowers, even those transplanted from the garden of Le Corbusier, in the brief oases of the desert nor are they merely to build serviceable shelters in that desert for the lower income group or the Pennsylvania Railway, but to irrigate it, to make useful and fruitful those vast resources of the spirit which our industrial wasteland conceals but does not destroy.

We must, I suppose, recognize the boundaries which divide into a dozen new professions the age-old profession of architecture; but we should not divide our art. I would have all of our students, whether they call themselves architects, engineers, landscape architects, city planners, decorators, developers of real estate, or prefabricators of houses aware of a collaborative art of which all are practitioners and to which their several bundles of apparatus and mystifications are merely costume and convenience. They should share one intention and one loyalty and they should go through our beautiful gate as soldiers in one army.

Their ministry will be less arduous if we temper that faith which we give them with a seasoning of realism. A clear view, free from confusion and mirage, of that field which they are to cultivate will anticipate some of those discouragements which embarrass their success and prevent at the start those facile illusions which haunt the dreams of architects and cramp their usefulness. Of course I know that the students in our schools of architecture are no longer concerned with palaces in Algiers; and yet I think that we might give them a somewhat more objective conception than that which they habitually entertain of the landscapes which lie beyond our gate and a clearer view of whatever role may be accessible to architecture in the American scene. We should show them this desert, infrequent of understandings and of applause; allow them to breathe its inhospitable air; armor them against its indifference; and even as we do this persuade them of that high office which is yet possible to architecture.

People are sometimes surprised when they visit the Harvard School of Design by the somewhat pedestrian nature of our programs, so rounded with actualities of site and expense and homely use. Our purpose was not, as some suppose, to reduce architecture to a technical service—although architecture is a technical service—but rather through a constant awareness of service to make sure that at every step of the student's progress his expanding art should be rooted in reality.

There are many practical difficulties imposed by such a principle. The number of planning programs lying actually within the range of a student's experiences, a house for his own parents, a building for his own school, is sometimes surprisingly small. On the other hand, it may seem curious that we should demand, even if the theme be one of these, an interpretation of life from men who have scarcely begun to live—all the more so if this interpretation is to be made in the unfamiliar and intractable shapes of buildings. Some conventions are obviously necessary, as they must be in any formalized system of teaching. For my part, I think that a program will suffice if two conditions are met: first, that it lies in the immediate life about the student; and, second, that it is accessible to him through observation and analysis. What I have in mind is empirical and direct knowledge of the thing to be done, even though this cannot in the nature of things go to the heart of the matter. The student is to visit an actual site, learn for himself the form and movement which life is to assume there, discover and formalize its economic basis and from that knowledge work out a pattern of ideas to be later translated into a pattern of structures. Such investigations are, in my opinion, more useful than those general surveys in what are called, somewhat quaintly, the *social sciences*. These are apt to interpose a screen of idea and theory between the student and the substance of architecture.

The other day I heard one of our students explain to a jury his design for "A Coöperative Farm." His explanation began with an account of the services such a farm might render, included next some data relating to potato growing and the care of bees, and finally some considerations relative to buildings as tools for these "social and economic objectives." This explanation was assisted by charts, diagrams, reports, and photographs. The student had, it appeared, projected himself into the life of his farm. The habits of rural society were in part at least known to him —the conditions of farm labor, the changes wrought by recent inventions, and the impact of these on the forms of shelter—and it seemed to me that by that means he had attained, not perhaps a practical knowledge of farming, but the sympathy and insight which gave his design a surprising eloquence. If, now, it should happen that his hypothetical farmer could not make out quite so well with his potatoes as my student planned, some essential economic or human factor having been overlooked, that would not be important. What is important is the anchor to reality implied in the method. This farmer is a better client than those ambassadors, archbishops, and captains of industry who were my clients in my student days at Columbia: a truer friend of architecture even than that eccentric, affectionately remembered old gentleman who, "finding himself in possession of four antique columns," decided to build a museum.

I should like our students to leave our schools of architecture with a wider vision and a broader range of interests than those which I had when, armed with my comfortable medal, I passed through that beautiful gate. I should like them to feel a deeper comradeship for those who, although architects in spirit and in way of working, are yet practitioners of an affiliated art. I should wish them to be armed with a practical and immediate technology, but they should have also minds that are curious and awake to every new discovery and invention; and they should be resolute to use their art, woven into actualities and yet addressed to the spirit, for the reconstruction of our ravaged world. In that direction lies the recovered authority of architecture.

CHAPTER TWENTY-ONE

blueprint for a university

I BELIEVE that our universities—or at any rate some of our universities—ought to participate in the evolution of a new social order in our cities. There should be such an evolution; and it should be a prescriptive task of the university not merely to record and to comment upon it, but to assume an active and generous responsibility in its promotion.

It should be understood that I am not advocating socialism or communism. What I have in mind is some new grouping of men, some new relationships and responsibilities of institutions, which may overcome the excessive standardization which now obtains in human activity and thought. This standardization, in part the consequence and in part the cause of our immense industrial expansion, has so impoverished the civic spirit that, unless its effects are in some way mitigated, it will surely defeat the democratic process. I am advocating a scientific attitude towards the problems thus created and the enlistment of intellectual forces in the effort to resolve them.

We are not concerned with a present pattern of community life. No such pattern exists, or has existed since the rise of mechanized industry shattered the placid, semirural order of the eighteenth century. Nowhere is that change more clearly exhibited than here in the United States, where our cities reached so rapidly their vast proportions, unembarrassed by the ancient autocracies. We know how the institutions, the habits of thought, the social orientations of the old world were confounded in these

cities with giant new machines and new ways of life; how uprooted and conflicting cultures, and long-established habits of
conduct and of patterned thought, were jumbled together with
new relationships and moralities. The consequence was not a
pattern but a conglomeration.

The mass-production system, invented in Detroit, completed
this social disintegration. The giant factories escape all social
surveillance and yet shape the life of the city. They transform
the city into one great machine for productive activity. The
machine grows daily more automatic, its movements more co-
ordinated, its elements more regimented. The beliefs, aims, and
values of the city dweller become each day like the houses in
which they live: so many uniform points in a fabric of monotony.
If you fly over Detroit you will see endless miles of standardized
houses: they are like the waves of a limitless sea and as eloquent
of spiritual waste. Out of this sea, like islands in an archipelago,
rise the factories, inhuman in scale, receiving and disgorging,
like Charybdis, their tides of men.

Nevertheless, living demands a pattern. We must have a
boundary to our lives. There were communities as soon as there
were men, and we know how every natural impulse of mind or
of conduct had its origin and its form within a framework of
social purpose. The movements of the human spirit are intol-
erably cramped without the communal environment and without
the social loyalties confirmed by a million years of experience.
Our new cities have conferred on man his deepest indignity by
making him an automaton. You will not build a democracy with
automata. Democracy implies a social system and the exercise
of the social function. When the vast majority of city dwellers
form, as they did in ancient Rome, an amorphous mass having
neither structure nor status, they become the facile material for
demagogues and tyrants.

We cannot compress our industrial civilization into one of the ancient patterns—feudal or monarchial or mercantile. We have more than once tried to imprison the stream of our culture, as we have imprisoned the stream of architecture, only to create new floods as our feeble barriers of romance gave way. The past will live with us as behavior, custom, common sense, and binding tradition, but these must be built into a new fabric and made valid within it. The creation of that fabric is the central problem of our time.

I do not suggest that a social pattern can be created by an act of the individual will—still less that it may be discovered through the researches of scholars. It will not be invented. It will be the consequence of an evolutionary process, anonymous and unpredictable, contemptuous of our theory, no doubt, and manifested not in literary or graphic form but in political action. There is nevertheless an art, however obscure, in politics; and political action, even when violent, is often a translation merely of currents of thought which lie very far beneath the appearances they shape. Such currents are sometimes set in motion by discontent and the self-interest of classes but, being set in motion, they may be guided, restrained, and given a rational end by intellectual forces. Such a guidance is, it seems to me, one of the responsibilities of science; and if of science, then surely of the university.

It should be our task to know this growing crisis in the affairs of our cities. We should discover the causes and the nature of our social disintegration and try to comprehend as a whole its direction and processes. We should try to express clearly and persuasively whatever we may discover and to give our expressions currency. We should sketch the patterns which might point the way to new equilibriums and lay at the feet of the city programs of action intended to resolve in part at least some urgent problem of civic life; and for my part, though it be academic heresy, I should include also the making and the use of whatever political instruments might be necessary to implement my programs.

I do not, of course, propose that the university should neglect its ancient functions. The university should continue to be the guardian of funded knowledge and the discoverer of new knowledge. The university's role as a vocational training ground should be extended rather than abridged. Nevertheless, these do not comprise all of our responsibilities to the social order. Ours is an evolving tradition which must be constantly reoriented to new necessities. The university, which was once a training ground for the aristocratic vocations and which became presently a laboratory of scientific and humanistic research, has already become a social and political institution integral with a democratic way of life. We should not try to arrest that evolution.

I think it probable that this evolution will be most evident and most congenial to those universities which are built into our great cities. There the demands of the city will be exigent, its crises apparent. More than one type of university is in the making: we have in America *urban universities* quite distinct from the tradition of Paris or of Oxford, having a proud history, advancing to new fields of endeavor. The discipline in these universities does not strictly comprise the fifty greatest classics of humanism, nor are there available resources wholly adequate for the mounting costs—already a heavy load for the largest industrial corporations—of chemical and mechanical research and invention. These universities have discovered a new dignity in an immediate serviceability to the great cities which nurture them. They are, in part at least, shaped by that serviceability and are daily made more integral to their civic environment. They could not undertake the training of thousands of young men and women, drawn from that human sea which breaks constantly over their shores, without a growing consciousness of unity with that sea.

First among the many solicitudes of this evolving university

set in the framework of a city must be the making of citizens—
I mean the development in the minds and hearts of students,
whether young or adult, of such attitudes as will fit them for the
collective life of the city. Citizens are not made through the
advancement of science or through the spread of literacy, still
less by precept or by laboratory experiment or by the development of professional aptitudes. Citizens are made when men
begin to feel a responsibility for the general welfare; when their
interests include not vocational matters merely, or personal gain
and adventure, but the destiny of that group to which their individual destiny is bound. Citizens are made by the experience
of citizenship. Every student in our urban university, the greater
number of whom will be adult students, should feel himself a
part of an institution actively promoting the life of the city. He
should experience the fact of participation, brought home to him
not only by the basic assumptions of his curriculum, by the daily
attitudes and thought of his teachers, but also by the habitual
and widening contributions of the university to the civic good.
He should see the university reaching out into the city, promoting
the general education and the public health, assisting the efficiency of administration and finance, of security and justice,
encouraging the arts and the public taste, mitigating the conflicts of classes and of economic interests. And the university
which has thus made known to him the dignity and joy of service
should follow him beyond her gates to confirm his faith and
uphold his hands.

I should think it strange if a university made in this way a
function of progressive civilization and sustained by civic life
should be indifferent to the physical aspect of the city. I dare
not suggest that city planning—I mean the conscious and guided
evolution of the outward aspects of cities—should be the prin-
cipal concern of a university; and yet, it seems to me, the indifference of universities to this art, especially the indifference of

a university addressed to the fuller life of a city, presents a curious contradiction. Education is a planning profession. Planning is a term which includes both foresight and responsibility for change. Very little foresight is needed to recognize the consequences of physical disorder upon social health; nor can that sense of responsibility be either deep or clairvoyant which will not recognize physical realities, not less than ideas, as a proper field of university interest. We shape our cities, and then our cities shape us (if I may paraphrase Mr. Churchill). Our present cities are clearly the consequence of social and spiritual disintegration; they may become also the cause of such disintegration.

The trouble is that we do not have a clear idea of the objectives and processes of city planning. We think of planning as something concerned with boulevards and plazas, with river esplanades and the magnificent grouping of public buildings. It is to most of us a pageant art, its objective a civic façade only casually related to work and to social usage. We need perhaps a new word to denote that scientific attack upon the disordered structure of our cities which is the essential process of modern city planning. The materials of this science are not vista and monumental ensemble but the home and its environment, the community and its institutions, the balance and rhythm of populations. It proceeds hand in hand with municipal research. It is a tool of social reconstruction, contributing to that reconstruction the demonstrated influence of environment.

The plan of Detroit, the artistry of Judge Woodward, was built of abstractions: of radial avenues and *rond-points* copied from the park at Versailles. These had introduced order into the garden of Louis XIV but were found less suitable in the course of time for citizens than they had been for trees. We should be glad that the expanding city refused that geometric corseting. The wide, amorphous city now offers us on an immense page the materials of reconstruction unembarrassed (except at the center) by inherited ideals of form. We are going to build out of this material—not arbitrarily, as the consequence of some new synthesis theoretically arrived at, but slowly, through processes of social adjustment and experiment—new vistas conformable to a changing order of civic life. That is what we mean by city planning. In that evolution the university, and especially the urban university, cannot be merely observer and analyst.

It is probable that our great industrial cities are about to undergo a process of decentralization. The factories move outward into the countryside, drawing with them the homes of the workers and their institutions. Satellite towns spring up all around the nucleus of the old city, inviting new loyalties and relationships in the community life. These satellite towns will have in time local colorations and local structures; the great industrial city will expand into a mosaic of smaller communities separated, it is hoped, by wide belts of greenery and tied together by swift, well-organized avenues of traffic. Already one can see in Detroit the shaping of that new pattern.

What will happen to the old city when that reshaping is accomplished: when the people leave untenanted the crowded and obsolete center to live in shining new communities in the far suburbs? Will they leave behind them vast ruined acres like those of ancient Rome? Shall we demolish these rusting skyscrapers and molding pavements to make room for wide, green playgrounds and forest vistas? We have been shown such a city in the plans of a great American architect: the site of the present Detroit a meadow, dotted with pleasant groves and ringed with thriving new towns. Given the developments in manufacture and communication promised by recent new techniques, such a new physical reality, providing every facility for economic and biological survival is by no means impossible.

I share my colleague's love of playground and forest; I am as firm as he in support of a new organization of dwelling and working place; but I cannot share the complacency with which he views the operation of that civic explosion which is to shatter the city into divergent fragments. Whatever his new pattern might be, it would not be a city: a city is not merely a collection of buildings or an aggregation of people; a city is made by the form and content of society. That form and content must be expressed in the institutions which are the functions of society. The civic soul is not nourished by the physical well-being or the prosperity of its citizens but by the cultural interests and the political order to which these are only background and accompaniment. Nor is it possible, as some believe, that cultural interests and political order can be sustained by newspapers, radios, and motion pictures, useful as these are; you must have institutions which invite participation and responsible action.

I think of the urban university as the first among such institutions. That life which the cathedral gave to the medieval city, that beauty which the palace gave to the city of the Renaissance, the university will give to the American city of tomorrow. It will form, with museums of science and art, libraries, concert halls, theaters, and schools, a great cultural heart out of which will flow the currents which inform the life of the city with dignity and meaning. A training school for the civic vocations, its uncloistered halls shall be crowded with citizens.

I cannot think of such a university built at the edge of a city; it should preside at the center, affirming by that relationship its leadership and serviceability. It should be conscious of its high place in the scheme of the city; conscious not of its relation to street and traffic merely, to the homes of faculty and students, to coördinated institutions and facilities, but more urgently conscious of those less immediate and less visible factors of city life, unobserved by the practical-minded, which create its usefulness as a civic force. It will build itself into the city. It will be a part of the city plan.

My university should be a city in itself. Like the medieval University of Paris, it should be a city within a city; and it should be a planned city, by which term I mean a city guided by that communal intelligence which seeks a harmony between man and his environment. The order and unity which it promotes in the pattern around it should be exhibited also in its individual pattern. That, also, should teach not by precept merely, but by example.

Our buildings and avenues and open spaces must be so organized as to make evident their participation in the totality of the university. They must remind us of that participation not only by consistent architecture but by their attitudes and arrangements. They must confront the city as a unity, not as a collection of fragments. A formless aggregation of anecdotal styles such as we have at Harvard may attain some romantic unity through history and long association—there is a spirit there which reconciles many monstrous discordances—but you may be sure that such an expression cannot be deliberately arrived at. To our new universities, which have yet to crystallize into indissoluble shape, architecture offers a true and invaluable companionship. Our buildings and the communal pattern which they may form will, if we will admit them to this service, facilitate in a thousand subtle ways the fulfillment of our mission.

The students and teachers who feel daily the impact of architectural order and unity experience through that impact the order and unity of the institution which these express. They know themselves to be a part of an organic whole; they are citizens and form the more readily the habit of citizenship. They perceive the intention of the university—the idea, the mood, of those who framed it—and its wholeness and its march are brought home to them in a moving symbol. The people of the city, also, are aware of that symbol which confirms in their hearts a faith in the university idea. There is no need to remind practical men of the value of order in the operation of a great institution, whether that institution be devoted to education, business, or government; nor is it necessary to affirm again the importance of an order based directly upon efficient and economical operation. That principle should be extended to our architecture. We must know how we intend our university to operate and provide a machine for that functioning. Though we cannot foresee every form of serviceability or provide in advance for every contingency, we can yet have a policy and plot its general directions and objectives; and our buildings can assist that policy. Most university buildings obstruct both operation and growth. Haphazard aggregations show clearly the lack of foresight and firm guidance; things happened to them and they await more happenings. Because universities had no policy, they became encumbered by sentiment and medieval mummeries: not in the detail of their buildings merely, but in the organization and relationship of these.

We are not sufficiently conscious of our present opportunity and its greatness. If we knew the commanding place which a university might occupy in our industrial cities, if we were truly aware of the city's anxiety and hunger, of its need for direction and guardianship, we should be more anxious to fit our universities to the actualities of time and circumstance. We should not think of the university then as the curator of ancient cultures merely or as an experimenter in the sciences—still less as a fortuitous collection of vocational schools—but as that light which is to rekindle the collective soul. We should then understand the necessity of affirming in the persistent and eloquent language of architecture our unity in that purpose. We should then yield ourselves to the city, identifying our destiny with the city's destiny, our health with the city's health, our form with the city's form; and we should affirm that wholeness by making our plan an inseparable, necessary part of the city's pattern.

CHAPTER TWENTY-TWO

the art in housing

SEVERAL years ago I asked an architect who had just completed a housing project to tell me the principle upon
which he had designed his façades.

"I got them," he said, "from the plates in Ramsey's *Late Georgian Houses.*"

For some reason the remark seems less preposterous after the
passing of years than at the time it was made. Not that the
eighteenth-century flavor he gave his designs has grown more
congruous to the busy life which they enclose, but rather because
these façades, whatever may be their absurdities, reveal at least
the consciousness of *an art in housing:* of a need for feeling and
for expression, as well as for science, which is too often unac-
knowledged in our more recent projects. Strange as it may seem,
these Georgian exteriors were added on with love; a love which
was no doubt misdirected but which was nevertheless real. The
architect, I think, built with his heart, and the structures he has
erected tell us so. We perceive beneath the veneer of his scholarship an intention to convey a mood, a thought, and that perception seems to lift his work above the arid materialism which
clothes so often the more advanced science of our own day.

Not less of your ingenuity, gentlemen. Not less of your admirable common sense and practical genius, your commendable
solicitude for the public purse. More of these, not less; but could
you not, without abridgment of your zeal for firmness and commodity, include also that sympathy for the human no less than

the technical objectives of your program which, fused into your buildings, might illumine their dismal efficiency? I do not suggest that this light should be made to shine from Georgian or Tudor adulteries or from trimmings and furbelows added on, whether in the name of taste or of scholarship, still less from the application of principles and rules of form gathered from the textbooks of aesthetes. I suggest, rather, that even in housing projects the architect should discover and guard some deeper purpose in his work than that of mere shelter and sanitation and that he should find the means as an essential part of those practical processes by which materials are assembled and shaped for use to make this purpose evident. I mean, in short, that housing should be, not an agency for social reconstruction merely, but also a theme for art.

It should be understood that I am not speaking of an abstraction. I do not use the word *art* in the drawing-room sense of something to talk about. The art I have in mind is essentially a process of giving spiritual content to things made by man. That is, in a housing project, something real and very much to the point. I shall go so far as to say that without such art (which I will call *architecture*) the housing project will fail as an agency for social reconstruction. Those true and compassionate persons who in their zeal for cleanliness and fresh air, for decent sanitation and comfort, for economy and sound construction, have ignored the arts of expression little know the subtle force of idea and emotion in human affairs. They would persuade us with argument when the way to our hearts lies open before them. It has yet to be proved that mechanical refrigerators have power to promote the good life; but the power of window boxes has been proved a hundred thousand times.

To be scornful of the utility of the arts, especially when these are warmed by sentiment, and to be by that means dressed in a reputation of militancy and stern realism has become the fashion since Pearl Harbor—as if an interest in civilized living were inconsistent with democratic faith and the practical administration of the agencies of war and peace. We flatter the Nazis too highly by so gratuitous an imitation. I am not for frills in housing; and yet even in the most temporary of "living units" I would admit some considerations other than the possibility of erecting these in nine and a half hours. That "lower income group" for which public housing is erected will not be made less discontented by a too Spartan economy practiced upon their wives and children, and while we assure the workers in our industries of our intention to defend the American way of life our promise might well be made visible and persuasive in the forms of the dwellings we build for them.

I have seen few landscapes more depressing than those areas devoted to temporary houses put up hastily for the use of our married veterans—especially those for veterans who are also students in our colleges. These dreary boxes must be very helpful in promoting a devotion to the nation's cause among wives and children. "The Japanese," said the great philosopher, Ch'iu Tsai, "are a naïve people: they think that wars are won by soldiers."

Heaven knows that I would not shelter that "lower income group," or any other group for that matter, in ornamental buildings, and yet I think we have been somewhat too resolute at times to be simple, functional, and modern. A balcony or two should not disturb our conscience, a canopy over a doorway here and there, a curved line, a panel, a spot of color. Stringcourses are not so expensive as to tax the resources of a government truly intent on human happiness; and although I am not a lover of cornices, I see no reason why we should not cap our walls with some material which would contrast with their texture and color. We should consider more curiously the nature and use of materials, and especially of the materials of walls. Red brick is practical and wholly respectable, but it is not the only material available to the architect; and even if red brick were the only material it would yet be susceptible to a hundred variations in texture, coloring, and pattern—few of which our architects have even hinted at. There should be broad planes differing in materials, colors, and textures and these should answer each other in considered sequences. There should be also a liberal use of white wherever that is possible, of a white which captures and holds the changing tones and radiances of the sky. Doorways, even in the plainest buildings, ought to have some emphasis; doorways of stone or wood can give life to the brick walls upon which they are placed. These, as well as the other details I have mentioned, could be made less costly by a reasonable degree of standardization and they could, as Mr. Albert Mayer has suggested, develop in the course of time their own idiom, not a "watered-down version of the middle class"—a sentiment in which I heartily concur.

We could do much more with windows than as yet has been attempted. I am not for variations made to avoid monotony— these only make the monotony more evident—but rather for a more sympathetic consideration of proportion, spacing, and treatment. Those antique buildings in the Harvard Yard—Holworthy, Stoughton, Hollis—owe their serene dignity almost entirely to their windows. It is surprising that we have learned that lesson so haltingly here in Cambridge. This corner of the Harvard Yard is very like a housing development: built for the use of men who certainly had as little money as we have to spend on architectural fripperies. The priceless ingredient in these houses is a nice sense of spacing and of relationships, of scale and rhythm. There is no plan or structure of so intransigent a nature as to prohibit in some measure such feeling and care, nor should such feeling and care be confined merely to matters of form or of appearances. We should depend upon windows more than on any other element in our design for that residential (I almost said homelike) quality which the façades of a housing project ought to have. People live behind these windows, and the sense of that life should and can be made to shine through them. Windows are like eyes: they can reveal a soul.

The character of buildings depends, more than most of us realize, upon such details as window treatment and the materials of surfaces; but I do not need to remind architects that these are after all only minor media in expression. That architecture is an art of three dimensions is a truth never more evident than in the designs of housing projects. The elements of those designs, the expressive elements no less than the useful, are solid objects (buildings) set in space. It is with these that the architect builds his patterns and the character of these patterns is chiefly determined not by materials or details but by arrangements: that is to say, by the shapes, proportions, and relationships of buildings, and by the shapes, proportions, and relationships of the spaces between and around buildings.

Now the most usual and most obvious fault with housing projects, considered as patterns, is their extreme monotony. The buildings are too much alike, too equally spaced. Their dreary repetitions seem to go on endlessly. I am persuaded that this monotony is as unnecessary as it is fatal to good design. I cannot believe that there is any science so tyrannous as to impose so iron a discipline; nor can it be excused entirely by considerations of economy. In an enterprise made up of so many human factors, of so many and so nice questions of economic balance, there can be, I think, no formulation of physical requirements so definite as to prohibit all variations in the forms of buildings. Our faith in "expert opinion" is much too naïve. Expert can be balanced against expert, as every lawyer knows, on any topic under the sun, and if it be heresy I will yet declare my suspicion of a code of procedure so precise in every part as that of the housers. Never, never—try as they may—will they devise that four-family apartment suitable for every family of four, Irish or Polish, Yankee or Middle West, Catholic or Puritan, tradesman or industrial worker, nor will they ever suppress (I hope) the influence of individual taste and irrational preference in the design of homes.

I remember an argument, fought out to an extreme of bitterness, over the height of buildings in a certain housing project and no one knows to this day, and no one will ever know, whether these should have been three or four stories in height. Why not, then, have some of three stories and some of four? With the variations in heights, variations in positions would follow (they should follow anyway) and these could be so managed as to afford not only a variety of sequences and groupings but also new contrasts and new harmonies in the shape, scale, and character of enclosed spaces. A quality of suspense or surprise is essential to all vitality in form, and this is never more true than in the forms of spaces. These spaces, it must be remembered, are as important elements in pattern as are the buildings and their forms and relationships must be as subject to our control. Our housing projects are too often like hospitals blown up to insane proportions, with ward after ward following in an endless march, and they lack even those central elements of administration and common services which in hospitals sometimes pull these wards into a tenuous unity.

It isn't their monotony merely, the tedious multiplication of standard units, which gives housing projects so inhuman, so antiseptic an aspect. It is even more their amorphousness, their indeterminate shape as a whole. They begin in the most casual way, zigzag endlessly over open spaces nervously dotted with trees, and end nowhere. You could double their size or reduce them by a third, and still they would be the same. Nothing is there other than the deadly concord of color and shape, and the fact that they have foliage and grass about them, to give them totality and coherence, to make of them a distinct and definite identity such as could be grasped and appreciated as a whole. Without such identity there could not, of course, be any satisfactory pattern.

I think of housing projects as inward-looking groups. I mean that they should have at their center some interests which are shared in common by all and which are expressed in structures or open spaces shared by all, so that the life of the project would be focused towards the center and away from the boundaries. The residents should of course share the life of the greater city of which they are a part and the life should flow in and out of the area at many points about its perimeter but, beyond this, they should feel themselves also a part of a smaller community, of a neighborhood.

This dual rhythm, like that of a great heart, should be expressed in the pattern of the whole. It is all very well to "discourage" outside traffic through residential areas, but one should not carry the principle so far as to create labyrinths. I have seen housing projects which resemble nothing so much as rabbit warrens, so confused and intricate are the spaces, and I wonder that any one who gets into them ever finds his way out. Something other than traffic, I think, was discouraged.

I am equally depressed by those designs which go to the opposite extreme and provide a single wide avenue or vista, open at one end and leading straight into the center. The unity here achieved is that of an institution, not that of a neighborhood. No scheme is more likely to invite an outward, rather than an inward movement; and this is made more rather than less obvious when, as sometimes happens, the vista is ended by some imposing dome or portico or commemorative monument. What is wanted is a heart which belongs to the neighborhood alone. Your heart is no longer yours if every Tom, Dick, and Harry can look into it.

I think that there should be *streets* and that these, with the exception of a few circumferentials, should lead from the perimeter towards an open space at the center and, whenever such an arrangement is practicable, the walls of buildings should follow the lines of streets. I would restore the street as the basic element in my pattern. The street—a term which implies a public thoroughfare lined with buildings—is a setting for a habit of life invented near the beginnings of social growth, and perhaps we should think at least twice before we decide that zigzags in a park are truly more appropriate to a habit of life thus embedded in history. And how, without history, shall we hope for expression in architecture? Every one will agree, I think, that the most beautiful part of Boston is that part lying on the western slope of Beacon Hill; and yet it will be thought strange that I should find in this area a lesson useful for the architects of housing projects. Heaven forbid that they should copy for the unsuitable pleasure of a "low income group" the elegant complacencies of Bulfinch, and yet they might, I think, observe that unmistakable quality of neighborliness, of people aware of each other and of a common sentiment, which is in part at least the consequence of a pattern shared by house and street. The houses are designed for the streets, the streets for the houses. Certainly I would copy neither the streets nor the houses of Beacon Hill but I would have our buildings grasp the pattern of our streets in a similar manner and so attain a similar unity, a similar clarity and definition, a similar humanity. I would have that sense of scale and articulation and, yes, there should be backyards "decently confined" and recreational areas clearly set apart from those spaces meant for circulation and service. I should like those persons who determine the orientation of our new houses to consider if that might not be worth some abatement of their strict regulations. For my part, I am not so avid of the sun as to wish its rays to fall on every inch of my façades.

I think it most unfortunate that housing projects have so little
relationship in their outward aspects with the patterns of their
environments. If you fly over them they look like bright new
patches on the worn fabric of the city. They will never become
integral with the city, so opposed are they to its prevailing lines
and scale. And yet they are parts of the city and not institutions
set into it. I would restore the *street* if only to recapture in part
the unity of neighborhood and surroundings; and for the same
reason I would establish definite boundaries for my play areas
and see to it that play did not overflow these boundaries. I have
seen more than one housing project in which boys of the noisy
age flow in from all the adjacent streets and fill the air with the
clamor of their games so that the people who live there are in
effect living in a playground—a very moth-eaten playground and
one too often cut into little pieces, like a jigsaw puzzle, by
squirming lines of concrete pavement. The street is among the
most pleasant and most beautiful creations of man.

People sometimes imagine that streets and playgrounds, shops
and institutions, are not the immediate concern of housing authorities—or of those great corporations which are building such
huge concentrations of apartment houses in the midst of our
great cities. It appears that the problem of housing has been set
aside from the wider problems of the city and must be attacked
with strictly limited tools and limited powers. We set our housing projects here and there in the vast matrix of the city with
little concern for the relationships of these to the city's life as
a whole.

This attitude of mind is largely responsible for the compactness of housing projects. There are no doubt practical advantages in compactness, especially when one is concerned exclusively with a single economic group; but in any comprehensive
view these advantages must certainly be outweighed by the social cost of such irresponsible planning. Little islands spring up

over the wide waste of the city, separated, not only from institu- ?
tions and from commerce, but from the general pattern of the ?
city's society.

If I had my way I would spread each housing project over
wide areas, leaving many sites within their boundaries—if they
must have boundaries—for houses occupied by the little-less-
than-lowest income group. In every project for public housing
such sites might be left for development by private enterprise.
In that way my project should be seasoned by many variants; it
should be tied into the city, commingled with the city; and if as
a consequence it lost some of its architectural unity and formal
impressiveness that loss might be generously compensated by a
relevance to social objectives which far transcend mere "decent
living standards"—important as these are. I am inclined to think
that the housing project thus scattered might actually gain in
architectonic qualities. Certainly it would gain in human interest.
I would invite a few accidents in my design.

New England villages, in the days when New England possessed her unique culture, had at their centers a *common*. I would
have a common at the heart of every housing project—but let
me hasten to add, before some illustrator draws a picture of my
common as elm-dotted field and picket fence and white church
spire that it is the idea and not the traditional form that I have
in mind. My common should be an open space with the shopping
center at one side and the neighborhood institutions at the other.
The housing authorities should assign sites for these, to be sold
at reasonable prices and controlled by reasonable rules. You
have a city now without a city's amenities; a place to live in
without that which makes life tolerable; technique without end,
and no soul whatever.

I would not place the shopping center outside the housing
project "at traffic junctions," as so many experts have suggested.
I need no expert to show me what havoc automobile traffic plays

with a shopping center. Shops are unifying factors; yes, and civ-
ilizing factors, too. There are few activities more pleasant than
spending money and when you spend money in the company of
your neighbors—to buy food and other things for your husband
and children or, for that matter, to give a party—that is a social
activity even though it has not yet been identified as such in the
quaint vocabularies of sociologists. These, and some housing authorities, are much too snooty about shops and markets. Shops
and markets, with their colored letterings, bright windows, neon
lights and the murmur of crowds, disturb their antiseptic calm—
and that is precisely what is needed.

My institutions should include a school, and I am inclined to
like the idea of a school district whose boundaries are cotermi-
nous with that of a housing project. I should suppose that, with a
little good will on the part of boards of education, that should
not be impossible of realization. I do not like the idea of a club
for grown-ups in the school but perhaps that is only my prejudice. I go to my club to escape, not to find, restraint and guidance, and I imagine that low-income folk feel much the same way.
I should have a public library and a gymnasium and, above all,
a church—if not one church for all, then several churches and a
synagogue. I don't see how we can expect to create any social
cohesion or any community spirit, still less an affection or loyalty of residents for their neighborhood, if people must go outside its limits to meet together in prayer or to attend a wedding,
a funeral, or a christening. These things of the spirit can be made
to illumine our new social fabric even though this is patently
an artificial and in some ways an unnatural grouping of human
beings; and, while they give internal strength and direction to
the common life within its boundaries, they should provide also
that symbol and focus which will pull into unity all the diverse
elements of our design.

The trouble with most of our housing projects lies in the *idea* which the architect sought to express. Architects have been, with notable exceptions, too concerned with techniques, too intent on economy, lighting, and sanitation, to give much thought to the human significance of their undertaking. Their science has been competent and active, but their insight and understanding have been neither deep nor sure. This is the true reason for that quality of unreality, of deadness, of alien manufacture which most housing projects seem to possess. Because the *idea* which is the spring and life of every work of art was too little understood to admit a deep expression, the search for form, which was genuine so far as it went, did not carry the architect beyond an intellectual satisfaction in distribution and arrangement. You can make any number of entertaining patterns out of the buildings of a housing project without endowing these with the faintest breath of life. You can play with these buildings in the way a child plays with blocks—or, what is quite the same thing, in the way an academic architect plays with peristyles and domes—and you cán delight the aesthetes with no end of balance, symmetry, rhythm, coherence, and every other quality admired of schoolmasters, and yet achieve not the slightest imaginative command. For that command you have to look far beyond the immediate practical exigencies of your problem; you must discover, far below surfaces and appearances, the true intent and significance of that which you are doing; and then you must be resolute to bring that to the surface, to make it express and visible. Your form must grow directly out of that discovery: out of the totality of the thing to be done.

I do not wish to end this chapter without an affirmation of my faith in public housing. There is no more promising manifestation of that new will to use our collective strength to promote our collective happiness, of our determination to reshape our world to a form fit for human living. We did not expect to create that world without initial failures and disappointments, to overcome with a single blow that terrible genie which has been released from the stacks of our factories. We see now that our science alone will not be adequate to that task. We must put more art into our housing.

CHAPTER TWENTY-THREE

housing and the democratic process

NOT long ago I attended a conference on public housing.
I heard many speeches—and made one myself.

Nearly all of the speeches (I will say nothing about my own)
were devoted to some problem of practice: to planning and techniques, incomes and rents, tenant relationships and management, operation and maintenance. Very little was said about the
objectives of housing, the place of housing in the pattern of society. It appeared to be taken for granted that the causes and
consequences of housing, which in practice is an arduous and
uncertain art, were definite, well understood, and approved.
Everyone present gained some useful information and each left
the conference by the same door through which he had come.

Housing, and especially public housing, has to do with many
things besides planning, maintenance, and sanitation. These,
after all, are means, not ends. If we are able by these means to
promote the happiness of thousands of people, to give them
health and opportunities for their children, to bring some measure of security and peace into their lives, that is a very real
and important achievement; but we should not assume too casually that those ends are indeed being achieved—still less, that
they are the only consequences of our activities. I venture to
say that when these activities are finally appraised, these ends,
even if we attain them completely, will appear less important
than certain social and political consequences of our work to
which we are surprisingly incurious. We are making some very

far-reaching changes, not alone in the physical pattern of our cities, but in the social pattern as well. We are, within the measure of our activities, reconstructing the environment which is, in part at least, to shape the thought and vision of the generations that follow us. Our influence and our responsibility are not limited to the areas occupied by housing projects. However restricted may be the localities actually cleared and rebuilt, their presence alters the rhythm and direction of civic life as a whole: alters it perhaps in ways that are more profound and less predictable than many of us imagine. Housing projects are not merely incidents in the vast fabrics of our cities. They are organic alterations. That is true whether they are conceived as integral elements in a broad plan of development or whether, as happens more frequently, they are scattered casually over the disordered city.

Our housing authorities and those agencies associated with them are destroying an environment which is the outcome of one way of life in order to substitute an environment which will be, no doubt, the cause of another way of life. Since human thought and conduct have been shaped, in part at least, by an environment created by man, they may suffer a further change through changes in that environment. That is, to put it mildly, a somewhat daring hypothesis, and yet it is one which appears to be confirmed by the history of mankind. Certainly it deserves our notice quite as often as does that compassionate attitude toward human suffering which is the more usual justification of public housing, or that aesthetic need for harmony in the city which takes so persistent a command over the imaginations of planners.

I should like to examine a little more definitely the nature of at least one of these social changes. I should like to forget for a moment the mechanisms of housing, important as they are, and consider the broader consequences of these mechanisms. To be frank, I am not deeply interested in the mechanisms themselves.

I care very little for what goes on under the hood of my car—the operation of spark plugs and carburetor, the number of gallons burned to the mile—but I should like very much to know where we are going.

Housing projects are at the best unnatural phenomena. Housing projects do not spring spontaneously from the free interaction of social or economic forces. They are, rather, products of theory —things contrived by men who, however anxious for social reform or for the relief of suffering, yet stand a little aside from the forces engendered by social conflict. No one in the lower income group could, I think, have invented the housing project. That group, as I remember it, was at first even a little resentful of our efforts—or at least of our attitude—and had to be teased into our shining new paradise with the promise of mechanical refrigerators.

To say this of the housing project is not to condemn it. Cities themselves are, to some extent at least, works of art. Cities are shaped by the clash of economic forces but they are also shaped by idea and conscious guidance. If that were not so, they would be intolerable. Nevertheless, it must be obvious that those aspects of cities which are the result of deliberate thought invite a more jealous examination than those which appear to have had a spontaneous origin. Because they are by their nature more submissive to our control, they lay a heavier burden upon our conscience. For my part, although I acknowledge the rightness and the human usefulness of public housing, I should feel more certain of my judgment in this matter if public housing had had its origin in the economic class which it is meant to serve: if it had been demanded, fought for, and finally achieved by the very poor.

We should have had very few housing projects had it not been for the crisis created by unemployment. Housing projects—at least those for the lower income group—are agencies for relief. They are also a means for promoting economic activity. They have been shaped by intentions which have sometimes only an incidental relation to more permanent social objectives and these intentions are stamped upon their character. This accounts for the wholesale nature of our enterprise, its machinelike processes, its tedious uniformity and explains the lavish expenditures for labor, the strict economies in the purchase of brains. What was wanted was a standardized industrial product capable of being turned out rapidly in the largest possible units and with the maximum utilization of labor.

Heaven forbid that I should in these days identify labor with the lowest income group, and yet it seems to me reasonable to suppose that labor, rather than industrial capital or a government in search of expense, might have been expected to promote the public housing program. Labor did not promote that program. There were, no doubt, many reasons for this; but one reason, more important than people suppose, was an awareness—felt, rather than explained—of social consequences unforeseen and feared. Whatever else it may be, the housing project is an act of segregation. It defines, separates and establishes economic and, to some extent, social stratifications. People in a certain category, arbitrarily created, are drawn out of the ferment of urban life, reëstablished on new sites cleared for that purpose. These new sites are as clearly demarked from the larger complex of the city—by arrangement of buildings, by a uniform architecture and landscape treatment, by the nature of intercommunications—as though solid walls were built around them. Within that invisible wall a new habit of life is invited: not invited merely, but demanded and—by methods which have at least the color of science—guided.

Each day, as your techniques of control and management assume more definite and known conventions, the segregating nature of the housing project becomes more evident. These are institutions set into the city, not parts of the city. Their occupants are more like inmates than citizens. Their former living quarters having been proved sufficiently horrible, they have become *initiates* and may claim, so long as they do not suffer an increase of income, a special right of asylum. Thenceforth like orphans they live apart, blissfully havened from the tumult and peril of the city's streets. In that environment, their lives shaped by a special Providence, the underprivileged suddenly privileged, men are surely less likely to feel that immediate responsibility for their own destiny which is the tried motive for self-improvement —still less that responsibility for a collective destiny which gives vitality to the democratic process. I know quite well that a certain degree of social segregation is inescapable in our great cities; but I am not thinking now of those vast unredeemable distances which will always, I suppose, separate the very rich and the very poor; I am thinking, rather, of those many narrow fissures which constantly corrupt the central core of democracy. These are encouraged, I fear, by the principle of economic segregation which appears to be fundamental in the present policies of housing authorities.

These tendencies are encouraged also by the compact and specialized character of housing projects and by their remoteness from the commonplace activities of city life. I read recently a pamphlet, written in that glowing language which architects use to describe their favorite children, which makes a great to-do over the "suburban-like atmosphere" which is going to prevail in a housing project to be located in the center of a great city. Surrounded by lilacs, dwarf yews, and hawthorns, the dwellings painted to "look like a collection of private houses," the people who live here will never suspect that actually they are living in the congested heart of Chicago. The author-architect takes it for granted that no one in the lower income group would live in Chicago if he could help it, that only a lack of funds prevents that group from moving *en masse* to Concord, Massachusetts.

There is, it appears, something perverse and unnatural about a preference for crowds and streets, for the drama of business, for neon lights and the adventure of shopwindows.

Now, if housing authorities would take one good look at the habits and tastes of those for whom they are building, if they were to consider those things which people do like as important as those which they ought to like, if, in short, they were willing to admit history and custom into their designs, they would think twice before they decided that low-income people are really made happy by plumbing, fresh air, and prophylactic calm. Housing authorities, when they plant their hawthorns and sycamores, are at pains to study the kind of soil which these have preferred. Trees, it appears, are less apt than tenants to survive the rigors of an abstract philosophy.

You have, to be sure, a science of housing, but it is a science more biological than social. The housing project in Chicago to which I have just referred is illustrated by an air view, in no way different from the air view of every other housing project, which certainly has more the aspect of a chicken farm than that of an environment for human life, so angular, separate, and schematic is its stark parade of multiple cells. Hygiene, economy, and good eggs are obviously the ideals. There is, no doubt, a biological science as apposite to men as to chickens, but in practice its conclusions should be somewhat tempered for the larger and less tractable of those species.

I know that the streets of our great cities are full of clamor, confusion, dust, germs, smells, and ill-mannered people—and yet there are moments when I would rather live in the meanest of streets than in the most sanitary of housing projects. The air there is less pure but more invigorating. There the life of the city is channelized; I can share its strange irregular rhythms, its moving power. I would not exchange the crowds and the traffic, the bright lights and the noise of streets for a wilderness of spirea and honeysuckle, of near and well-kept lawn, of façades saturated with the charm of colonial days. I am sure that people in the lower income groups will agree with me and I submit that their preferences, confirmed by centuries of experience, are likely to be founded upon something more fundamental than caprice.

Of course I know that our streets can be improved. Of course I know that the treatment, arrangement, and control of streets are matters grievously neglected by municipal authorities. I know how the lunatic industries of the nineteenth century distorted that once beautiful theme, and I have noted the dire consequences of land exploitation, of the undirected growth of cities, and of that strange encouragement which our fathers gave to architectural indecencies. I know that slums must be cleared and cities replanned, but I know also that this can be done without fostering segregation, either social or economic. Nor do I expect all of mankind to share my desire to live in a little apartment at the corner of Broadway and Forty-second Street. You can have good housing without eliminating the street: the street, which is integral with the tradition of cities, the most active channel of human intercourse, the oldest theater of democracy.

I would return the housing project to the streets of the city and I would return it also to the city's institutions. You are not apt to develop any sense of social solidarity in a scheme which excludes the church, the theater, and the school. I have never seen a housing project which included these except by accident, and yet I cannot imagine any device which could make more evident the separatist nature of these enterprises. That is surely an artificial—I almost said inhuman—neighborhood where men cannot feel the continuing presence of these ancient and vast traditions.

What I miss most of all in your housing schemes is a spire. You must make room for that symbol, if only to relieve the

deadly monotony of your roof lines. Next to the spire I miss
the promise of the schoolhouse, the relaxation of the clubhouse
and the gymnasium, the invitation of the theater; and, to tell the
truth, I am not long in a housing project before I begin to miss
the barroom also. You have fresh air, plumbing, vitamins, and
landscaping no end—yes, and good planning sometimes—but you
have left human nature outside your gate. If I had my way, there
should be no residential district in a city inaccessible to the
church and the school, no area in which these are not provided
for. I cannot believe any other scheme to be a wholesome one—
either for those inside of it or for those outside of it; and the
doctrine that a certain self-respect, engendered by an escape
from squalor, affords a compensation for these things of the spirit
leaves me very cold indeed.

I should have a group of institutions at the center of each
neighborhood—the size of which should be determined by history
and experience. I seldom visit a housing project without wanting
to open a great hole in its center—by a good charge of dynamite,
if necessary—so as to make room for such institutions. But I would
not do that if I could not at the same time open many smaller
sites to be used for the dwellings of income groups other than
the lowest. Certainly I would not have institutions reserved for
the use of any one group, however low or high.

The more I think of the average housing project, the better I
like the dynamite idea. A good explosion would not only open
a space at the center but would, at the same time, scatter the
low-income dwellings out into the wider complex of the city and
open channels for an admixture of other dwellings. Some housers,
I suppose, would consider the method drastic; and yet I wonder
whether, in the long run, it would prove more disruptive than
their own.

I hope that housers will understand that I am on their side.
I believe in public housing. I believe that we ought to use col-

lective resources in this way to destroy the slums of our terrible cities and, for the sake of our children and of our democratic way of life, give to every family the opportunity of decent shelter. That will be expensive, but we can afford it. Nor is such a program, in principle at least, a program for the benefit of one class at the expense of another. When you cure a cancer in one organ of the body, that is surely to the interest of all other organs.

I am discussing not so much an idea, but the way in which an idea has been translated into practice. Partly by accident, partly through errors of judgment, and partly by forces which are only incidentally related to our central objective, habits of thought and action have been developed, conventions formulated and crystallized, special interests entrenched, until there has grown up a pattern of behavior the rightness of which we take quite too casually for granted. Now, after the war has made necessary a pause in our practice, we ought to reëxamine that pattern. We should examine not processes and appearances merely, not tools and means merely, but, most searchingly of all, values and ends.

I think that much could be gained, and only a little lost, if housing projects for the lower income group could be broken up into many small units and if these could then be widely separated (not necessarily by dynamite) over a considerable area. No one unit should comprise more than two or three buildings—and sometimes only one—or provide shelter for more than, say, fifty families, and there should be normally not more than one such unit in a block. The buildings in each unit, planned in accordance with the highest standards, occupying not more than one third of each site, should yet be distinguished from other apartments in the city by no peculiarities other than excellence in design; nor should there develop any traditions in management other than those which have become customary and accepted in other apartment buildings in the same environment. There should be no trace of the *institution*, no acknowledged or implied separation, and certainly no "trained personnel" bustling about and ready to channel the lives of tenants into accepted molds.

If this policy were followed, many of the spectacular aspects of housing would, to be sure, disappear. We should not have the excitement—or the difficulties—which arise from the accumulation and exploitation of large areas of land; but we should be able to buy or condemn land in small parcels wherever it is to be had cheaply or wherever housing conditions are in need of reform. Those problems which arise from wholesale management might be made less difficult, and a wide range of experiment in plan and expression made possible. These are practical advantages; but far more important than these would be the social gain. Our smaller units, illustrating new and attainable standards, should not form segregated areas still surrounded by darkness but, as scattered stars set aglow the night, they should illumine and redeem the whole of the wide city. The people who live in these units should be invited to improve, not to change, their way of life, which would remain as before, integral with that of the community.

Housing authorities which have thus clarified their objectives should at the same time enlarge these in such a way as to include, not low-income housing alone, but all housing. Good housing should be their objective, whether for rich or for poor. They should not be thought of merely as relief agencies, but should be given as their responsibility the total problem of shelter, wherever this touches the lives of city dwellers. It should be their task to devise processes by which these problems can be solved and, wherever that is possible, they should carry these processes into practice—whether by planning and building, or by the encouragement of private enterprise, or by legal reforms, or by subsidies and other methods of financing, or by technological experiment, education, or propaganda. Perhaps also they might, if that is not too striking an innovation, lend their influence to the encouragement of *architecture*—a term which includes not only good planning and building but also a search for those qualities of form which are as essential to human welfare as are bread and shelter. Not least among the sins of housers is their indifference to that generous pursuit.

CHAPTER TWENTY-FOUR

only the living remember

FOR many years, my special field of study being the history of architecture, I have taken more than a casual notice of monuments—a term which connotes all those forms which architecture assumes when it seeks eternal life. The war being still so recent, these seem to invite an interest more immediate than that of an historian. Now, when the seeds of a million war memorials are warm in our soil, we ought to examine monuments more curiously than hitherto; and especially we should take note of those familiar strange shapes set up on village green and city square after each of our wars which, addressing the future in the commingled languages of architecture, sculpture, and letters, promise for those we love an immortality seemingly more evident than our own. Shall we again entrust to these the memory of our soldier dead? We should ask our philosophers to speak of these matters: to tell us what monuments are, why we build them, and if we ought to build them.

In the midst of an evolving and fragmentary world we are forever searching for permanence and completeness. The endless pattern of change perplexes us, deprives our lives of importance, frightens us as we stand each day nearer to eternity. Therefore we have taken eagerly to ourselves whatever appeared to be enduring, anchored, and yet apposite to human life. We see the hills, solid and firmly set upon the earth, but the continuity which these proclaim is not our own. Not so the pyramid which, smaller in bulk, is yet infinitely larger in human effort. Stable, balanced, incapable of collapse or fracture, of change or of growth, coexistent with the mountain after which it was patterned, the pyramid, most perfect of monuments, shares the energy of the mountain and yet announces our energy. Whoever builds a pyramid collaborates with the gods, perfecting their work with a model more conformable to our desires. They were most nearly gods who placed three pyramids side by side.

We have searched also for definition and finality—and we have discovered these also in the monument. Symphonies, poems, and philosophic pantologies console us with promises of order and completeness; they are walled Utopias having each its gate and secret key; and yet they may lift us out of this our uncongenial world with a force less compelling than that of the great obelisk which commands the Washington Mall or the arch which crowns the Avenue des Champs-Elysées. Lost in the jungle where no thing arrives at more than a momentary perfection, where even the systems and the suns must submit to the caprices of nebulae and comet, the mind clings to such symbols. The monument, geometric, arbitrary, and self-sufficient, stands before us evident and complete, accessible to the intelligence. Pure of form like a sonata the monument solicits our disinterested vision; we follow the lines, the planes that answer or oppose each other, the sequences and the harmonies, some of which reveal themselves subtly and after a sustained experience; we are for that moment free.

These are the first and philosophic gifts of the monument; but we demand a wider utility. We ask for shelter. The primeval monument was a heap of stones protecting the body of a departed hero: from that time to this we have tried to give such dignity to useful space. We ask for praise. The house of a god must be tall and more nobly built than that of his worshipers: from that source flowed the stream of architecture confirming through long generations the majesty of gods and kings, of democratic legislatures and of the Pennsylvania Railroad. We ask for

pleasure. The monument, clothed in anecdote and peristyle, deco-
rates the city; steeped in history it is the last refuge of the Academy. We ask also that the monument should remember.

This need for remembrance added effigy and picture to the
monument. The gods were the first to ask that favor. Although
they were well served by architecture (which worships them even
in the meanest house) they were yet not so confident of eternity
as to rely wholly upon an art of abstractions. They had need
also of statue and story explicitly to confirm their authority. The
autocrats, the conquerors, and the great kings, who always aspire
to be gods, then extended their dominions into time by the same
device. Like the gods, they loved monuments as simulacra of
that ordered world which is the natural home of the absolute
mind—a passion they shared with philosophers, themselves a
species of autocrat—but they could not rely merely upon solidity
and harmony of form. The monument must set forth more patently the nature and the causes of their grandeur. Queen Hatshep-
sut explains and warrants her temple with the story of her birth
carved on the granite walls of Deir-el-Bahari, and the renown
of the Emperor Trajan, secure in the magnificent sequences of
his Forum, must yet be defended by a ribbon of his soldiers
wound around a marble column. An infatuation with monuments
is the common trait of Pharaoh, Philip, Caesar, Napoleon, and
Hitler.

The people, to whom monuments are presumably addressed, do
not understand abstractions and care for them less. They will
look for picture first and for architecture after the story is told.
When monuments are big enough they will astonish the people;
when they are old enough they may capture the people's romances; associated with the dead they are pegs for the people's
piety; but without picture the people will not love them. Monuments must enact history: as does "Liberty," for example, en-
lightening the world in New York Harbor, and "Farragut," in

Madison Square, swept by the breezes of Mobile Bay. These are actors on a wide stage. The excitement they occasion as picture, the emotion they provoke as symbol, have little to do with form or taste or provenance, still less with their architectural harmonies. Rare indeed are the instances of popular approval of a monument "for its own sake," a work of art valued for that contemplative delight which we are told is the essential of the aesthetic experience. For that sort of thing we build museums.

The people want to see their heroes and to see them at the moment of their heroism. Saint Sebastian is not summoned to the people's mind by the slender shaft which leans against the abbey wall—they must see the cruel arrows bristling from his beautiful body. So Nathan Hale must look proudly into the British rifles and Stonewall Jackson flourish the sword of the Seven Days above southern tulips; and so must the men of Guadalcanal ride their tanks over fronded marble.

The monument confers dignity upon history. We approve monuments without liking them because they appear to give importance to our country. The people, as every politician knows, like to usurp the homage due the gods, and symbols of autocracy are translated into symbols of democracy with surprising facility. We know how Thomas Jefferson, himself an architect, fills the round imperial Pantheon with democratic sentiment: the two had made an appointment in Heaven to meet again on earth. In like manner the statue of Abraham Lincoln, lovingly homespun, is prefaced with that same peristyle which once promised us, not Lincoln, but the thearchy of Athens. A popular success necessarily arises from the fusion of themes so dear to our hearts with the cadences of an old and aristocratic art. The equivocal nature of this dignity will not offend those who know little Latin and less Greek.

Architecture has this advantage over sculpture: its absurdities are evident only to those who love it. A sculptor once unclothed

Washington and gave him, in an heroic statue confronting the
Capitol, the nude grandeur of a Roman god (the costumes of
gods being ever a sculptor's dilemma), and we know that the
renown of Washington might not have survived that apotheosis
had not Congress wisely sequestered Greenough's masterpiece in
the unvisited halls of the Smithsonian Institution. Such mummery is less often rebuked in architecture.

This then is the people's memorial. Raised by the gods to assure men of eternal life, the monument also illustrated in picture
and statue the legends which sustained their theocratic power.
The conquerors, who walk the stage of history less remotely than
the gods, made that symbol their own and, in order that the gods
might not claim them, covered their monuments with the picture
and inscription which recited the stories of their conquests. The
people, persuaded of the immortality of the memories entrusted
to monuments, adopted the tradition. The people's heroes, the
grandeur of their spirits and the story of their wars, were thenceforth described in bronze and set in frames of architecture.

Shall we ask now if we ought to build such monuments and
especially whether we should build them as memorials to those
who fell in the Great Wars? In what way do such monuments
honor our soldiers? In what way do they anchor in our memories
their devotion and sacrifice?

No picture, not even a thousand pictures, can show us war.
Pictures are at best peepholes revealing the merest fragments of
reality. The most candid of cameras—and of motion-picture cameras—selects, arranges, and distorts. There is no realism which
can compass war, this horror and madness, this confusion, pain,
filth, and waste; neither is there any symbol which will counterfeit the smallest part of it.

How then shall we portray our heroes? The warrior without
war? That is precisely what the conquerors have shown us. In

their monuments we see war, as Perseus saw Medusa, in a mirrored shield. We are shown the glamour, the adventure, the movement and heroic posture, but not the cruelty which gives these meaning; nor is there any realism of attitude, costume, or facial expression which can move these from behind the footlights. We know, for example, how Wolfe died at Quebec and Nelson at Trafalgar, their officers grouped picturesquely about, and every visual circumstance given emphasis by the sanctions of the Academy. We hear the music of the cannon; we see the sunlight on the stage; only war is missing. Not men, but sawdust fantoccini, are torn by the confetti shrapnel of Meissonier.

On his elegant horse, led by a delicate Victory, General Sherman rides out of Central Park. His cape falls in studied folds, carefully adjusted in a Parisian studio. What was it then that Sherman said of war? Who was the better witness, the general or his statue? Where now are the endless marches under the southern sun, the blackened villages, burnt fields, and uprooted gardens, white columns wrapped in red flames, the hatred and anguish and despair spread over half a nation? They are not on the monument; and neither, let me add, is Victory. They who have seen Victory give quite a different account of her.

High over Monument Avenue on his rococo pedestal rides General Lee, wrapped in his beautiful legend. We do not see around him the casuistry which provoked four years of useless and unnecessary conflict, the ungenerous rancor which sent him and the gallant men who followed him into their cruel struggle and more cruel disillusionment; nor do we find one hint of the ruin and bitterness which these scattered over the land. What is there here of war? A gentleman rides his horse on Monument Avenue.

It will be interesting to note how the sculptors of our day will represent generals now that our generals no longer ride their horses. Marshall answering the telephone? Doolittle at the con-

trols? Probably we shall not show them at all. In art generals
have gone out of fashion. The column of Trajan and the Arch
of Titus are classic precedents, if such are needed, for describing
in sculpture and in terms sufficiently ingenuous the common
soldier, certain to be the hero of this present war. Colonel Shaw,
cast in bronze on the Boston Common, rides his horse against a
panel of infantrymen; it will be the colonel now who will fill in
the background.

We have seen in Times Square the sculptures which tell us
how the G. I.'s raised the flag over Iwo Jima, a prophetic work
heralding a population of marble G. I.'s. The sculptor, without
being conscious of it, was as economical of war as were those who
cast the equestrian generals. You have not seen the flag raised
over Iwo Jima until you have seen the black smoke and red flames
of our guns, the terrible swift descent of our bombers, the enemy
tortured by tank and flame-thrower, the emergency operation,
the noise and stench, the loneliness and desolation which covered
that narrow island. The sculptor will fill our parks and squares
with faithful presentments of our soldiers, explicit of helmet,
bayonet, and button, and no homely circumstance slighted. He
will try to bring the grim business to your doorstep in a democratic guise. He will not succeed. The war will hide its head
behind the common man quite as easily as behind the trophies
of conquerors. Do not ask the monument what is hidden. The
monument does not remember.

We acknowledge the need to commemorate, to build some witness to this sacrifice and to our gratitude. If not the monument,
what then?

Whatever continues and sustains that for which our soldiers
fought is a commemoration more eloquent and enduring than
the loftiest monument. That man is most remembered whose en-
deavors are most imitated; whose words and deeds are published
by the words and deeds of other men; who lives in the lives of

those who follow him, their spirits kindled by his spirit. Lincoln is less honored by those who caricature however lovingly his gaunt figure and quaint costume than by those who repeat his generous soul; and Washington, I am sure, would give his obelisk to have a few pounds of his steadfast courage under the iron dome on Capitol Hill. So the Salvation Army youth, beating his drum on the sidewalks of the Bowery, continues William Booth; so the scout leader continues Robert Baden-Powell; and so the nurse in the alien Solomons continued and honored Florence Nightingale. Art cannot attain so just an expression.

Four hundred monuments, it is said, burden the field of Gettysburg; and yet they add no single leaf of laurel to those who died there. Gettysburg is transfigured, as we all know, by a briefer dedication infinitely less facile.

Now I do not suggest that we should let this present moment pass without some gesture which shall translate our hearts. I am for some act, immediate and unequivocal, repeated in every town and village, which will attest our faith in the cause for which these men have made so great a sacrifice. The flags and the bunting come down, the band plays for only a day, the bravest toasts are speedily drunk, and even the speeches end at last. Our lives resume their even rhythms, and the most recent war is hurled each day backward towards Château-Thierry, Appomattox, and Yorktown. Let us not turn to our ledgers without some durable achievement which shall give added life to that for which our soldiers fought.

I do not know what our soldiers fought for if it was not to guard and to nourish the spiritual energies of the people among whom they were born and among whom they hope to live. The Four Freedoms? Freedoms are opportunities. When we have won the Four Freedoms we have won only the freedom to build whatever civilization we may wish to build.

Let us build on the foundations our soldiers have laid a civilization fit for free men. Let us begin that rebuilding at once with something that is simple and considered, useful to the community, unaffected and full of a present happiness; some fine thing that we cannot afford and yet will afford. Do not wait for the completed plan of a city; take now the first utilitarian steps. A park in a neighborhood which is now a waste of asphalt and brick; a playground where children have only the streets; a schoolhouse to replace that dreary box so long overtaken by the progress of the art and science of teaching; a music hall, a theater, a library, a church accessible to all faiths. The role of these continues through the years; they are not make-believe; they serve; and they are always beautiful.

People tell me that in these buildings purpose and use will obscure the dedication. Our memories must be brief indeed if they are so readily distracted. People tell me that in building useful memorials we are exploiting the soldier, building in his name the things which suit our convenience. He is bankrupt of argument who calls me a knave. Clearly I am thinking, not of conveniences, but of that service to the spirit which gives meaning to useful things. I am not for Memorial Convention Halls or Memorial Baseball Fields or Memorial Waterworks—although it may be that my judgment in these matters is more a judgment of taste than of principle. There is no serviceability which does not give dignity to architecture, but there are degrees in serviceability as there are degrees in dignity. There are buildings which lift the communal life out of the narrow business of getting and spending. These I would illumine with that renewed purpose and hope which our men have surely drawn from their ordeal by fire.

It is that purpose and hope which I would commemorate; not war, for that is glorious only to conquerors and the ancient gods; not war, for that can never be recorded. If our soldiers remain anonymous in our useful buildings that is because they are already anonymous, being inseparable from the nation out of which they sprang. How then can you give them added life except in the life of that nation? The monument recites names, dates, events, and our own piety, but never the spirit. That also the monument does not remember.

I should like now to return to the beginning of this paper and to remind the reader of the basic nature of the monument which I noted there: I mean the monument as an essay in permanence and completeness. I should like to consider not so much the appearances of the monument as the quality *monumentality*. I would have the monument address us once more in the language of architecture, disencumbered of picture, legend, and conventional piety. Will it then have some meaning for us—and perhaps some quality apposite to the service of our soldiers— which in my comments on the more popular memorial I have overlooked?

It will not be easy to imagine such a *pure monument*, so overlaid are architectures with alien shadows and reflected suns. How shall we imagine the Invalides without Napoleon, Versailles without Louis? How shall we imagine Mont St. Michel free from the cadences and colors of the *Chanson de Roland*, now that Henry Adams has made these inseparable? And if we could disentangle the Colosseum from Rome and set it down like the Yale Bowl all crisp and shining at the edge of New Haven, would it not *be* the Yale Bowl? The crater of the Bowl has as majestic a sweep; only it does not, as it happens, contain the blood of Christian martyrs—well, at any rate, not so much of it.

Within the variable and uncertain meanings which time lays on architecture there are enclosed architectural ideas which are constant and universal: among these the *idea* of the monument. If the obelisk, free of Washington, stood before us a pure mathematical creation of the spirit, if it no longer decorated the city, conclusion and crown of the great Mall, it would nevertheless speak to us. What then would it say? It would reaffirm, I think, precisely that which the pyramids promised us: stability and finality.

Why is it that this message has had power over our imaginations? Is it not because we believed in and desired the peace that is promised us? Suppose that we came in the course of time to find less oppressive than hitherto the ideas of impermanence and change; if we were indeed to accept the actuality of a universe in evolution, of a mankind borne forward on a great tide whose distant end and present values are inaccessible to our imaginations; if we were to accept this actuality without fear and without rebellion; would we not then find somewhat less persuasive the story told us by the monument? Thus made modern-minded —less wistful of eternity, less enraptured of symmetry—we might cling less tenaciously to its consolations. Perhaps we should conclude that the monument, considered as philosophic expression, belongs definitely to the civilization out of which it developed: I mean the classic world-picture in which nature was finite and man the measure and fixed pole of the universe. It is not by accident that our monuments are so often dressed in the Doric mode.

These considerations will appear less fantastic if we will acknowledge, first, the principle of architecture as an art of expression, and, second, the necessity in architecture, so often affirmed and so little heeded, of a relevance to the genuine culture of its time.

If with these principles in mind we were to examine the American scene, we would, I think, discover a surprising dissonance between our present thought and the monument, a dissonance which began with the Greek Revival and continues to this day. A people in continuous and accelerated change covers its land with fixed and static symbols. Our giant and unpredictable ener-

gies which admit no impediment in science, in technologies, in
social progress, or in war submit in art to the imprisonment of an
arid ritual. Our techniques multiply; our powers widen; new patterns of thought and conduct, of valuations and loyalties, come
crowding upon us; we are free men and the world draws near us
—and we give outward form to our thought and feeling with
quaint adulteries of Greece and Rome.

It should be understood that I do not reproach the innocent
men who raised the Washington obelisk. They were speaking
Greek without understanding it. They had returned in their
dreams and in their oratory to the glories of antiquity; a co-
quetry with Rome seemed appropriate to a republic governed
not by a parliament but by a *senate;* and the future tinge of
democracy in the fabric of government could not have been
then discerned. They expressed not themselves but their doctrines, architecture being a dead art.

There must be many of us who, knowing the latent power of
architecture for human happiness, wish for an architecture which
is no longer a dead art. We should like to relate our architecture to ourselves in order that it may have meaning for us. Living in the midst of a becoming and an unfolding, conscious of
change and of the necessity of change, of the end of old systems
and thoughts and usages even when we love them ardently,
opening our arms to an unpredictable future, we, too, desire a
symbol. That symbol, if it is to command us, must be founded
upon our own thought. We do not ask for escape.

Useful buildings—useful in the sense that I have described—
will satisfy us with an ordered pattern which, if we understand
it, must be inherently more eloquent than any monument: not
from a dignity of service merely but from the share it assumes
in the march of our civilization. That relevance completes the
pattern which otherwise lacks the faith essential to all finality;
and if these buildings pretend to no eternity but like ourselves

are clearly to be dissolved into the stream of history, it may be that that, too, will bring them closer to our hearts. Long life is no virtue either in man or in his constructions.

Our soldiers will understand our faith. They fought for it. They will know that whatever we build for the happiness of our people—of their people—honors them; that we continue them in the structures which serve the ends they served. They will see that we believe in that which they believed in; that we have made the freedoms they defended the bases of new freedoms; that we have taken to ourselves their spirit and merged it into the crescent civilization which we share. This land is their immortality.

acknowledgments

The permission of the following periodicals and institutions to reprint material is hereby gratefully acknowledged: *American Scholar, Architectural Record, Atlantic Monthly, Columbia University Quarterly, Garden Magazine, House and Garden, Journal of the American Institute of Architects, Mademoiselle, Magazine of Art, Transatlantique* (England), Wayne University.